IMAGES
of America

JEMEZ SPRINGS

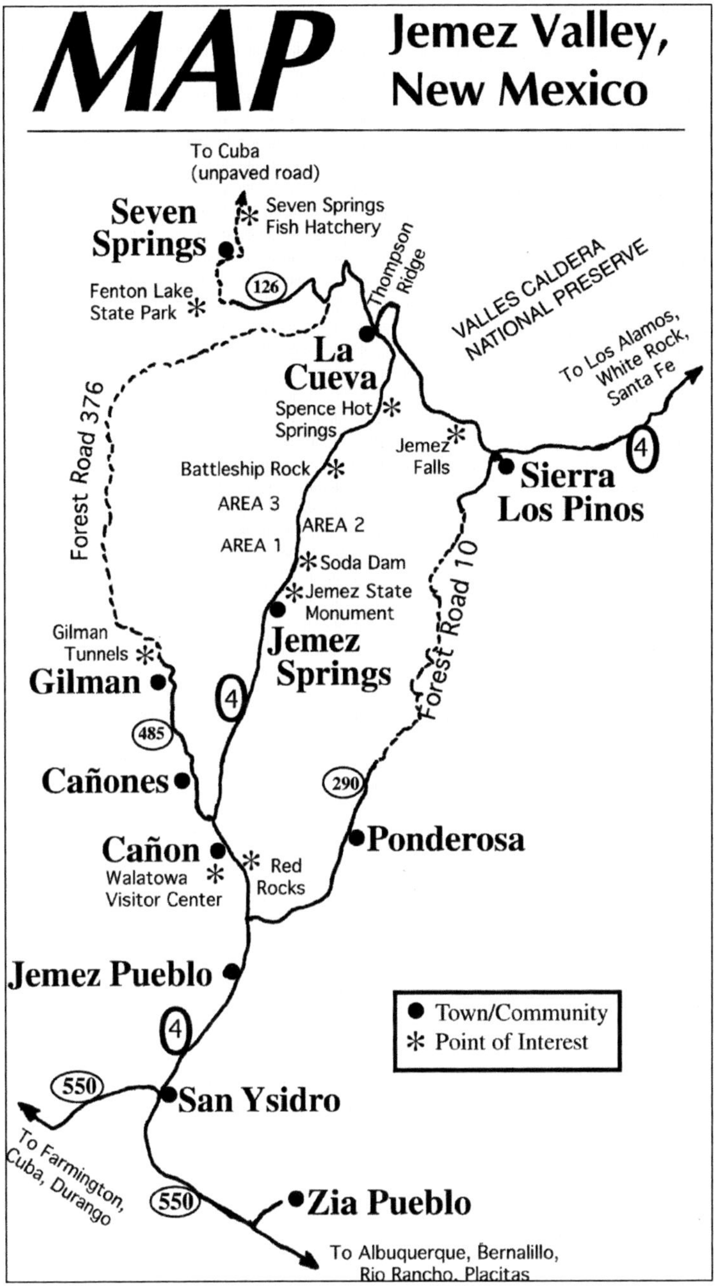

People just use the word "Jemez" to refer to Jemez Springs and its surroundings. All of these small, unincorporated towns and developments are almost like suburbs of the village. San Ysidro is the only other village in the Jemez Valley that is incorporated. (Courtesy *Jemez Thunder*.)

On the Cover: The head wrangler of Rancho Rea was Shorty Kelso, the Madison Square Garden championship cowboy for 1927. It was said that he once bulldogged a big steer from the running board of a 1927 Chevrolet Roadster. (Courtesy 2005 July 4 Committee.)

IMAGES
of America

Jemez Springs

Kathleen Wiegner and Robert Borden

ARCADIA
PUBLISHING

ISBN 978-0-7385-7055-6

Published by Arcadia Publishing
Charleston, South Carolina

Printed in the United States of America

Library of Congress Control Number: 2008934529

For all general information contact Arcadia Publishing at:
Telephone 843-853-2070
Fax 843-853-0044
E-mail sales@arcadiapublishing.com
For customer service and orders:
Toll-Free 1-888-313-2665

Visit us on the Internet at www.arcadiapublishing.com

To Elmer (Joseph) Routledge, the inspiration for this book, and the 2005 July 4 Committee, for starting the process.

Contents

ACKNOWLEDGMENTS

This book has truly been a labor of love for Jemez Springs. There were many individuals whose help made this book a reality. I would like to thank Jim Coad and Nancy Tucker for providing access to their beautiful postcard collections. I sincerely thank the Sandoval County Historical Society, Museums of New Mexico Palace of the Governors, USDA Santa Fe National Forest, Hummingbird Music Camp, and the Bodhi Manda Zen Center for allowing me to explore their vast collections of vintage materials.

Along with the many archives that provided materials, I would also like to thank local sources for their vast knowledge of Jemez Springs, such as the Servants of the Paraclete; the *Jemez Thunder*; Department of Special Collections and University Archives, Marquette University Libraries; and the Academy of Natural Sciences of Philadelphia.

The private photograph collections by Tom Abousleman, who graciously provided his time, were used. Joseph E. Routledge answered my frantic e-mails when I needed more information about the good old days. I would like to take this moment and thank Susan Diggle, Paul Adams, Julie Crook, Delores Garcia, Frank and Rita Slowen, Joann Dolk, Richard Sanchez, Jim Forcier-Call, Frank Sarnol, Steve Lucero, Esther Smedley, *Jemez Mountain Railroads* by Vernon Glover, and finally, Jared Jackson, my editor, for his good humor and patience, which made this process a joy to complete.

INTRODUCTION

The name Jemez Springs was not settled on as the name of the village until 1910. Prior to that, it had many names. The Native Americans called it Giusewa, meaning "land of boiling water." The Spanish referred to it as Los Ojos Calientes for the many hot springs found in the area. The Jemez Indians called themselves the Hemish ("the people"). The Spaniards changed it to Jamez or Jemez (pronounced Hay-mez). In the late 1800s, the name changed when the then-postmaster, named Perea, asked the U.S. Postal Service to name the post office after himself. Even when its name was officially Jemez Springs, it was often referred to as Jemez Hot Springs.

Both the Spanish and Native American cultures still exist in Jemez today. The Pueblo of Jemez lies 10 miles south of the village. Spanish names like Trujillo, Jaramillo, and Garcia abound. Only after New Mexico became a U.S. territory in 1850 did the Anglo presence become a part of the Native American–Spanish mix.

For a long time, Jemez was the place where people came to pick up their mail, buy some supplies, and enjoy a night on the town. For people living in the far-out rural areas, Jemez Springs was often a much-anticipated "trip to town." It wasn't much of a town.

At the dawn of the 20th century, Jemez Springs was an isolated rural community literally at the end of a dirt road. Only horse trails headed up the canyon. But the early 20th century saw the beginning of Jemez Springs as a tourist town, popular for its many hot springs. There were two bathhouses in Jemez Springs, and both operate today, although in altered forms. The story goes that during the summer, tents sprung up like mushrooms near the hot springs as people camped, hoping the hot water full of minerals would cure them of their ills.

There were hotels, as it was a two-day ride by horse-and-buggy to Albuquerque. Dude ranches appealed to the people "back east" who wanted to experience a bit of the not-so-wild West. They were lured by advertising that promised "fishing in the beautiful Jemez," "freedom unparalleled in hiking activity," and "food and food service par excellence." The Santa Fe National Forest provided places for fishing, hunting, and camping as well as just plain sightseeing.

While other Western communities became boomtowns because of rich mineral deposits, except for some copper and turquoise that was not good for jewelry making, Jemez Springs did not participate in the boom-and-bust history of so many towns. It was the green gold of the forests that provided the industry. Small areas like Ponderosa, Gilman, and Porter, which are south of Jemez Springs, were alive with logging activity. The lumber companies even built a railroad, blasting tunnels in the rock to bring the logs down from the rough slopes to the mills below.

North of the village, people hunted, farmed, and raised cows for milk, beef for meat, and chickens for eggs. Joseph Routledge, who grew up in the Jemez during the 1920s and 1930s, remembers some of the more interesting people who came by the family's cabin.

There was the "bee man," who not only sold honey but also ran a con game. He would disguise his racehorse as an old nag and then challenge people to a race—the stakes were both horses. Looking at the bee man's sad-looking horse, people gladly took the bet and lost as the "old nag" beat their horses.

Then there was Cox, "The man who trained burros." He had a corral, a campsite with a tent outside, a campfire for cooking, and makeshift chairs and stumps to sit on to eat around his cooking pot. He told one story about a con he had played on a "dude from Albuquerque" who came up to fish and had a fancy car. Well Cox took the battery out of the car and put it in his tent. When the man came back and his car wouldn't start, Cox told him that someone must have stolen his battery. By chance, said Cox, he had one in his tent. So the man paid $20 for his own battery.

Progress came slowly to Jemez Springs, but it did come. Electricity arrived in 1948 when Fred Abousleman and others set up a small electric generator and then joined with other rural cooperatives to become part of the Jemez Mountains Electric Cooperative. In 1949, Highway 4, which serves as the village's main street, was finally paved. The village was incorporated in 1955. Telephone service came in 1964. The first telephone still hangs in Tom Abousleman's house. In the 1990s, there was the new post office, clinic, and credit union.

The difficulty for Jemez Springs—or the blessing, depending on the person—is that it has almost no room to expand. The forest service owns large tracts of land that surround the village. A Catholic order owns 2,600 acres of land just north of the village. Most newcomers build or buy outside the village and come to town to a restaurant, for a dip in a hot spring, or to pick up their mail. The population of the village—currently 388 give or take a few—has remained about the same year after year.

Buildings in Jemez Springs don't get torn down as much as they are recycled; they just change names or functions when taken over by a new owner. The Laughing Lizard Cafe, for example, has been the stage set for cafés, dance halls, a union hall, a way station for goods from Albuquerque destined for places up the mountain, and boxing demos by Jack Dempsey and other boxers. As a result, a number of buildings in the heart of the village can lay claim to being over 100 years old.

For most businesses, tourism is still the main source of income. The busy traffic through the village in the summer (three million people by some estimates) comes from people driving to forest service campgrounds, fishing holes, hot springs, or hiking trails. And like other tourist towns, businesses cut back their hours in the winter and hope the money they made in the summer will carry them through.

One

Culture Clash

The Jemez Indians migrated to the Four Corners area and the Jemez Mountains in the 13th century. Speculation is that the migrants had once been residents of the great pueblos at Chaco and Mesa Verde, which were suffering from a drought so severe that the two pueblos could not sustain their large populations. A number of pueblos—some say as many as 20—were established by the Jemez Indians, the largest being the Pueblo of Giusewa, the ruins of which are now within the Jemez State Monument on the north end of Jemez Springs.

First contact with the Spaniards occurred in the winter of 1540–1541 when the entourage of Francisco de Coronado set up camp in the nearby town of Bernalillo. Coronado sent out parties of exploration, and one of the Spaniards reported back that the Jemez people were peaceable and furnished provisions to their visitors.

When Coronado found no gold, he returned to Mexico. The pueblos went undisturbed for the next 40 years, until another expedition under Don Juan de Oñaté arrived with the intent of colonizing all of the New Mexican pueblos. Oñaté assembled 31 pueblo leaders to swear vassalage to the cross and the king of Spain. By doing so, all of the pueblos came under the rule of Spain.

Mission churches were built. The Native Americans were forbidden to speak their own language and forced to learn Spanish, denied the right to practice their ancient religion, and made to become Christians.

But 82 years of coexistence came to an end when the pueblos arose in the "Great Pueblo Revolt" of 1680 and drove the Spaniards out of New Mexico. In 1692, twelve years after the revolt, the pueblos were retaken. Later the Jemez people living in numerous villages were forced to resettle at Walatowa under the Spanish resettlement policy known as "Reduccion." The Treaty of Guadalupe Hidalgo in 1848 concluded the U.S. war with Mexico, making New Mexico a U.S. territory.

To this day, the inhabitants of Pueblo of Jemez continue their dances and sacred rituals despite concerted missionary activity.

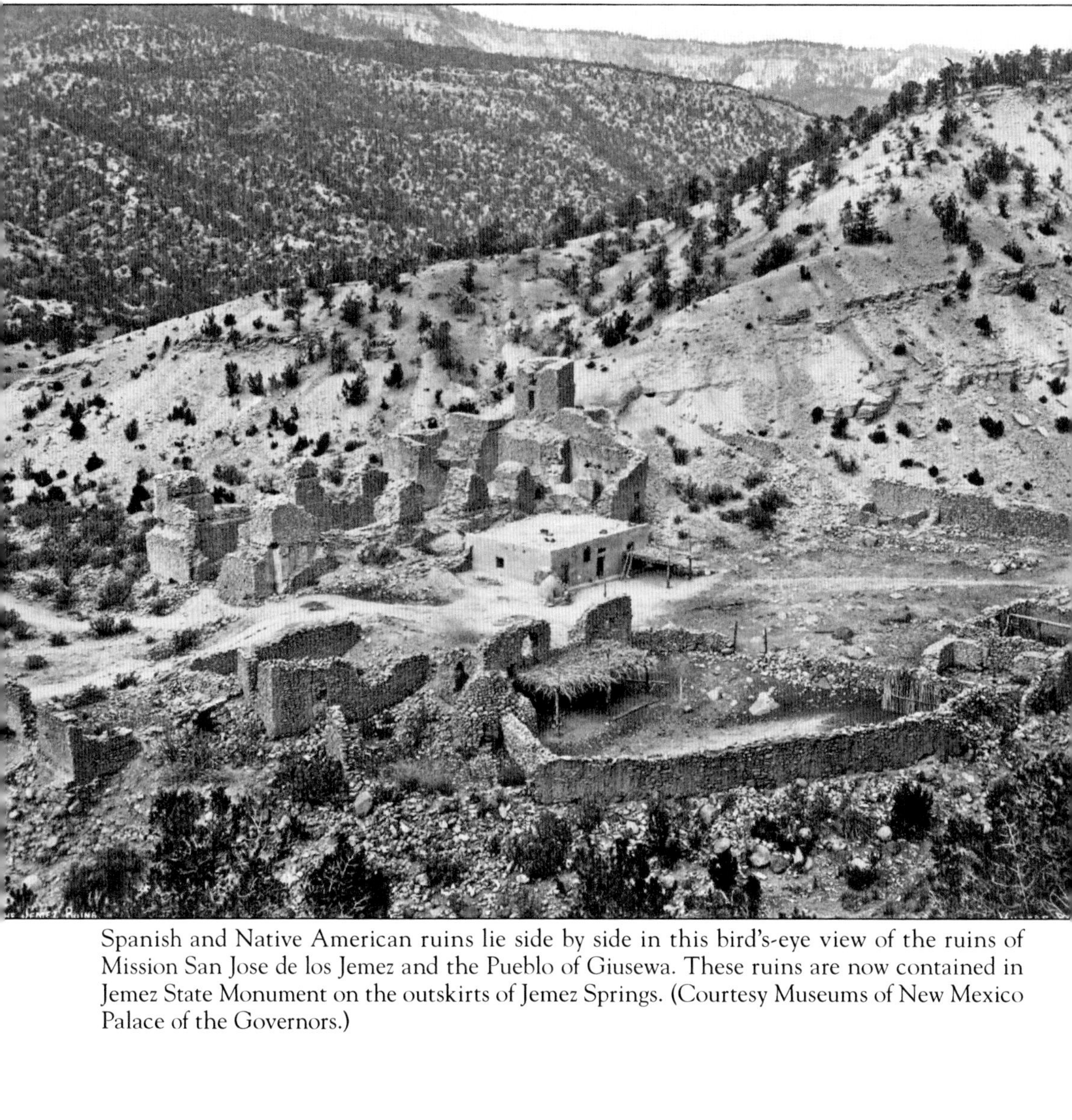

Spanish and Native American ruins lie side by side in this bird's-eye view of the ruins of Mission San Jose de los Jemez and the Pueblo of Giusewa. These ruins are now contained in Jemez State Monument on the outskirts of Jemez Springs. (Courtesy Museums of New Mexico Palace of the Governors.)

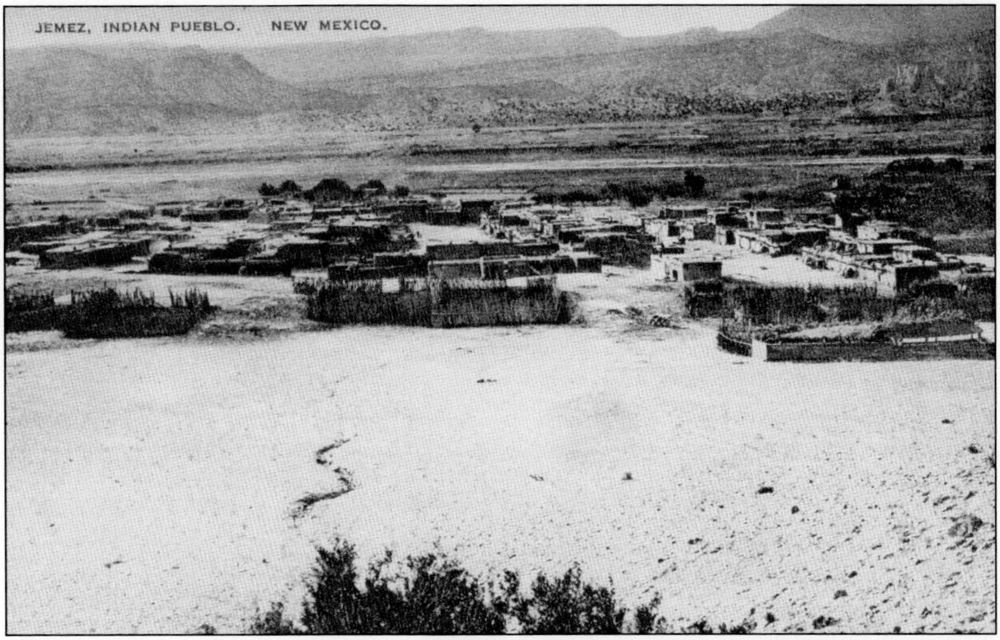

This postcard is of the Jemez Indian pueblo. Today the pueblo has many modern buildings, although the central plaza is still relatively untouched. (Courtesy Jim Coad.)

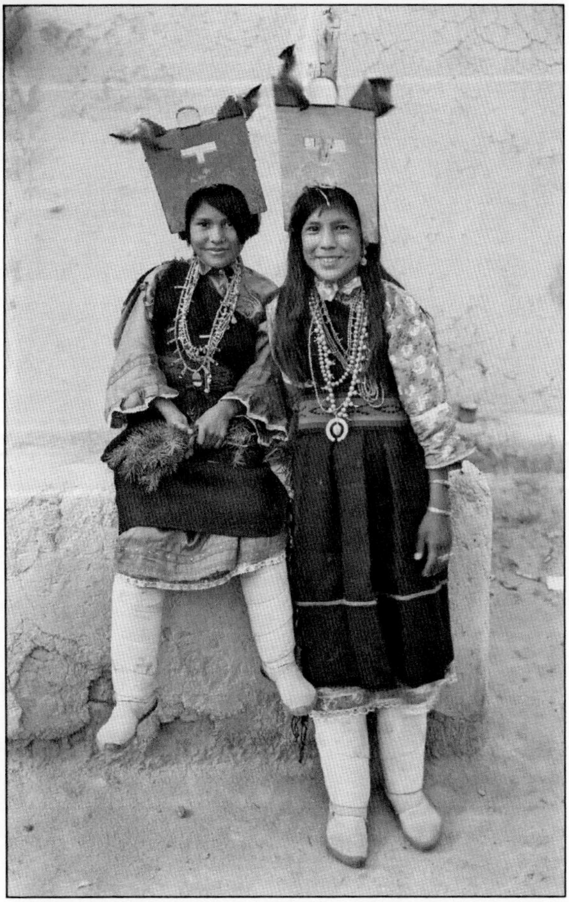

These girls are dressed for the corn dance. Dancing is still a very important part of Jemez Pueblo culture. On feast days, the general public is invited onto the pueblo to view the dances. (Courtesy Museums of New Mexico Palace of the Governors.)

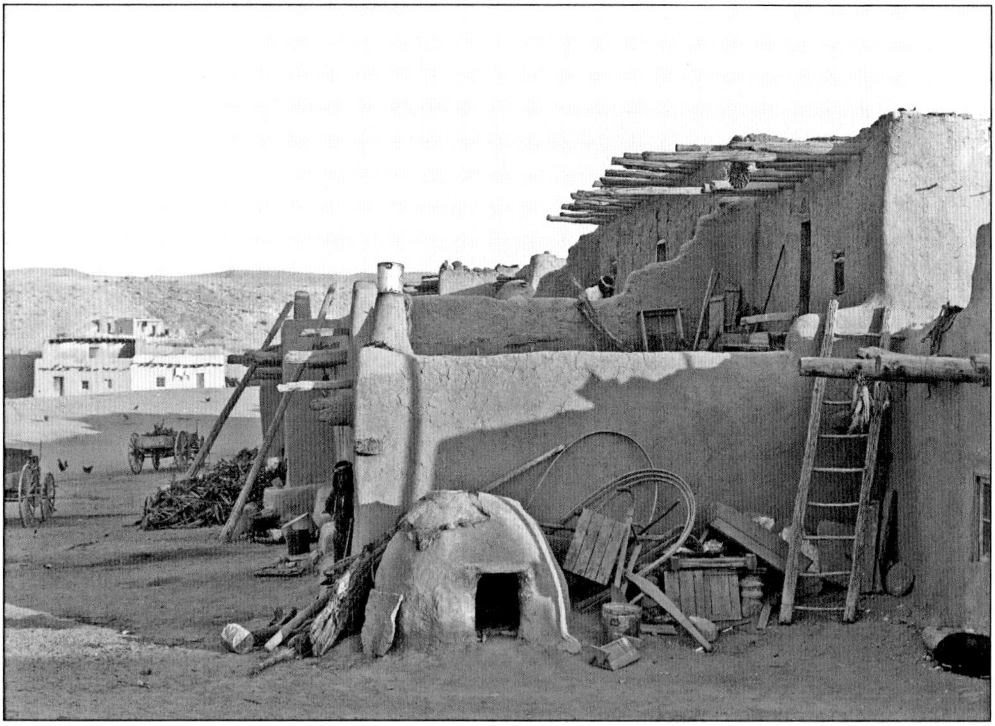

The main plaza of Pueblo of Jemez, looking west, includes a typical two-story building. *Hornos* (or adobe ovens) are still used today for baking bread. (Courtesy Museums of New Mexico Palace of the Governors.)

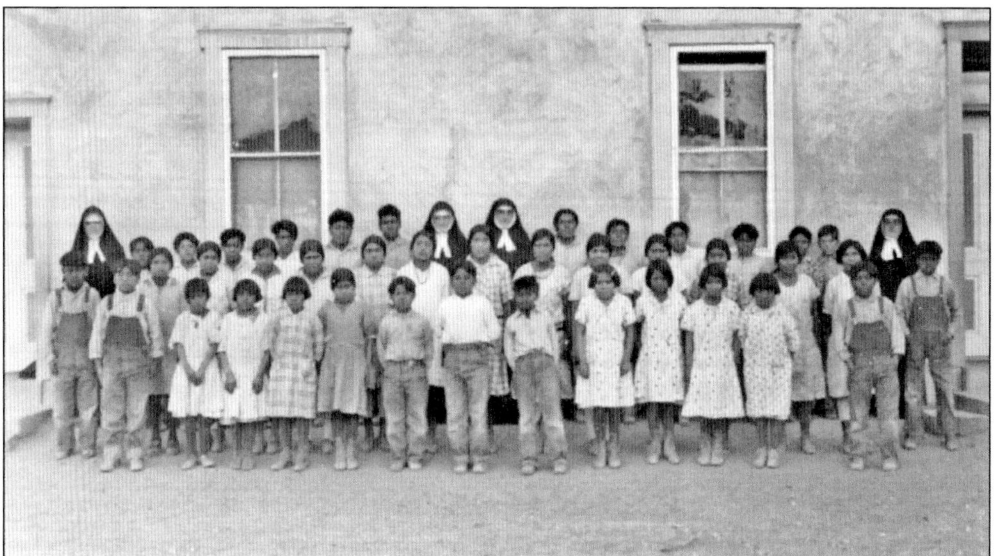

This is the 1931 graduating class of San Diego Mission School, which was founded in October 1906. It exists today as the San Diego Riverside Charter School. (Courtesy Department of Special Collections and University Archives, Marquette University Libraries.)

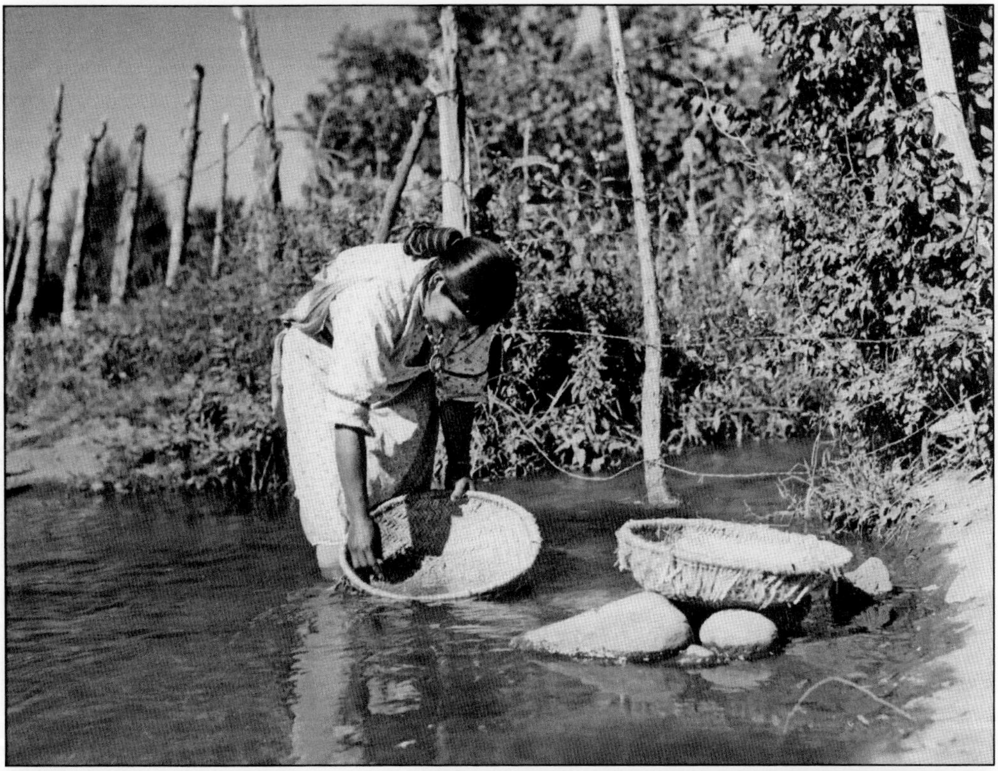

This *c.* 1936 picture of a woman washing wheat reflects a time when the pueblo was primarily an agricultural culture. Even today the Jemez Indians raise wheat and corn, chilies, and squash along with other crops. (Courtesy Museums of New Mexico Palace of the Governors.)

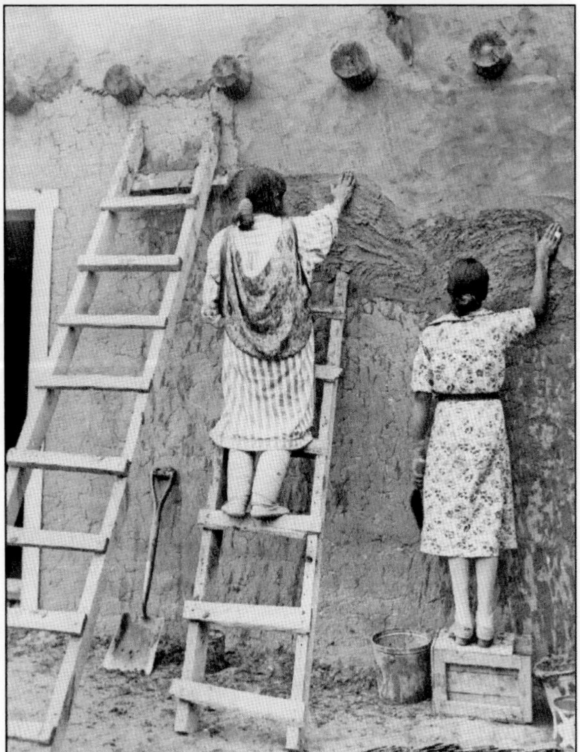

Adobe walls needed to constantly have new mud applied as the surface cracked and crumbled in the sun. (Courtesy Museums of New Mexico Palace of the Governors.)

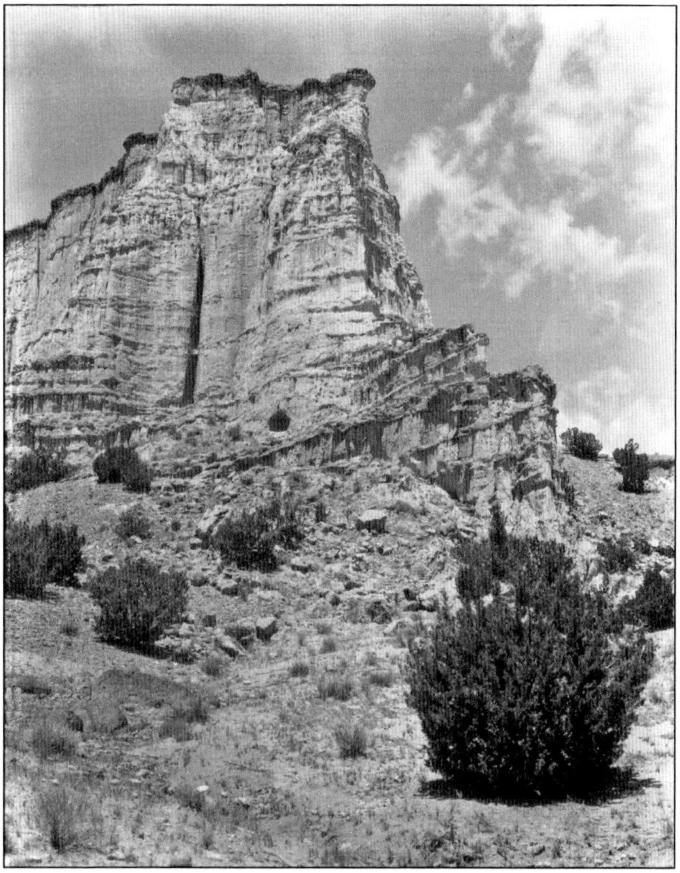

When attacked, the Native Americans often took refuge in the natural caves in the mesa. (Courtesy Museums of New Mexico Palace of the Governors.)

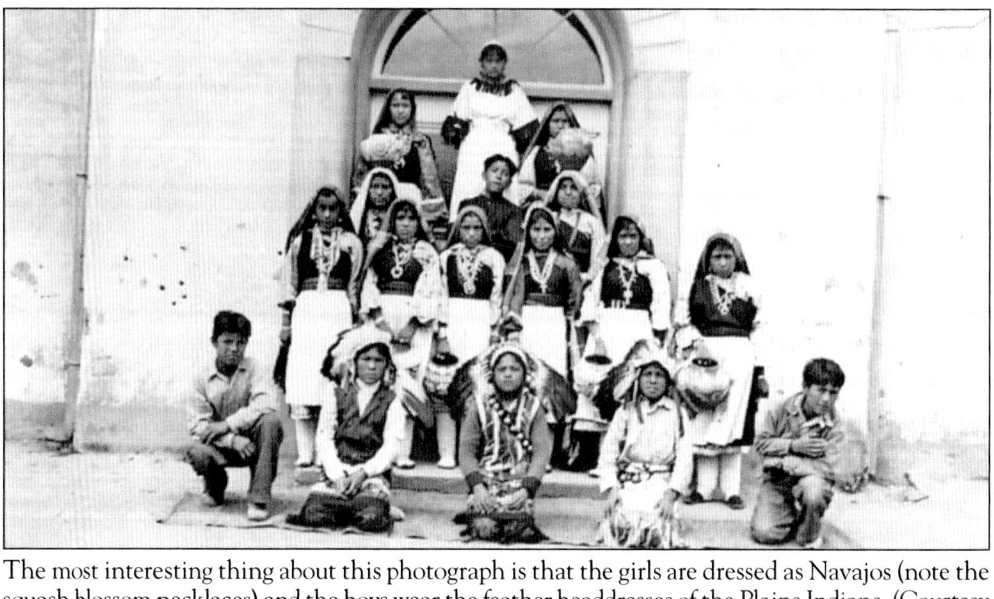

The most interesting thing about this photograph is that the girls are dressed as Navajos (note the squash blossom necklaces) and the boys wear the feather headdresses of the Plains Indians. (Courtesy Department of Special Collections and University Archives, Marquette University Libraries.)

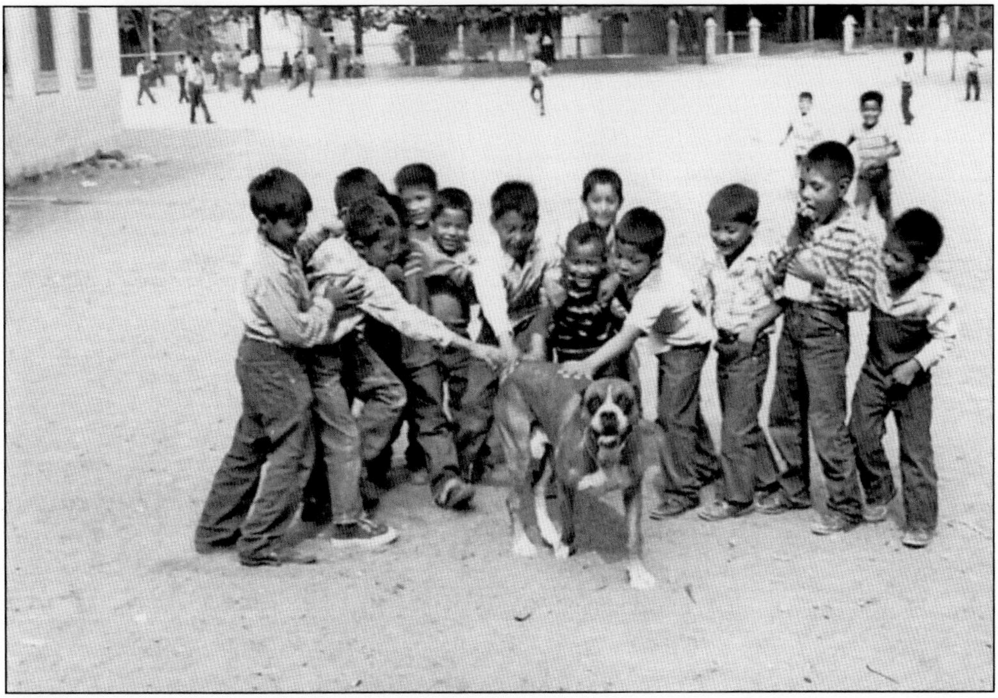

Children at the mission school welcome a new friend during recess. (Courtesy Department of Special Collections and University Archives, Marquette University Libraries.)

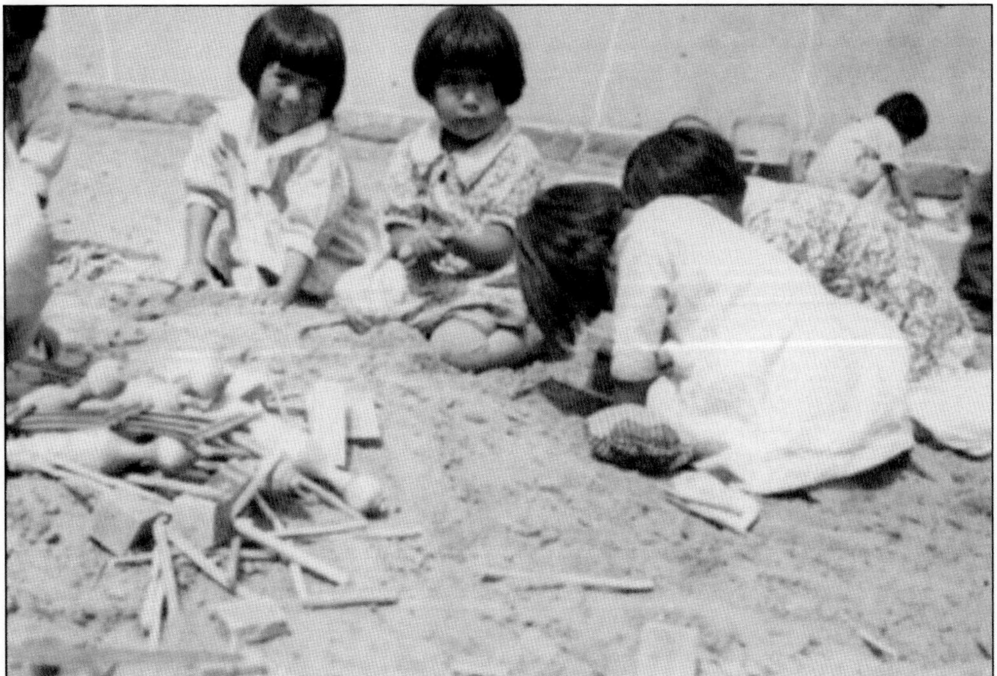

Girls play with wood scraps perhaps left over from the boys' woodworking class. (Courtesy Department of Special Collections and University Archives, Marquette University Libraries.)

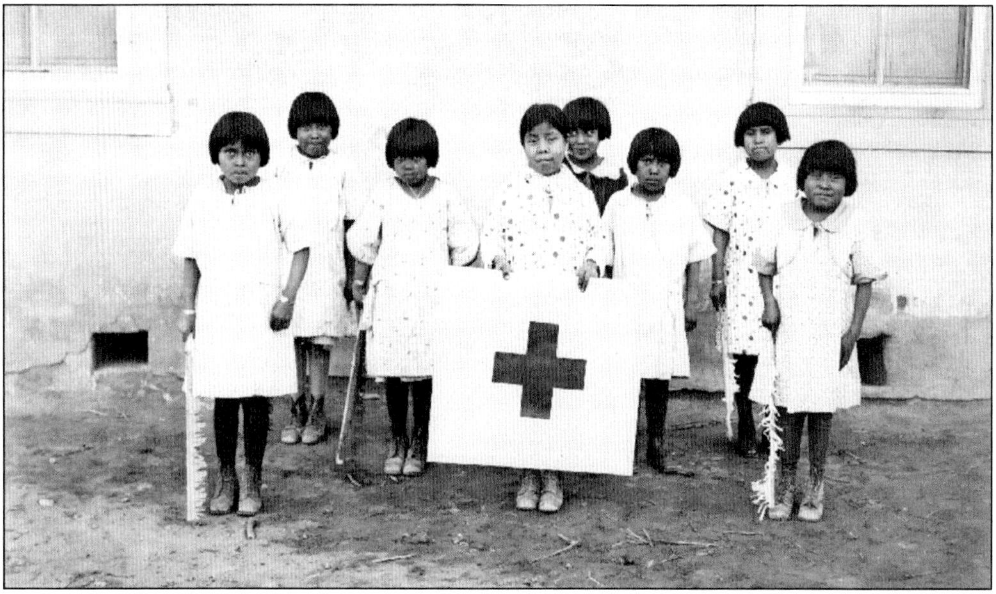

Pueblo children show their support for the Red Cross. The influence of the mission school is apparent. Children who had never heard of the Red Cross or other outside influences were schooled in their meaning. (Courtesy Department of Special Collections and University Archives, Marquette University Libraries.)

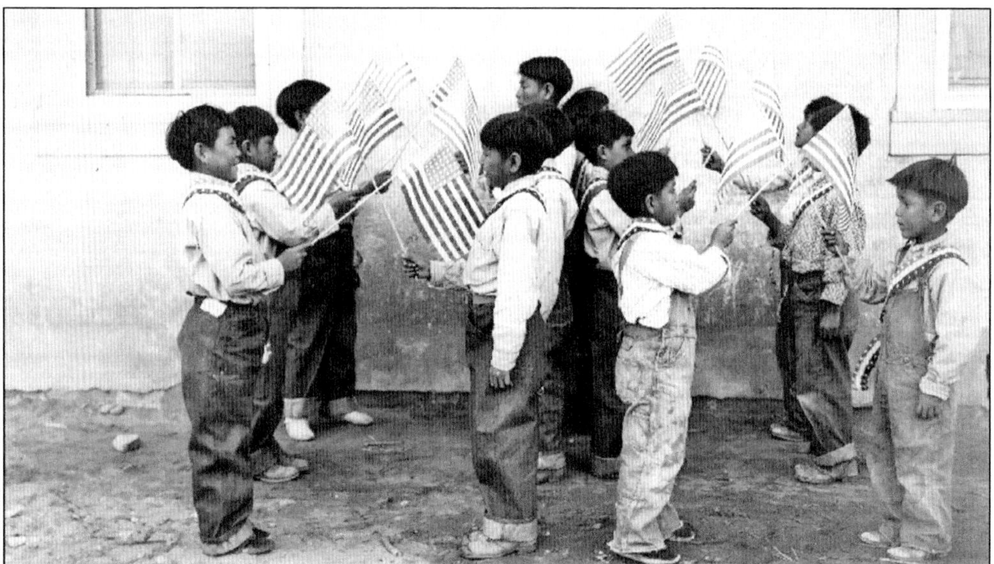

It is not clear what occasion caused such a display of patriotism on the part of these mission schoolchildren, but they wave their flags with enthusiasm. (Courtesy Department of Special Collections and University Archives, Marquette University Libraries.)

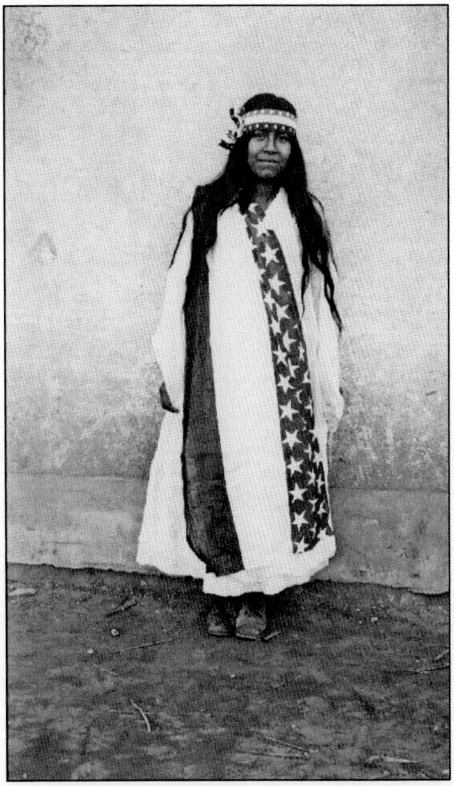

It is hard to know how this Jemez girl felt about being dressed in the stars and stripes. (Courtesy Department of Special Collections and University Archives, Marquette University Libraries.)

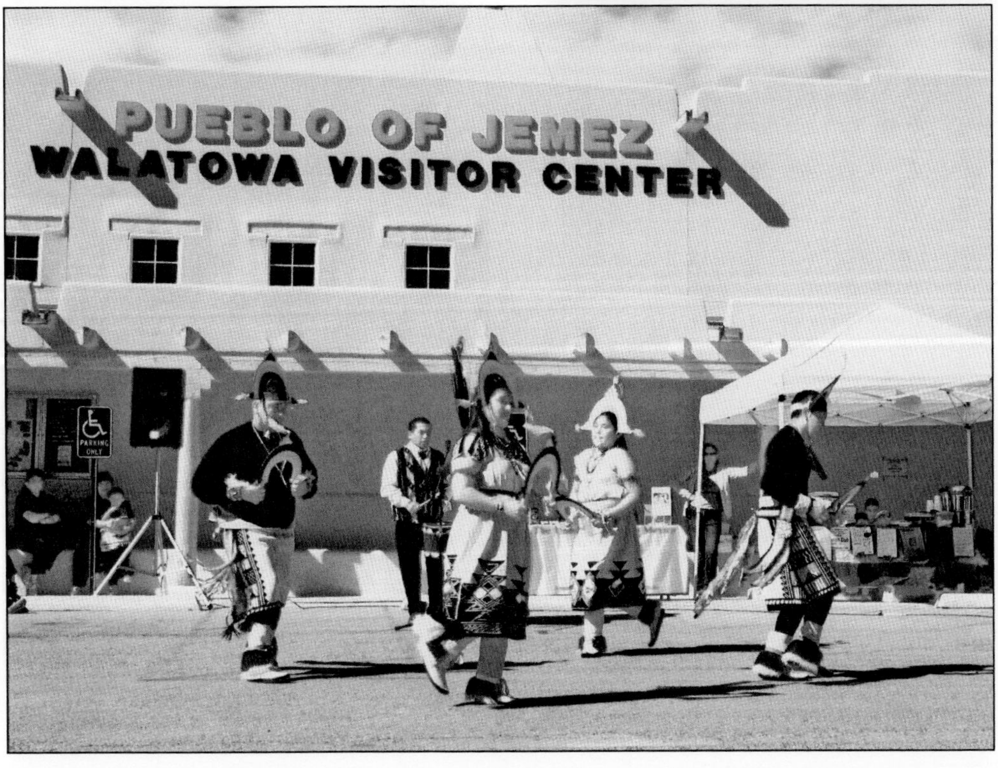

Buffalo dances take place in front of the visitor center. Since it is forbidden to take photographs in the Jemez Pueblo proper, the Jemez use a visitor/cultural center to provide access to Jemez Pueblo history and photo opportunities. (Courtesy Robert Borden.)

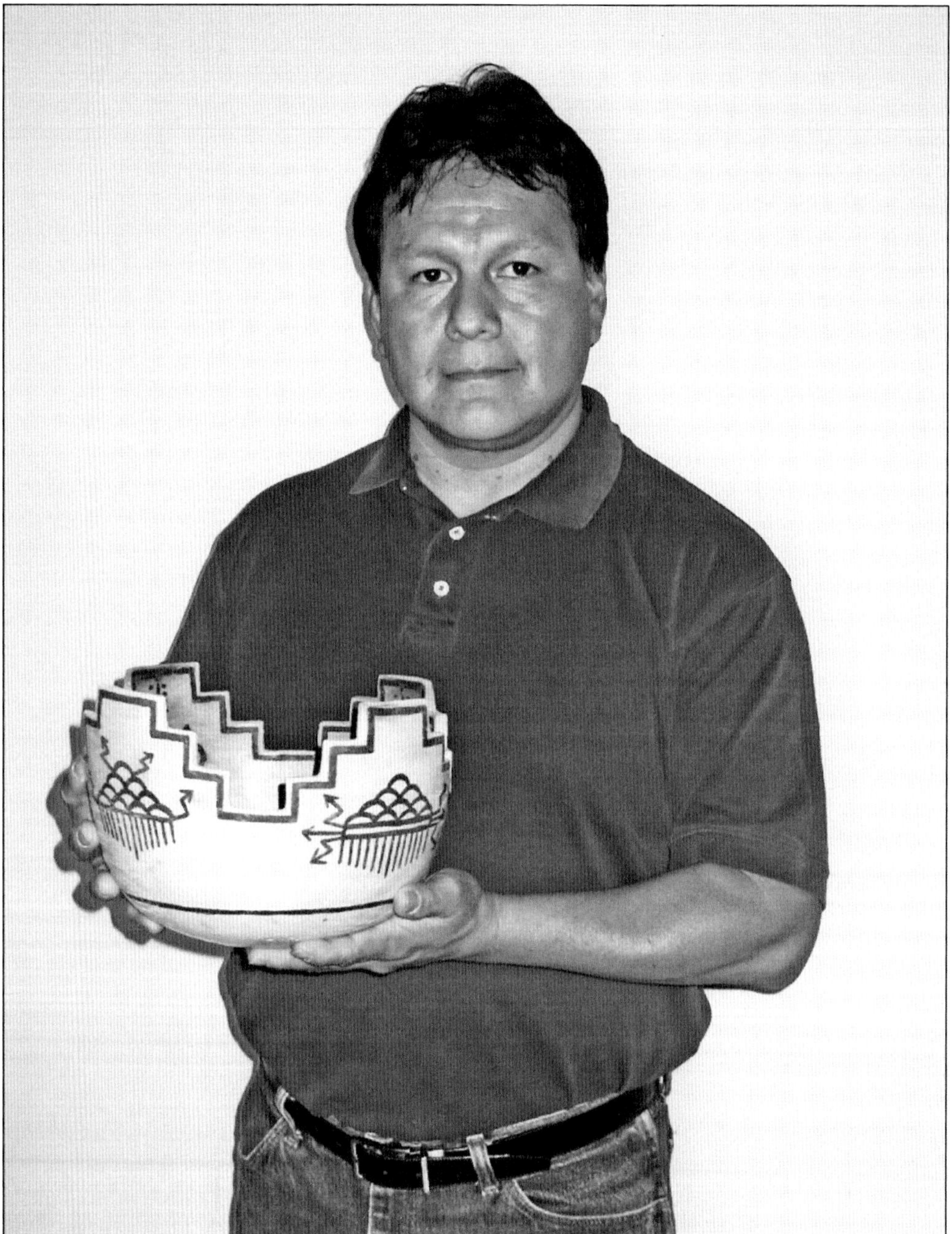

The Towa people carried black-on-white pottery to the Jemez Mountains in the 14th century. Theories vary as to why the Jemez abandoned their black-on-white pottery production. Soon knowledge of the technology was lost. In the late 1990s, Joshua Madalena began to search for the raw materials and the techniques to revive Jemez black-on-white pottery. Some of his pots are considered to be better than some of the originals from centuries ago. (Courtesy Robert Borden.)

This postcard shows Tony White Cloud, a well-known dancer, performing the hoop dance. Today the hoop dance is performed mainly at powwows. It is more closely associated with the Taos Pueblo. (Courtesy Jim Coad.)

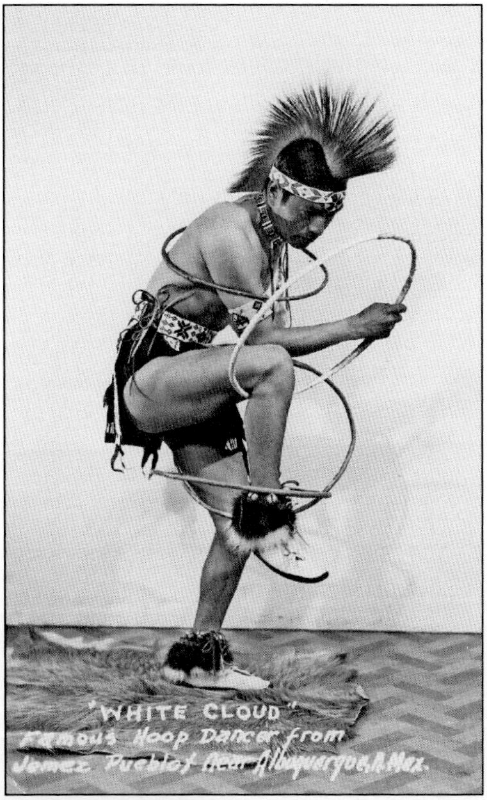

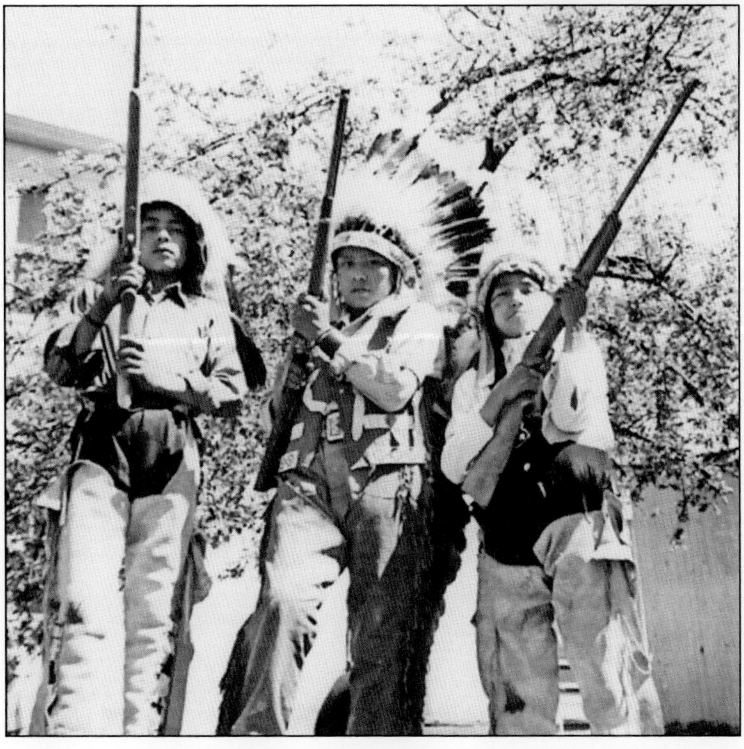

The Jemez people were not particularly warlike. These three boys in headdresses and carrying guns look more like they come from a warrior tribe. The Jemez, for example, do not wear feather headdresses of this type. (Courtesy Department of Special Collections and University Archives, Marquette University Libraries.)

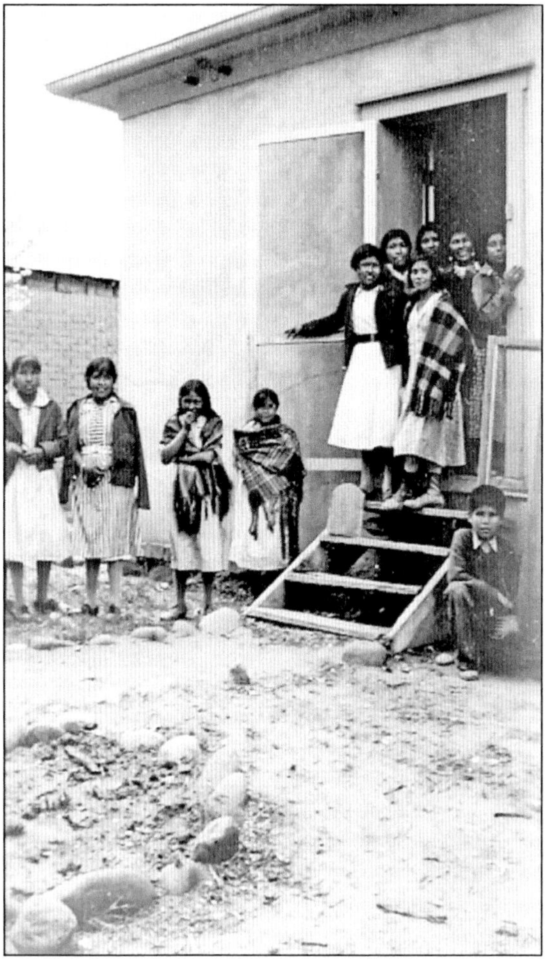

This is a sewing class in front of Old Convent School in 1945. (Courtesy Robert Borden.)

This drawing of the Jemez Monument ruins in 1849 by Richard H. Kern comes from a sketch by Edward M. Kern. Both Kerns traveled with the expedition; often Edward would do a sketch that was then made into a drawing by Richard. (Courtesy Academy of Natural Sciences of Philadelphia.)

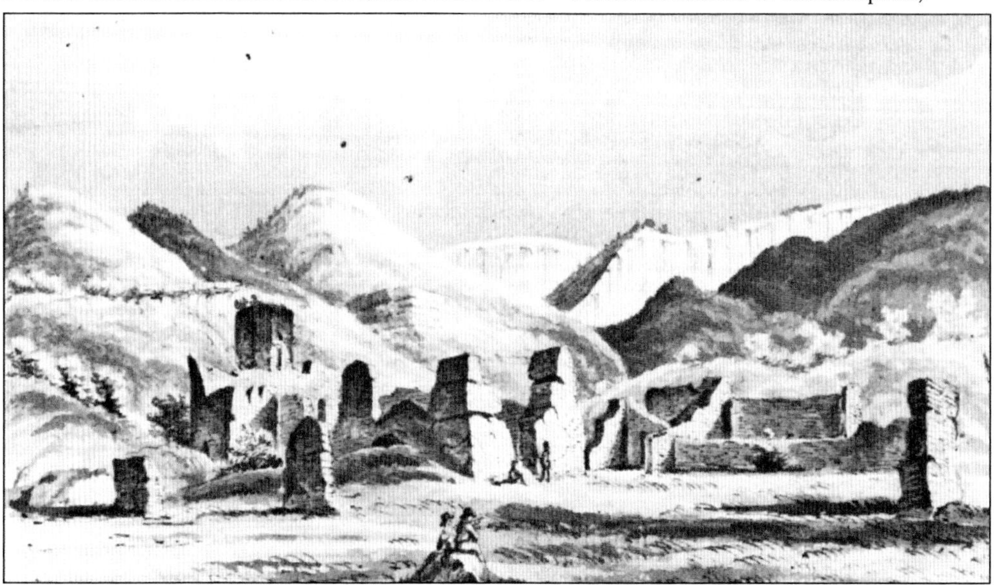

Two

Those Were the Days

Being a pioneer even in the early part of the 20th century was no easy matter. Those who did not live in Jemez Springs were responsible for providing most of their own food. There would be an outhouse and a dog and chickens living under the house porch. A cow not only provided milk, butter, and cheese for the family but something to trade for seed, flour, and other essentials. Water had to be hauled from the river, and clothes were hung on the bushes to dry. Life was lonely, broken only occasionally by a visitor.

Edwin Fluke kept a diary from 1913 to 1914, reprinted in *Jemez Mountain Views* in April 1976. This is a typical entry:

> Dec. 2—2 below zero 6:30 a.m. Clear. The sun is bright and very warm. Charlie is churning. Harry and George have gone to split and saw up a dead tree. Charlie got dinner and when we were eating Toney and Abram came. Toney brought the mail and 106 pounds of apples, the coat and gloves got here. We rec'd the bills from Korber tho made out in Fluke Bros. name. I sent the mail down with Toney. This is George's birthday. He is 21 years old. Pound, Pound. It snowed most all afternoon. Two of the traps were sprung. Commenced to feed the pigs rutabagas and turnips.

The Fentons and the Routledges were two families who lived in the outback, as it were. They often socialized, and their children grew up knowing one another.

Jemez Springs itself was somewhat more refined. The Blocks, one of the few non-Spanish families in Jemez, were entrepreneurs. They built a hotel, general store, and several residences. Block was the most important man in Jemez Springs by many accounts. He was a banker and military expert. If anyone had real estate to sell, Block would find a buyer.

Moses Abousleman, who was originally from Lebanon, came to Jemez Springs from the pueblo in 1910 and built the big white house in the center of town. He and his family were also people of means. Abousleman owned a store, a saloon, a livery stable, and a bathhouse.

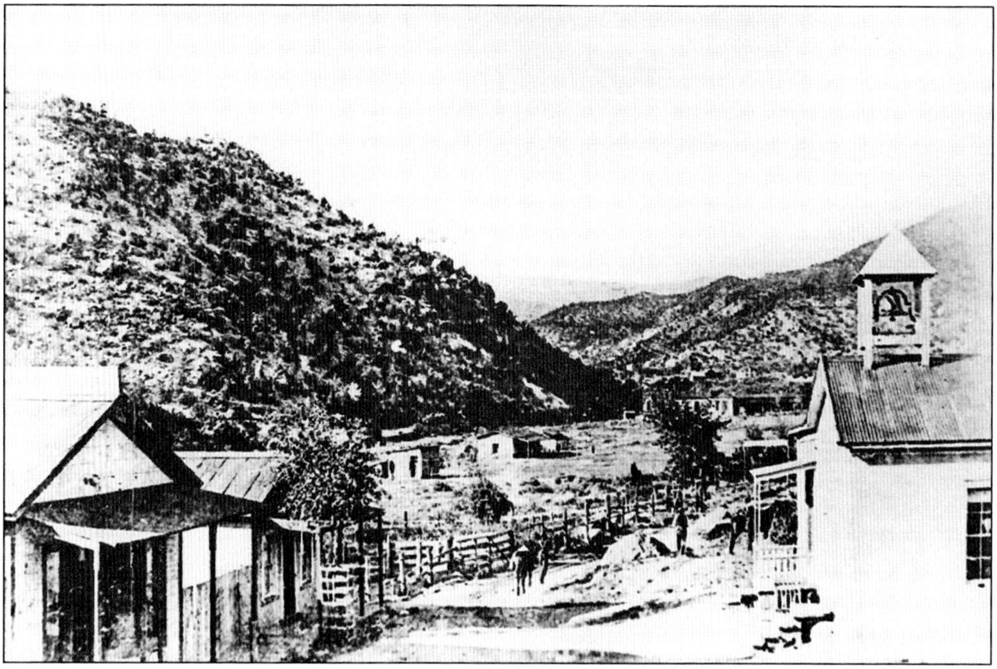

This picture of Jemez Springs in the late 1890s provides a good view of the newly built Jemez Springs Community Presbyterian Church. Across the street is the building that became the Jemez Mountain Inn. Where the village complex stands is all grassland. (Courtesy 2005 July 4 Committee.)

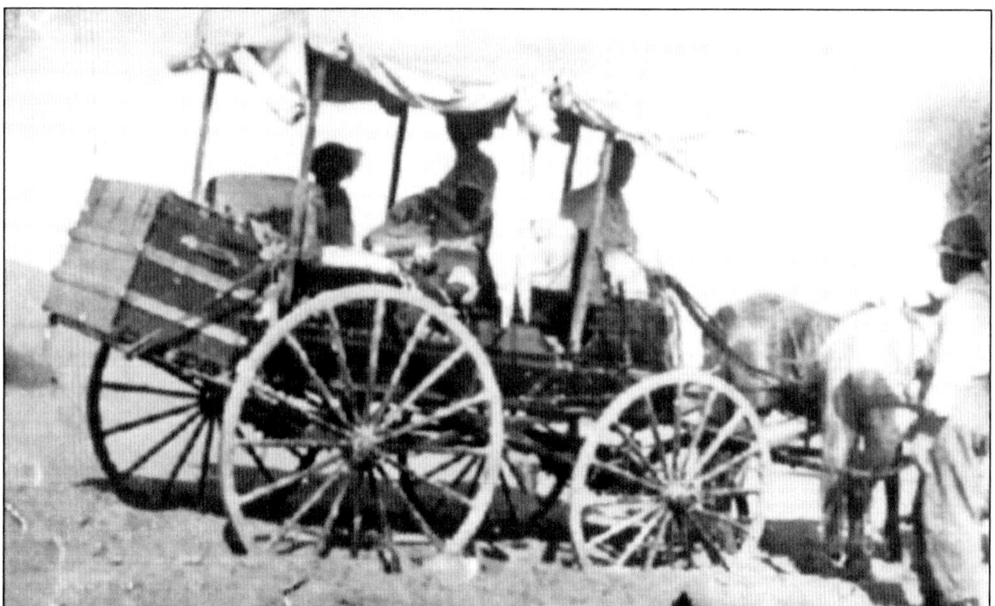

The trip to Bernalillo and back could take several days, especially when the wagon wheels got stuck in the dirt. (Courtesy 2005 July 4 Committee.)

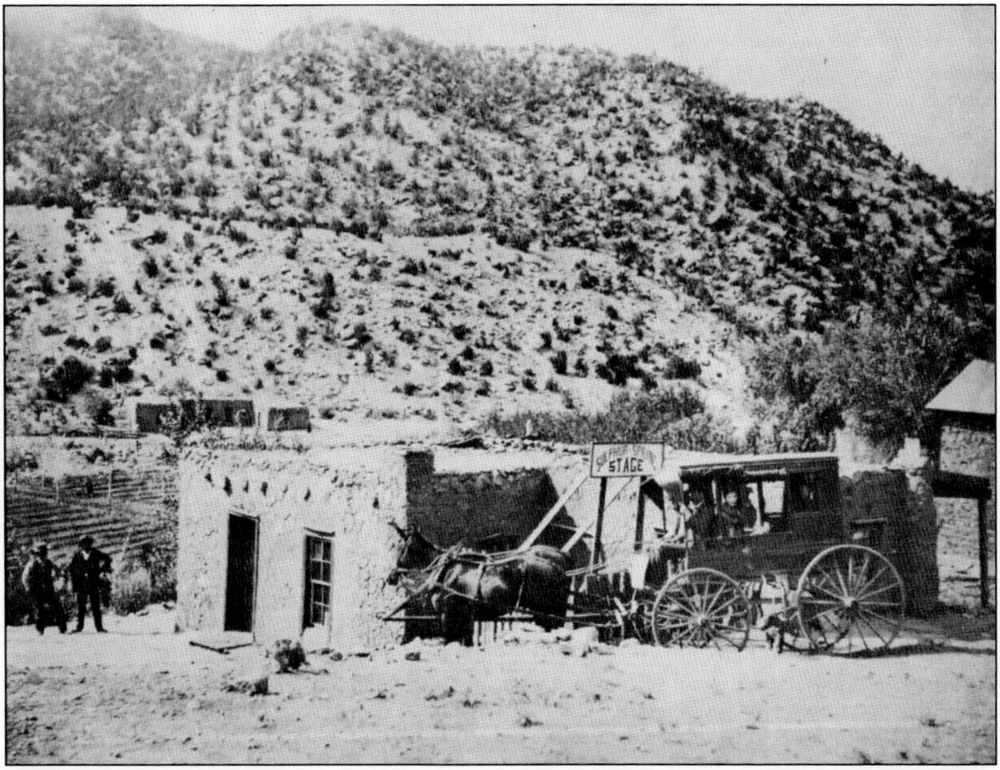

Stage stations have figured prominently in any number of Western movies. This 1897 photograph shows a real-life stage station near Jemez. (Museum of New Mexico photograph, courtesy Paul Adams.)

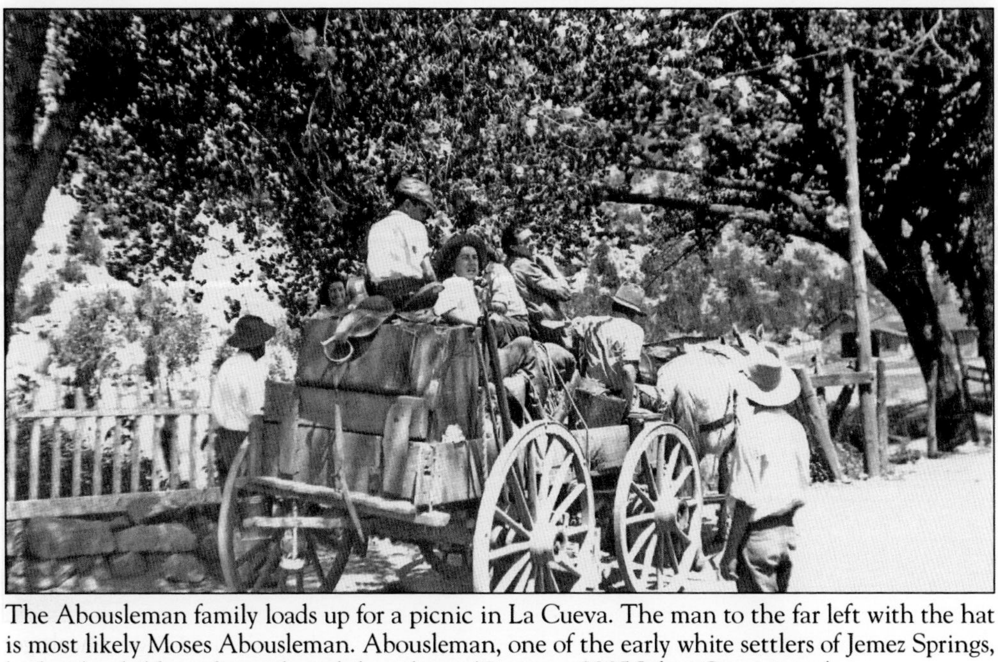

The Abousleman family loads up for a picnic in La Cueva. The man to the far left with the hat is most likely Moses Abousleman. Abousleman, one of the early white settlers of Jemez Springs, had eight children: five girls and three boys. (Courtesy 2005 July 4 Committee.)

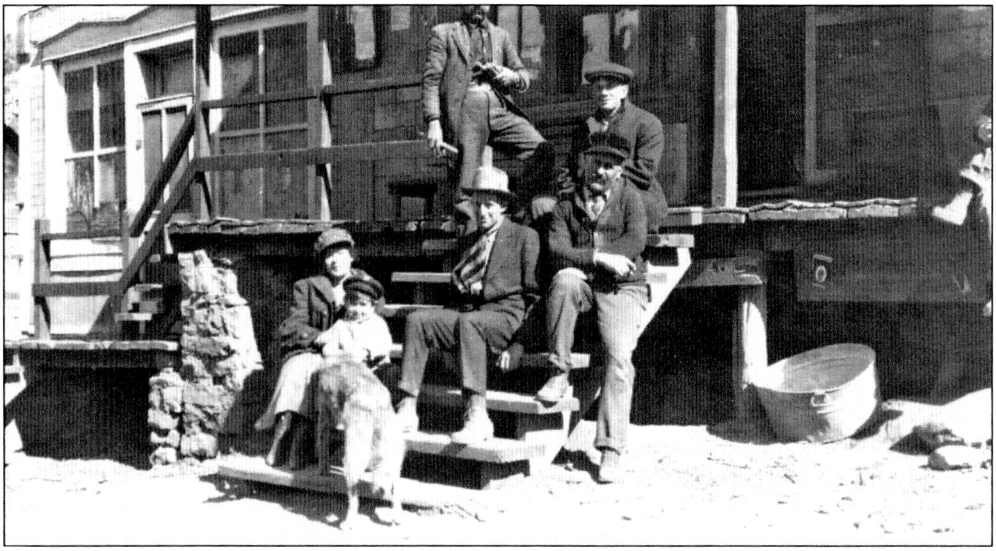

Moses Abousleman was an avid entrepreneur. He dealt in sheep (he once owned as many as 40,000), general merchandise, real estate, farming, cattle, a livery stable, a saloon, and a bathhouse. His house in the center of town is still standing. It is made of rock and adobe and has 21 rooms. Here a group of locals sit on the steps of his general store. (Courtesy Tom Abousleman.)

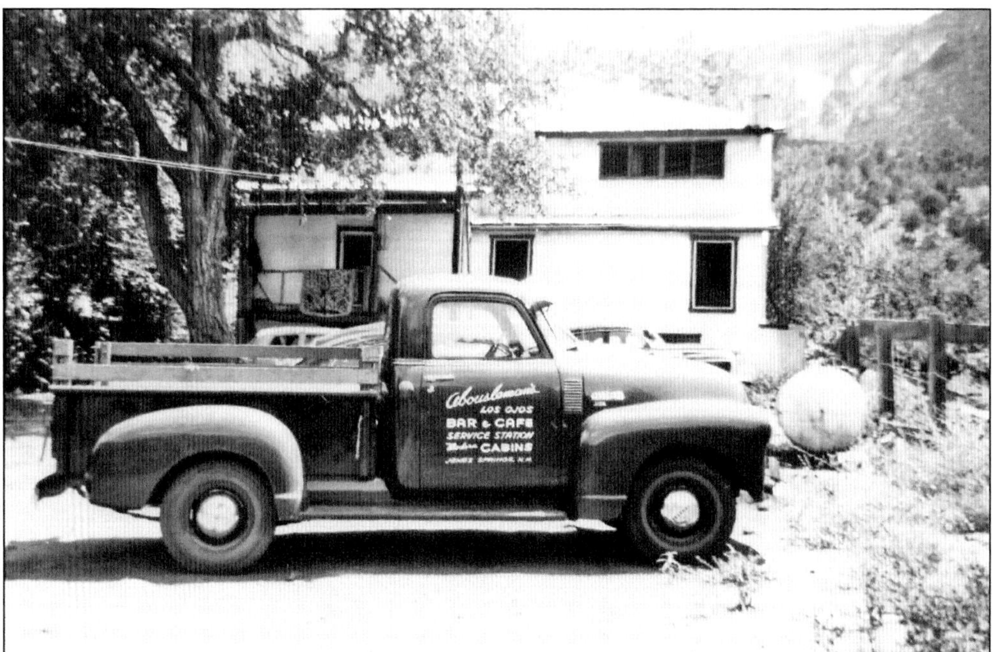

Even after World War II, the Aboușlemans had multiple businesses as attested to by the lettering on this truck parked in back of the Abousleman house. (Courtesy 2005 July 4 Committee.)

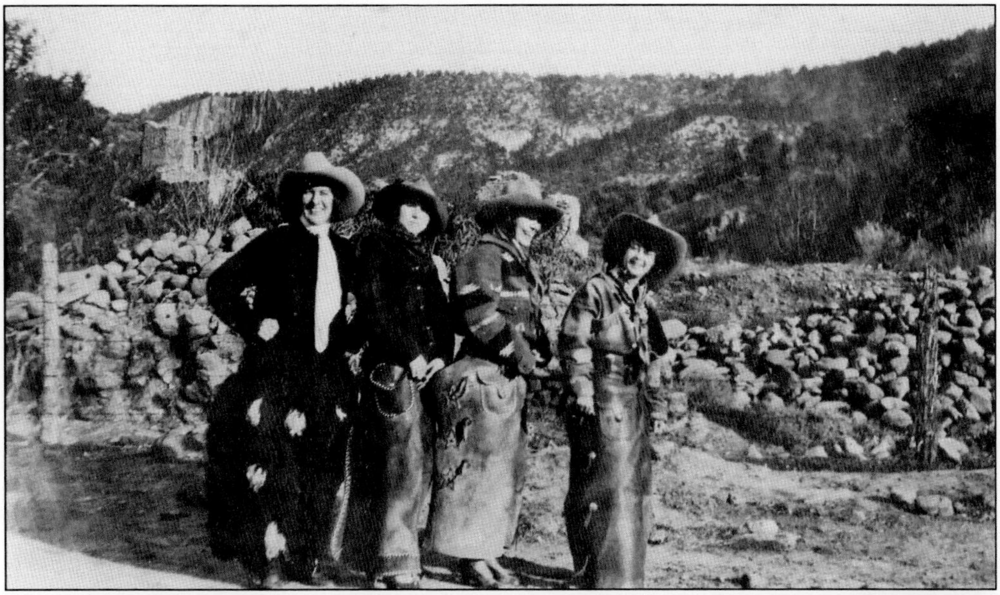

Some of the girls in Jemez Springs liked to dress up in fancy cowgirl gear and have their picture taken by some old ruins. These girls are in front of the ruins of the Esperanza Hotel sometime in the 1920s. (Courtesy 2005 July 4 Committee.)

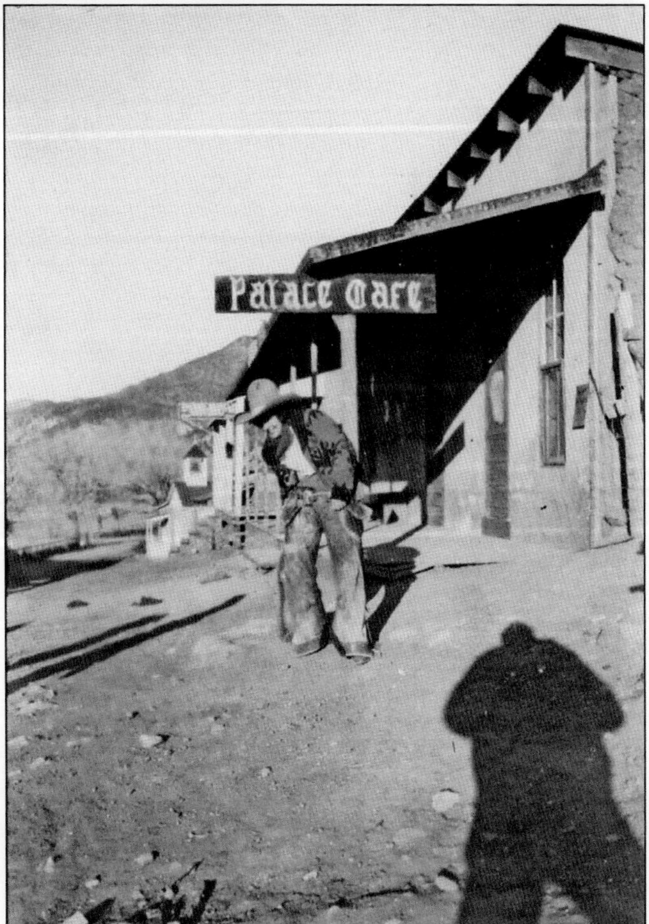

A cowgirl poses in front of the Palace Café, probably in the 1920s, just south of the Jemez Springs Community Presbyterian Church in Jemez Springs. The photographer casts his shadow in the afternoon sun. (Courtesy Tom Abousleman.)

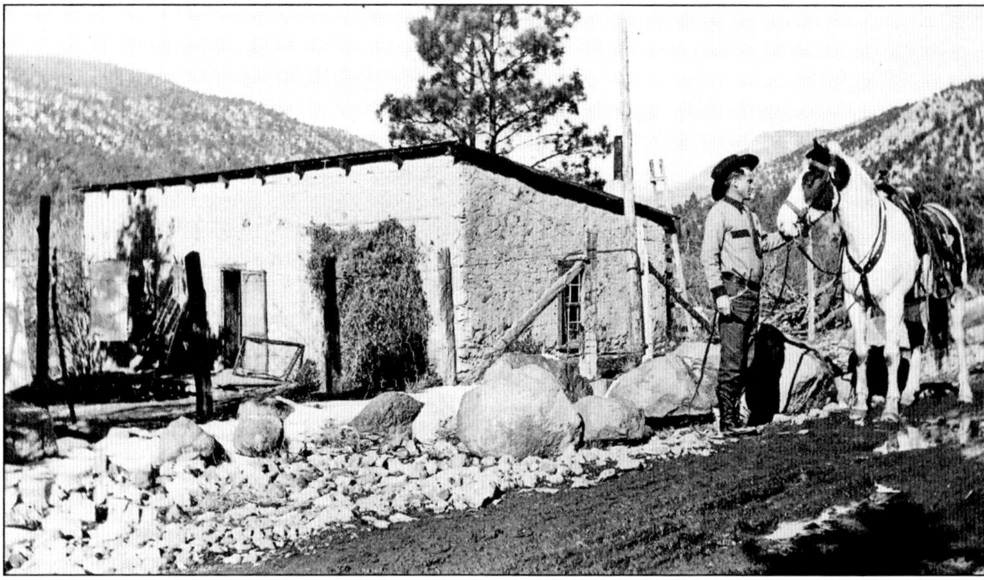

Shorty Kelso was known far and wide as an expert horseman and rodeo rider. (Courtesy 2005 July 4 Committee.)

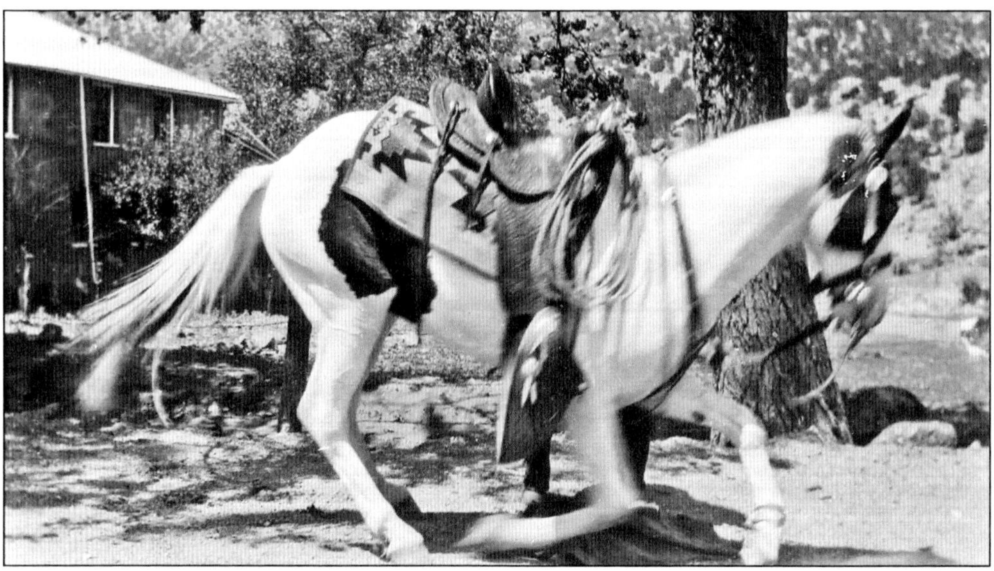

Shorty was good at teaching tricks to horses. Here he has his horse kneeling. (Courtesy 2005 July 4 Committee.)

Art Routledge, pictured here in 1910, was a fancy dresser who rode a fancy horse. He went to Hollywood to try to break into the movies. To impress Ethel McCloskey (who became his wife), he donned his buckskins and put on a Wild West show in front of her house. (Courtesy 2005 July 4 Committee.)

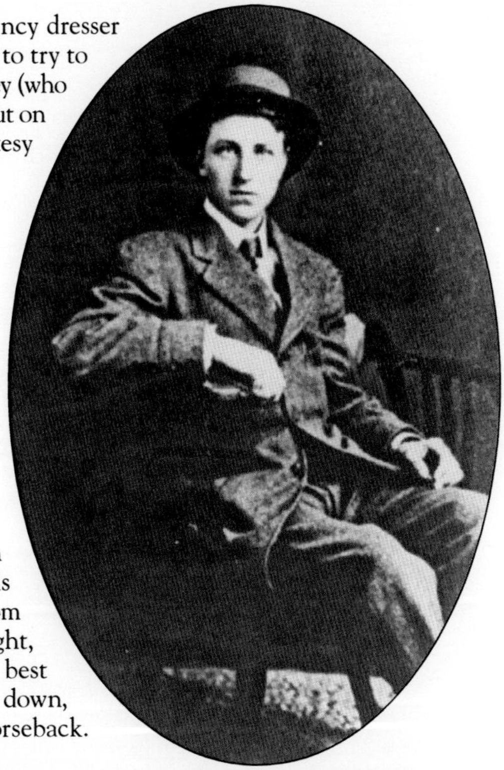

Art attempted to make a name for himself in Hollywood with his trick riding. According to his son Joseph, he could pick up a handkerchief from the ground and pivot to the left and to the right, bouncing to the ground and up again. But his best talent was with a rope. He could spin a loop up, down, and around and dance in and out of it on horseback. (Courtesy 2005 July 4 Committee.)

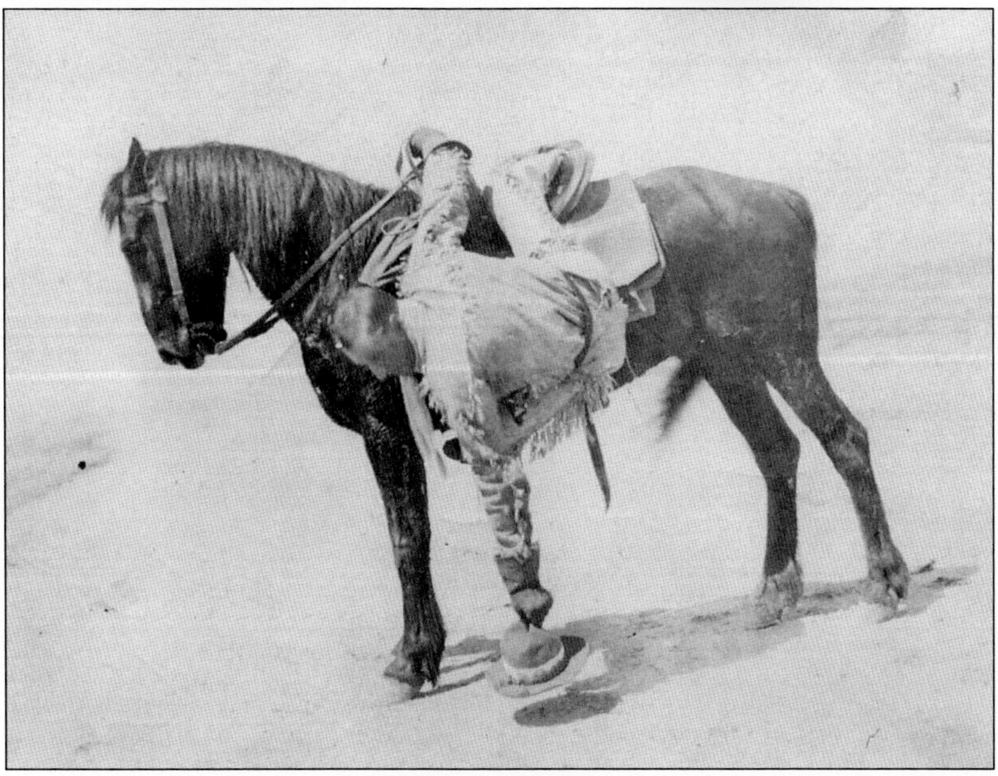

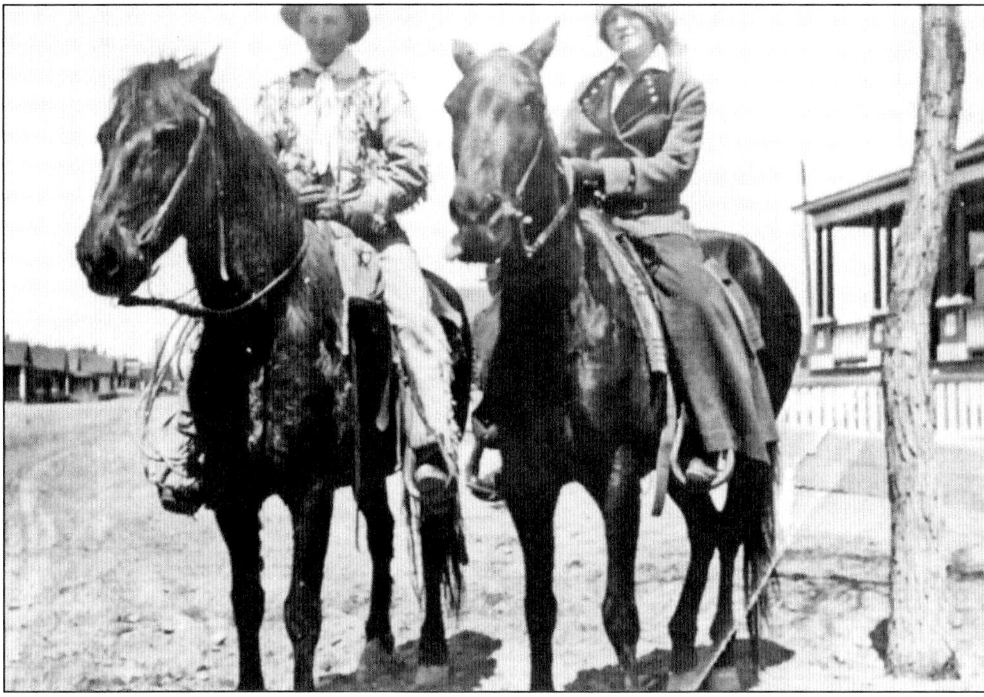

Art and Ethel Routledge moved to Bland, formerly a roaring mining town where Art had been born. Only a few people were left, hoping the mine would reopen. Ethel made quite a splash with her fine city clothes and genteel manner. (Courtesy 2005 July 4 Committee.)

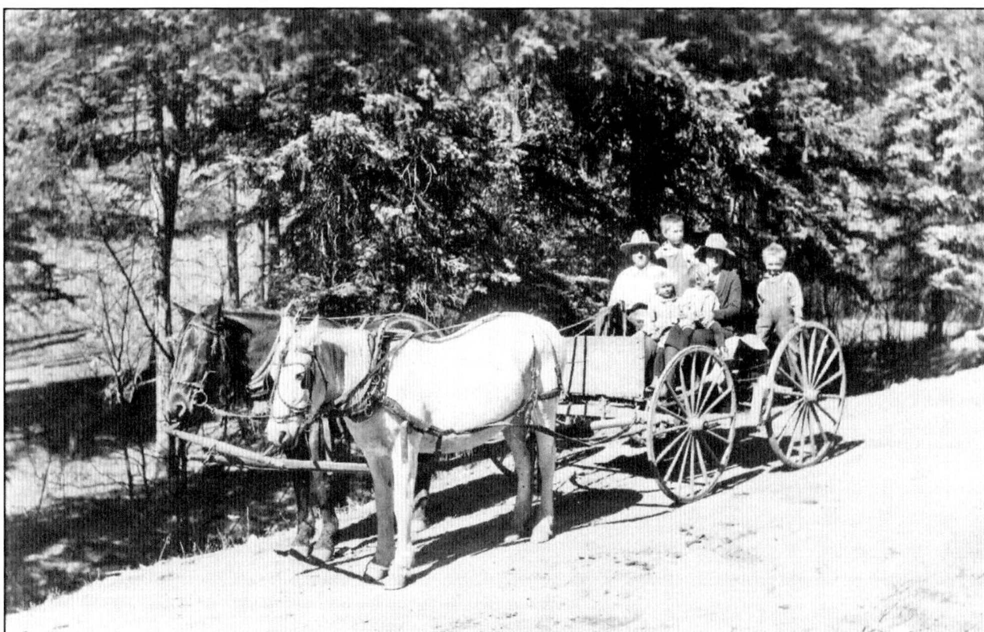

The Routledge family goes for an outing in their buckboard. The 150-mile round-trip to Albuquerque and back could be bitter cold or hot and dusty. The trip involved staying with a family at night, sometimes at the Indian Pueblo or with a Mexican family. (Courtesy 2005 July 4 Committee.)

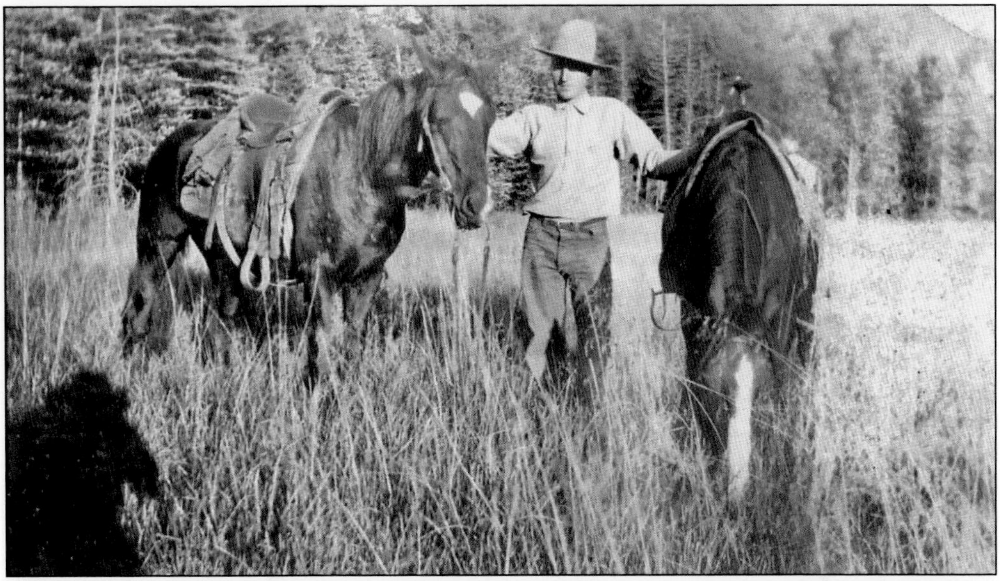

Art Routledge was part of an American Expeditionary Force that went into Mexico in search of Pancho Villa. Art drove a pair of mules pulling a supply wagon. This photograph was taken in 1920 after he returned from service. (Courtesy 2005 July 4 Committee.)

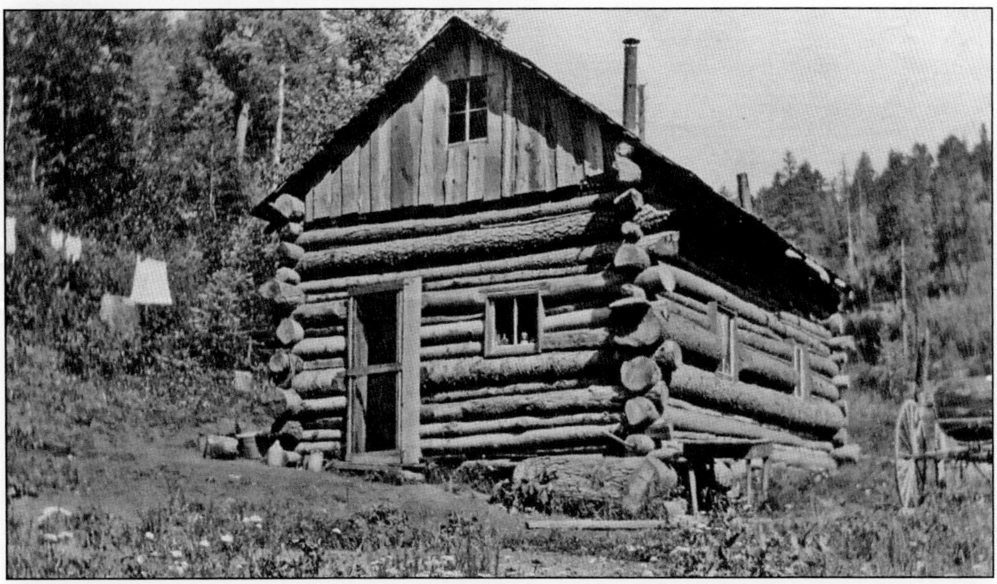

The Routledges' one-room cabin in Mediodia Canyon was on an unproved homestead. As it was too far to travel every day from Bland to the cabin site, Art took his axe, saw, camping gear, and the team and wagon. He got up every day at 4:00 a.m. and worked until it was dark. (Courtesy 2005 July 4 Committee.)

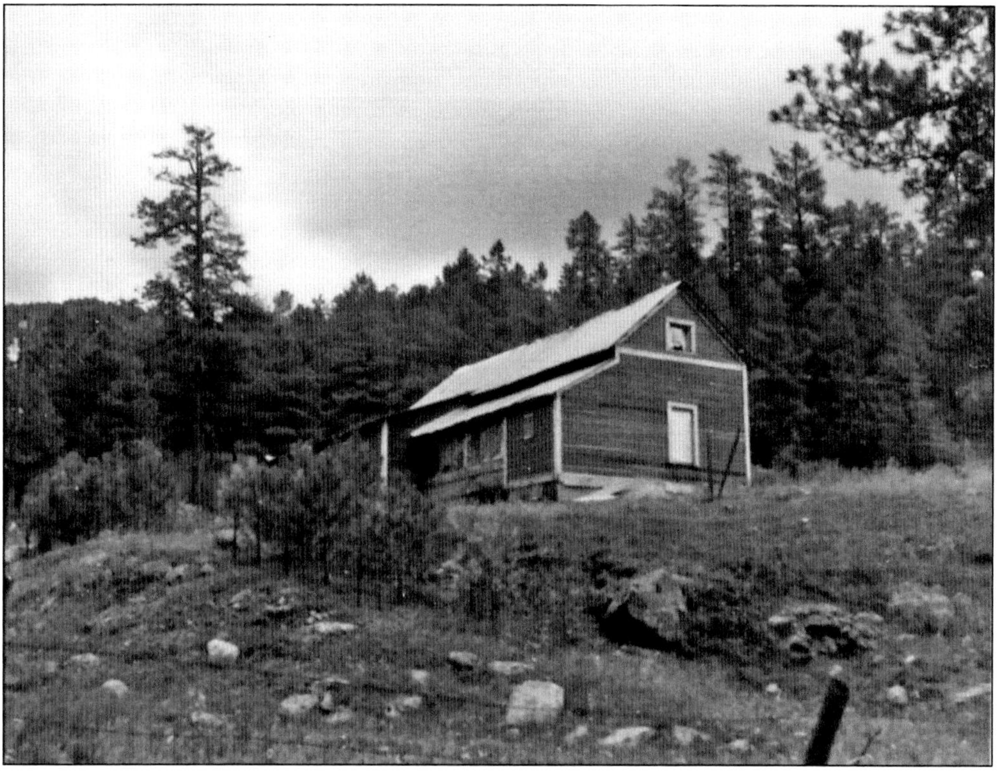

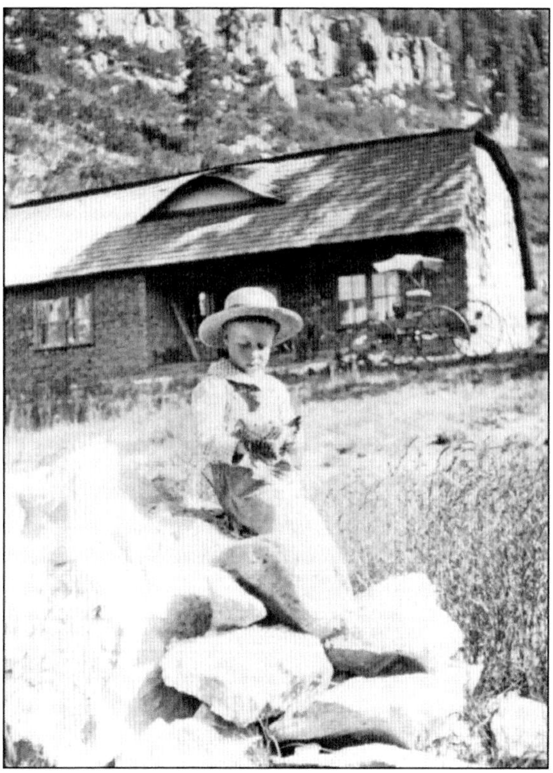

This was the Freelove Ranch that Art bought from Mr. Block. The ranch was isolated, and no one had any money to buy it. But Art worked out a deal to make payments of $25 a month for 100 months. This is the ranch on which the Routledge children grew up. (Courtesy 2005 July 4 Committee.)

Hugh Miller tends to an injured flicker. (Courtesy 2005 July 4 Committee.)

Daniel Garcia was an outlaw, or at least as close to one as there was in Jemez Springs. Rumor had it that he either killed a man or was wanted by the law. Friends smuggled him out of town. Daniel got as far as Colorado and was never heard from again. (Courtesy Delores Garcia.)

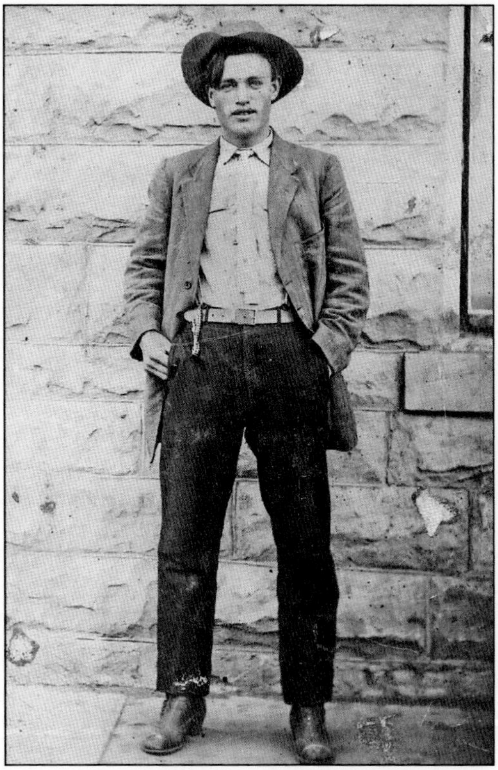

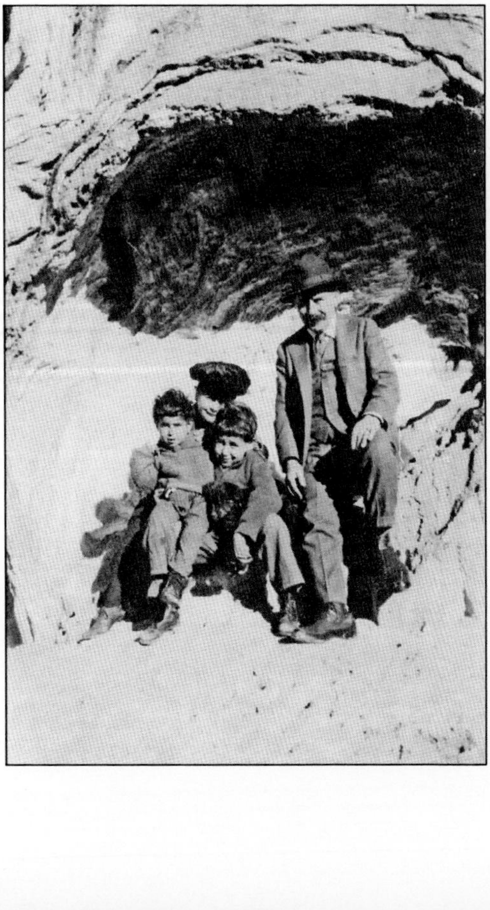

This may be Moses Abousleman and some of the Abousleman children at Soda Dam. The dam was a popular place for photography. (Courtesy 2005 July 4 Committee.)

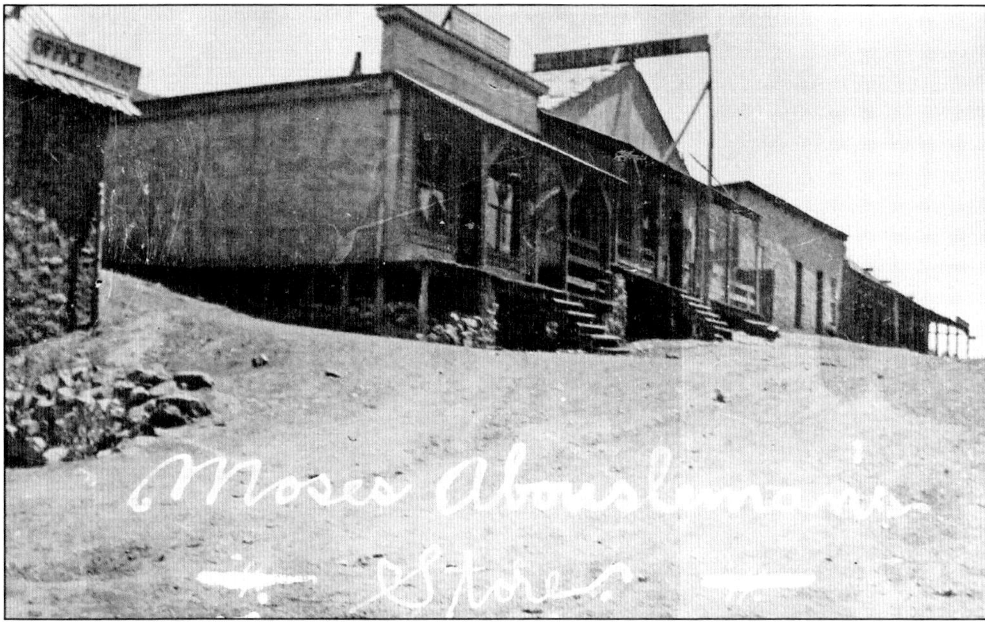

Moses Abousleman's store was in downtown Jemez Springs. (Courtesy Paul Adams.)

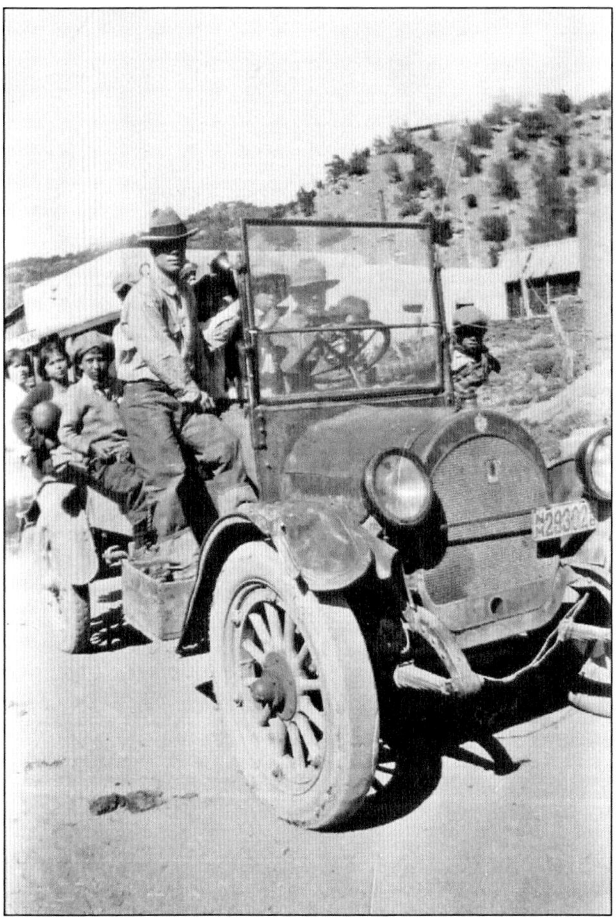

The Abousleman children take a wild car ride through downtown Jemez Springs. (Courtesy 2005 July 4 Committee.)

Elijah McLean Fenton Jr. was known as "Mac." His father, Elijah McLean Fenton Sr., came to New Mexico as a missionary, stationed at the pueblo. But en route to his parishes, he discovered areas that were open for homesteading. In 1892, he filed claim on 160 acres. He increased his holdings to 640 acres, buying the homesteads of relatives. Fenton Lake, now a state park, is named for him. (Courtesy 2005 July 4 Committee.)

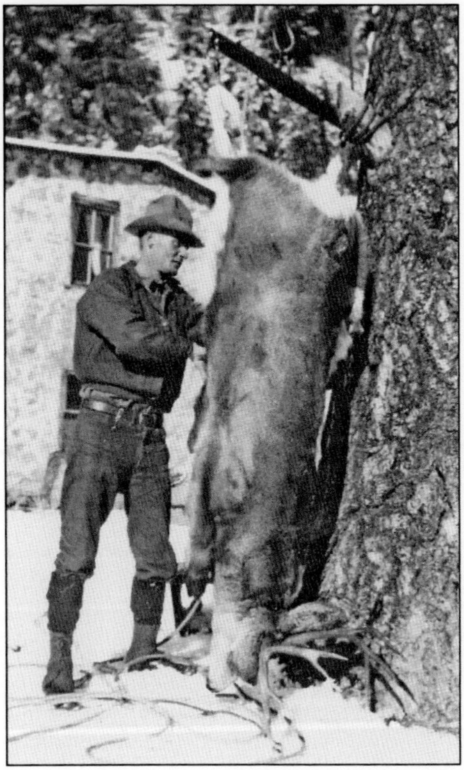

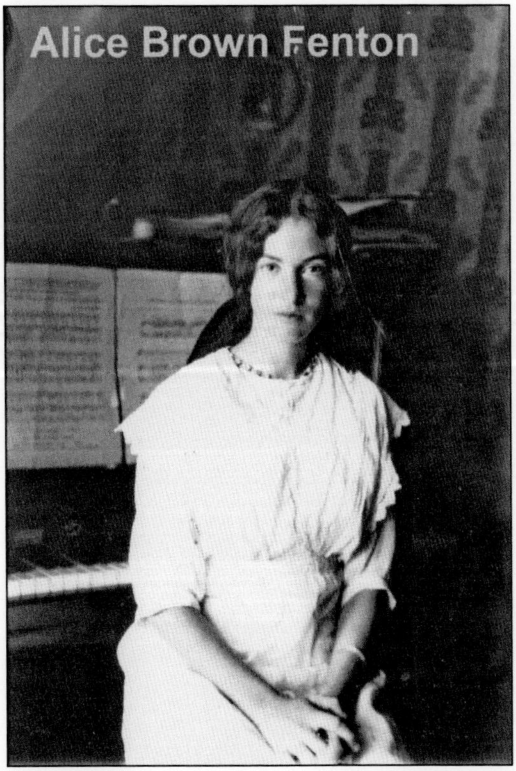

Alice Brown Fenton was the wife of Mac Fenton. She and Mac had five children: Stewart, Charles, Bob, Jessie, and Mary. Mary married Lew Caldwell, who worked in the lumber business, and they now live in Ponderosa. (Courtesy 2005 July 4 Committee.)

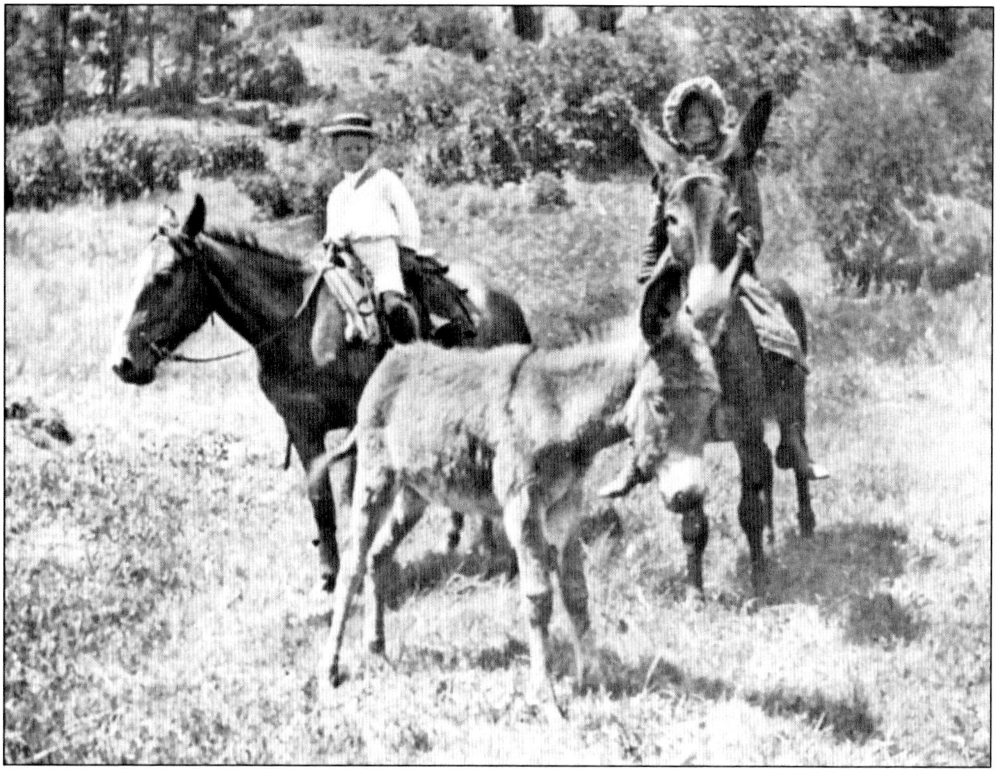

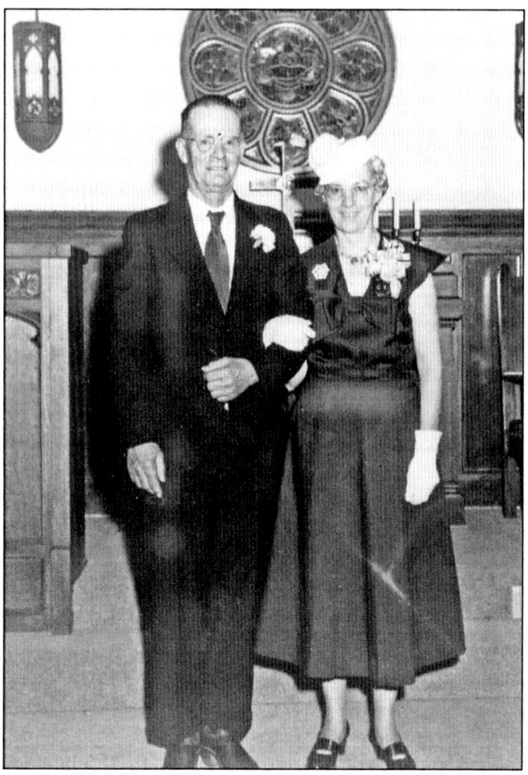

Mac and his sister Jean had horses to ride when they were young. (Courtesy 2005 July 4 Committee.)

Mac and Alice Fenton are pictured here in 1956. (Courtesy 2005 July 4 Committee.)

Tom Abousleman believes this photograph is of his brother Fred Abousleman and Shorty Kelso (left). Shorty may be teaching him to ride. (Courtesy Tom Abousleman.)

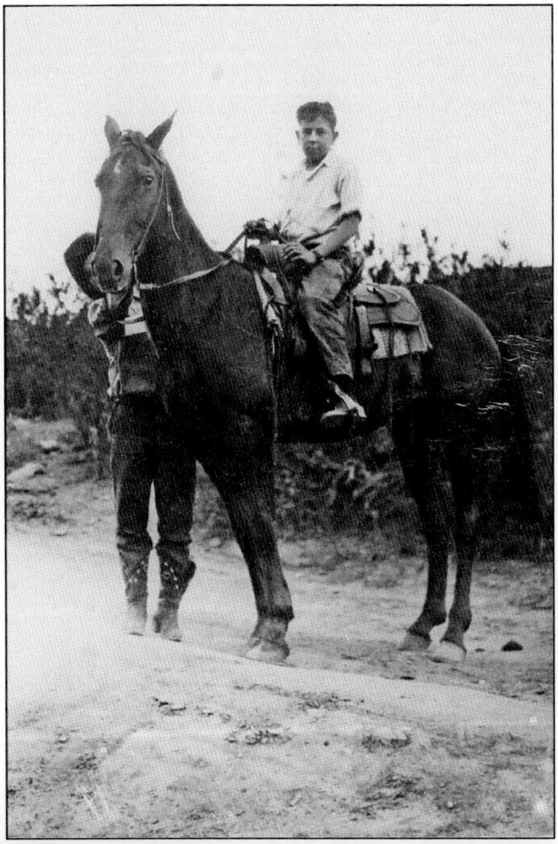

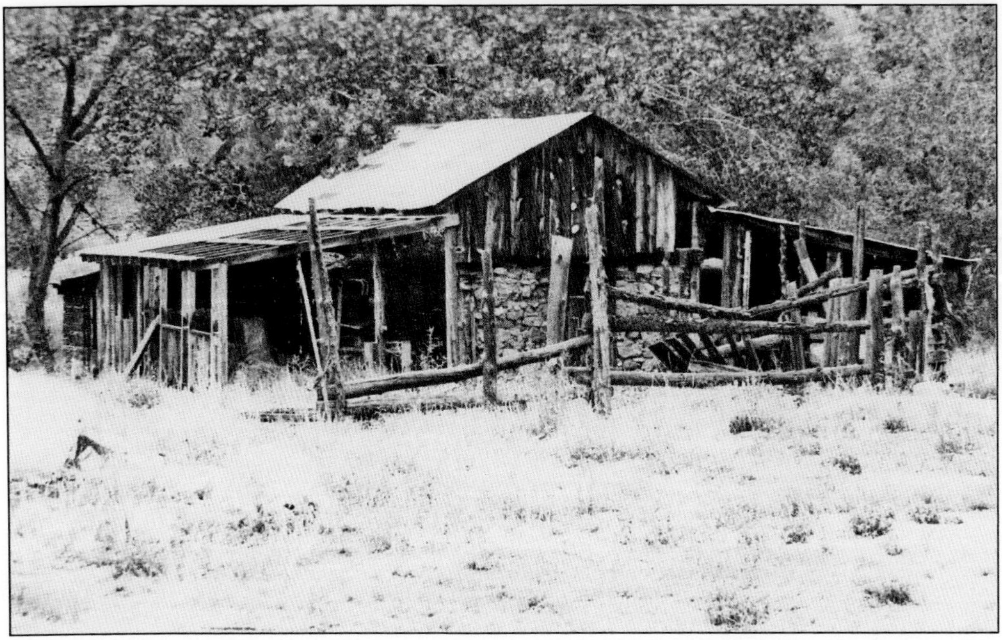

This old barn, near the center of town, is over 100 years old. It may be falling down, but it has one occupant inside: a horse. (Courtesy Robert Borden.)

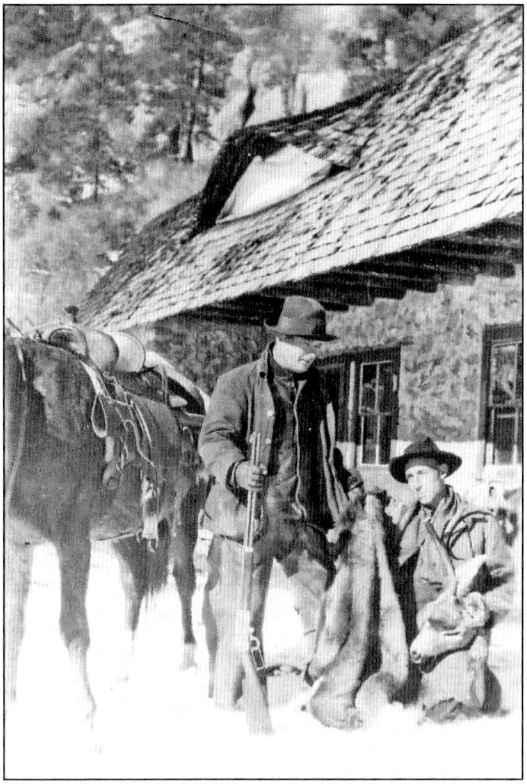

Stamps and Fluke display their hunting trophies. (Courtesy 2005 July 4 Committee.)

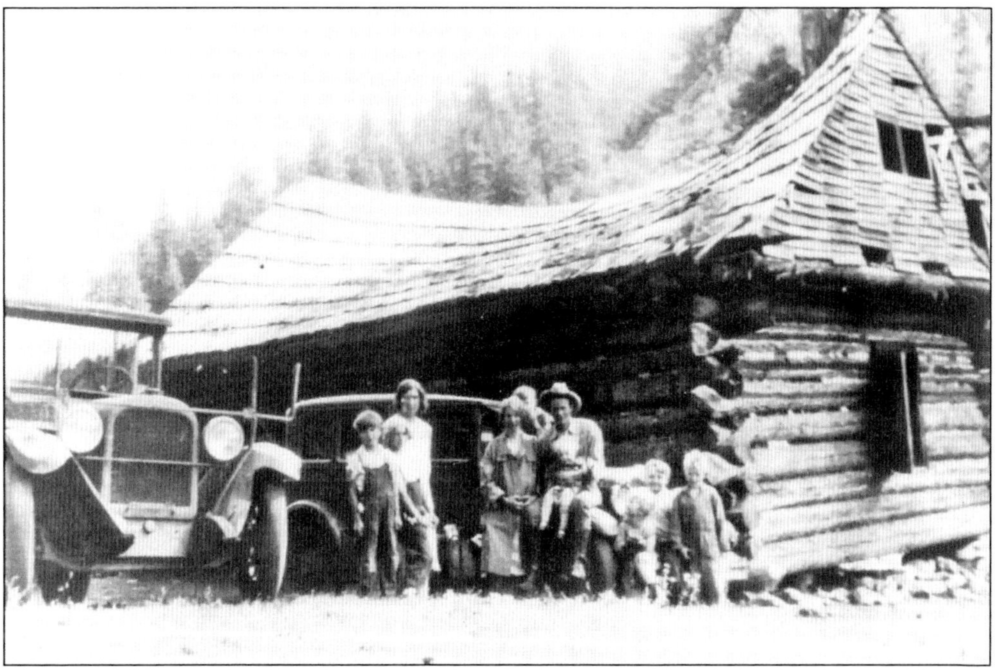

The only children within 12 miles of each other, the Fenton and Routledge children would travel by horse-and-buggy to play with the others. Often they were invited to dinner at one place or the other. (Courtesy 2005 July 4 Committee.)

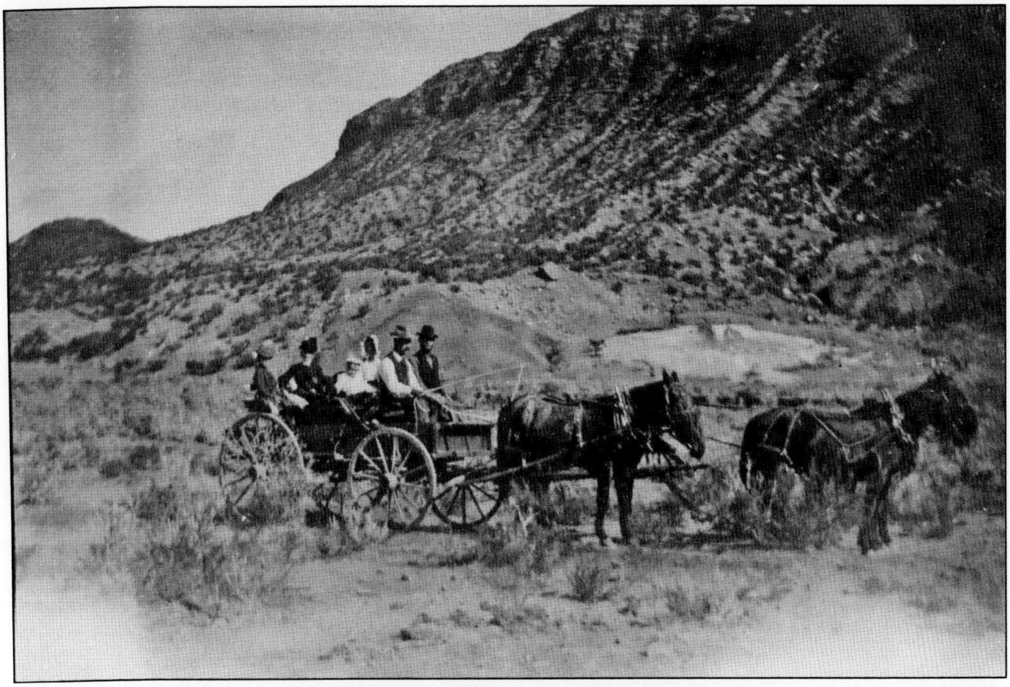

A picnic in the Jemez in the old days could be a significant undertaking. (Courtesy 2005 July 4 Committee.)

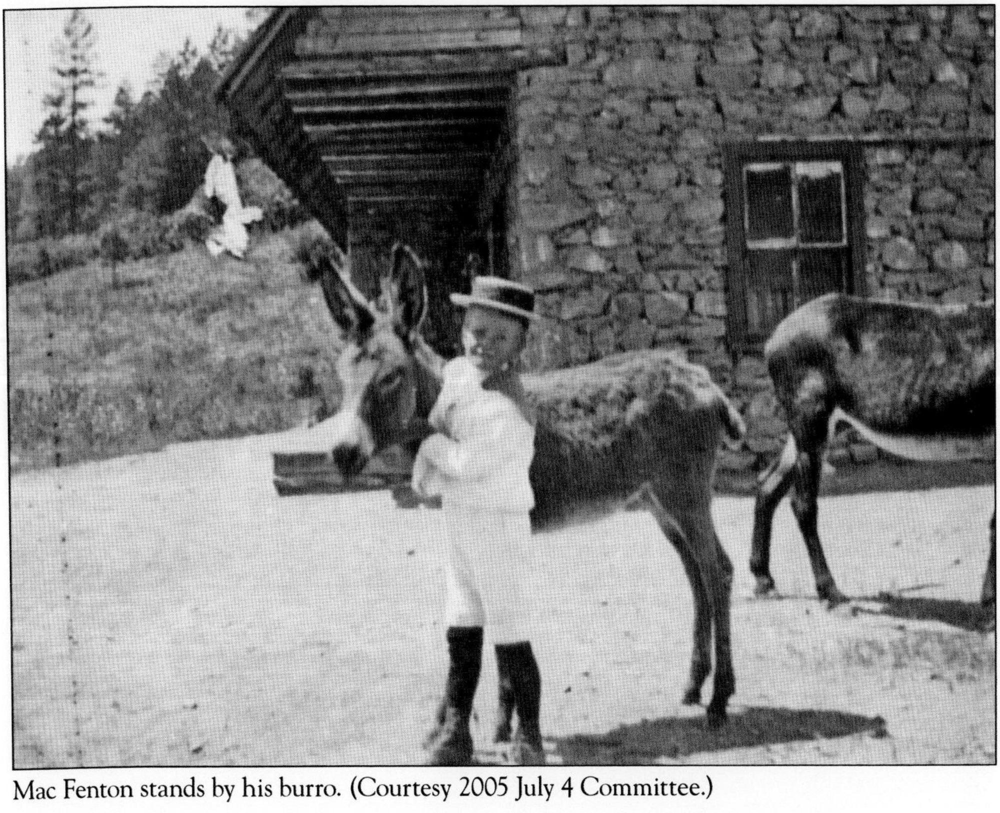

Mac Fenton stands by his burro. (Courtesy 2005 July 4 Committee.)

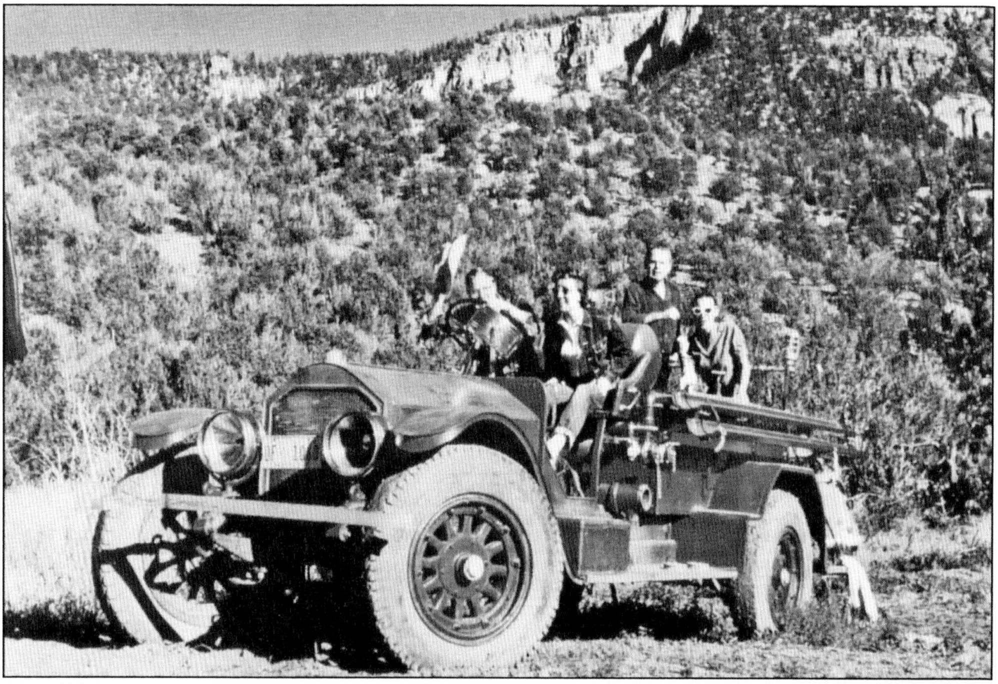

This 1921 American La France fire engine was given to Jemez Springs, but the village soon retired it, parking it at the American Legion. Because of vandalism, the village sold it at auction for $100 to Tom Abousleman, who kept it parked behind his house for 10 years before reselling it. (Courtesy Frank and Rita Slowen.)

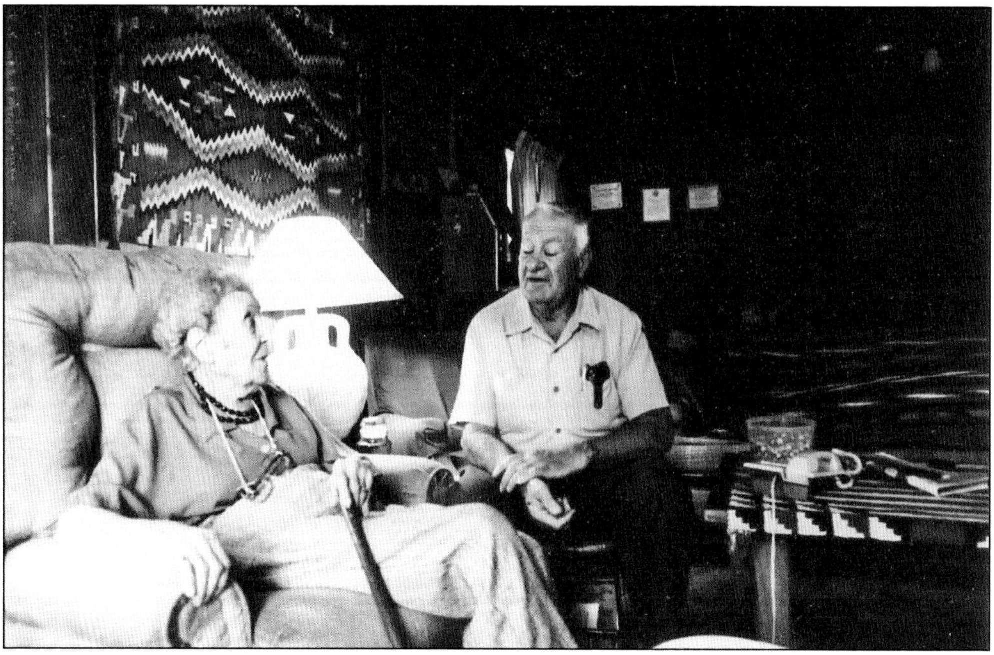

Tom Abousleman and his sister Josephine relax in the home their father built. This picture was taken in the Abousleman living room when Josephine was 88 and Tom was 77. Josephine died at the age of 94. Tom turned 90 in 2008. (Courtesy Tom Abousleman.)

Three

THE SPRINGS IN JEMEZ SPRINGS

The existence of hot springs in Jemez Springs and the surrounding area had been known for hundreds of years. The Jemez Indians knew about the springs, naming one of their pueblos "the place of boiling waters." When Juan Oñate visited Jemez in 1599, he sent a letter to the viceroy in Mexico praising the health-giving waters he found there. Richard Kern made a sketch of the hot springs of Jemez Springs in 1849 as an artist with the James Hervy Simpson expedition.

The hot springs provide Jemez Springs with several tourist attractions. There is Soda Dam, which lies just beyond the village's northern border. This magnificent natural dam began forming approximately 5,000 years ago when dissolved calcium carbonate from limestone was heated and then rose to the surface and precipitated as a marble-like substance. At the dam, it is possible to put one hand in hot water and the other in cold water. As a side note, the Soda Dam rock and its traces of algal filaments have been used in studies of how ancient Martian life might be detected.

In the early part of the 20th century, the numerous hot springs were crowded with people up for a long weekend or more. Like Oñate, they believed the waters were good for healing. There is a story that Chicago gangster Al Capone, who some say used the Jemez as a hideout, soaked in hot springs to see if it would cure his syphilis.

Some of these hot springs have been developed to allow people to soak in the mineral-rich waters. There are three hot springs on forest service land: Spence Hot Springs, McCauley Warm Springs, and San Antonio Hot Springs. In Jemez Springs proper, there are two hot springs that have been developed to provide easy access without an arduous hike. The Jemez Springs Bath House is housed in a historic, century-old building run by the village and provides tubs for soaking. Giggling Springs is an open pool that was once the site of Abousleman's bathhouse.

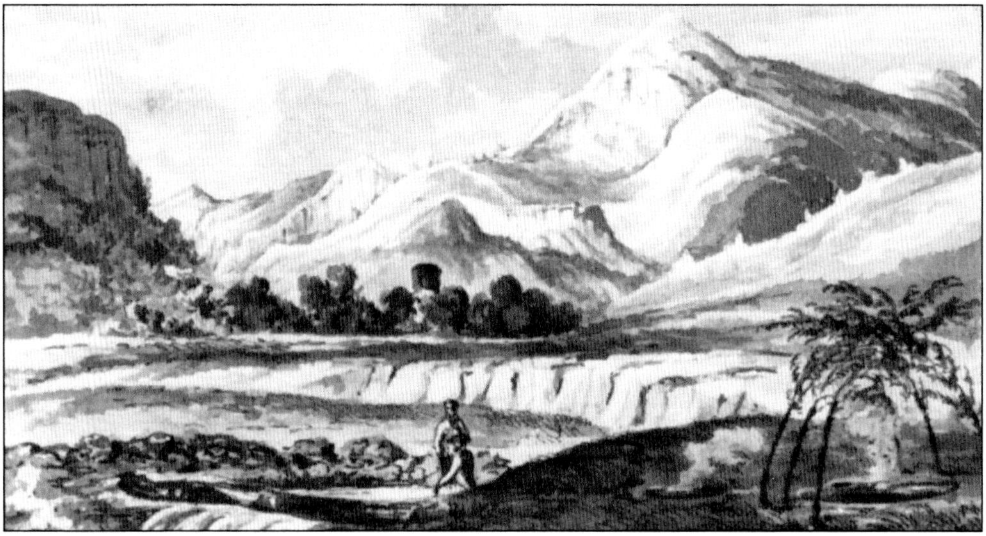

The first picture of the hot springs in Jemez Springs was drawn by Richard Kern, who was an expeditionary artist with the James Hervy Simpson expedition. The hot spring is probably the one feeding the Jemez Springs Bath House. (Courtesy Academy of Natural Sciences of Philadelphia.)

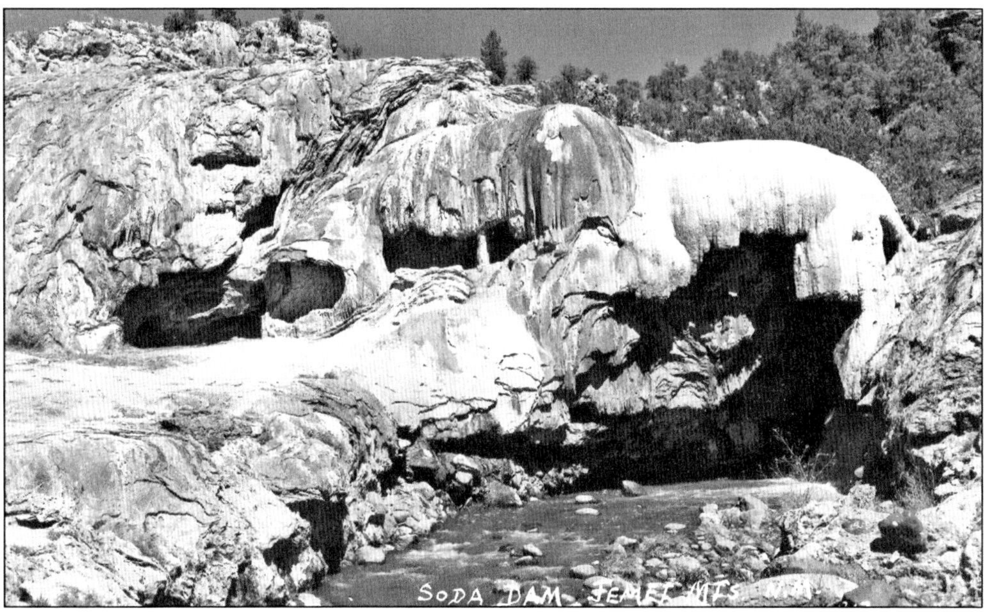

When hot waters, rich in dissolved calcium carbonate, issue at the surface, they begin to cool. As the waters cool, not as much calcium carbonate can stay dissolved, and so the springs deposit travertine, a calcium carbonate hot spring deposit. Over thousands of years, repeated deposition of calcium carbonate as the spring deposit travertine has formed Soda Dam. (Courtesy Jim Coad.)

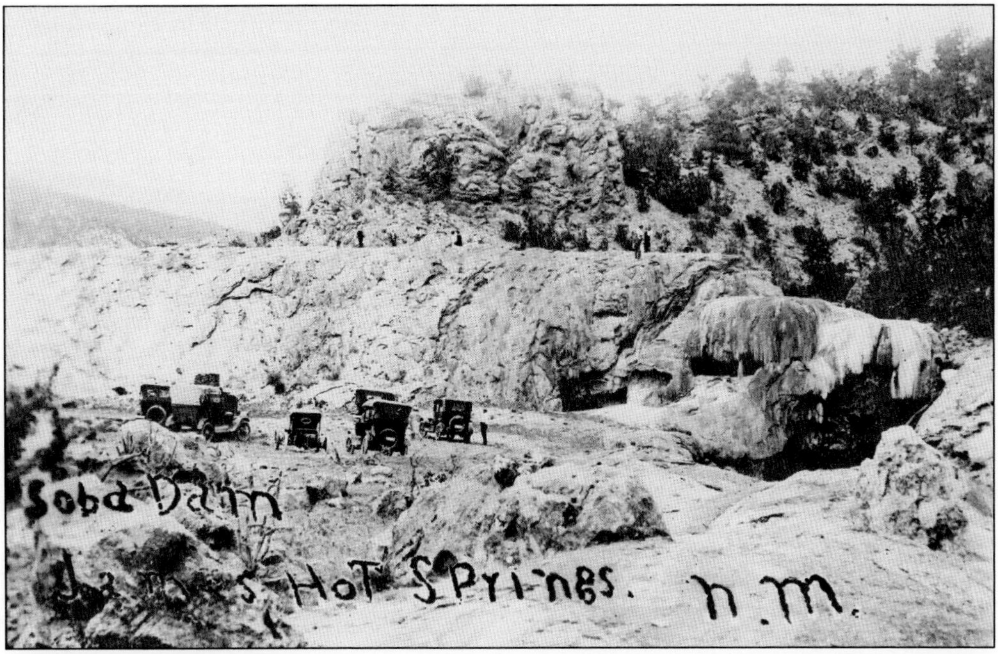

Soda Dam has always been a tourist attraction. People enjoyed climbing the strange structure and having their pictures taken on the dam. But in the 1960s, a notch was blasted through Soda Dam to get rid of the large hump in the highway where it crossed the dam. The blasting unfortunately destroyed almost all of the natural plumbing of the springs that formed Soda Dam. (Courtesy Jim Coad.)

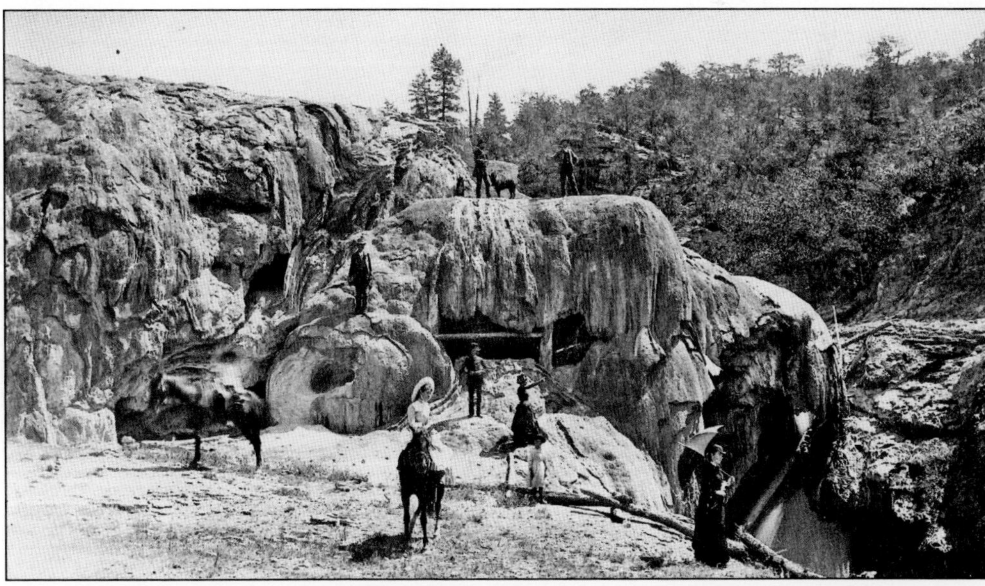

People dressed up even for a day in the country. The men wore suits; one woman holds a parasol, and the woman riding uses a sidesaddle. This old postcard is probably from the 1920s. (Courtesy Jim Coad.)

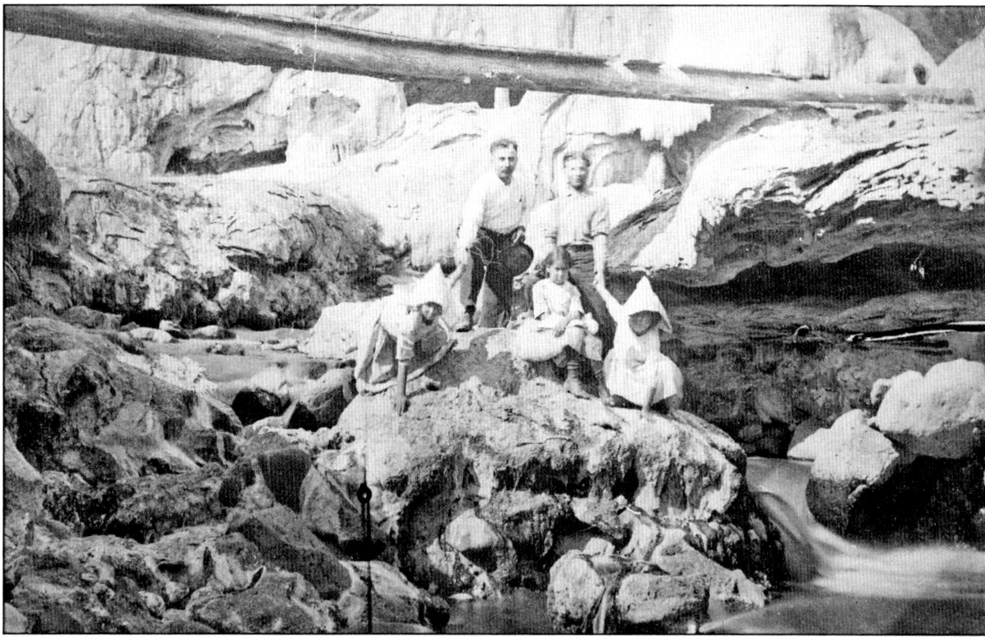

This 1920s postcard shows a family on Soda Dam. Not knowing much about geology, people marveled at the dam and of course had to have a picture taken. (Courtesy 2005 July 4 Committee.)

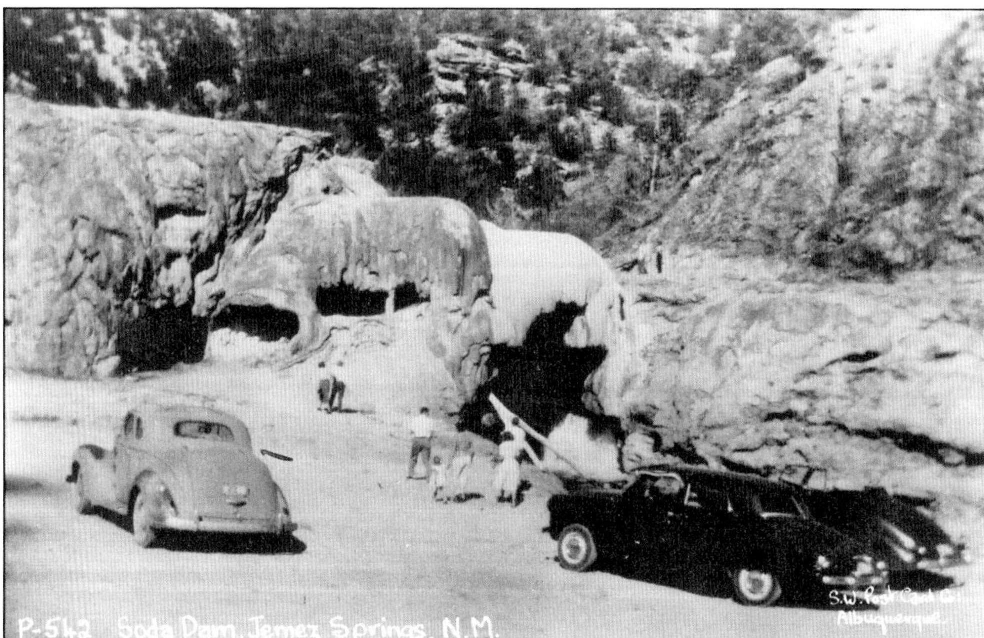

Soda Dam's popularity continued through the 20th century. Note the cars parked in front of the dam. (Courtesy Jim Coad.)

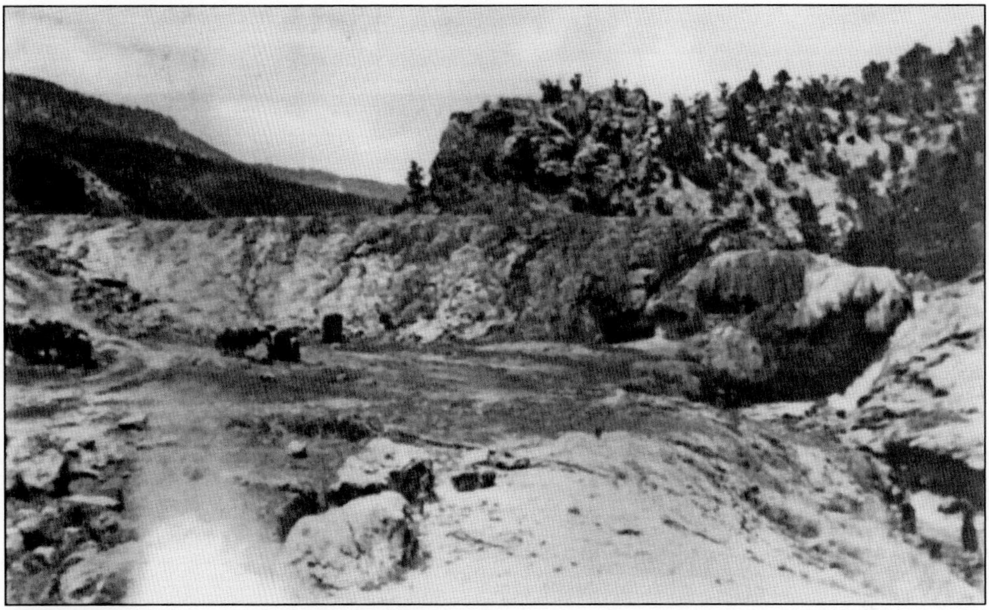

Horses and wagons stop in front of Soda Dam. This postcard shows the barrier Soda Dam created for automobiles. This was the barrier that was blasted through to lengthen Highway 4. (Courtesy 2005 July 4 Committee.)

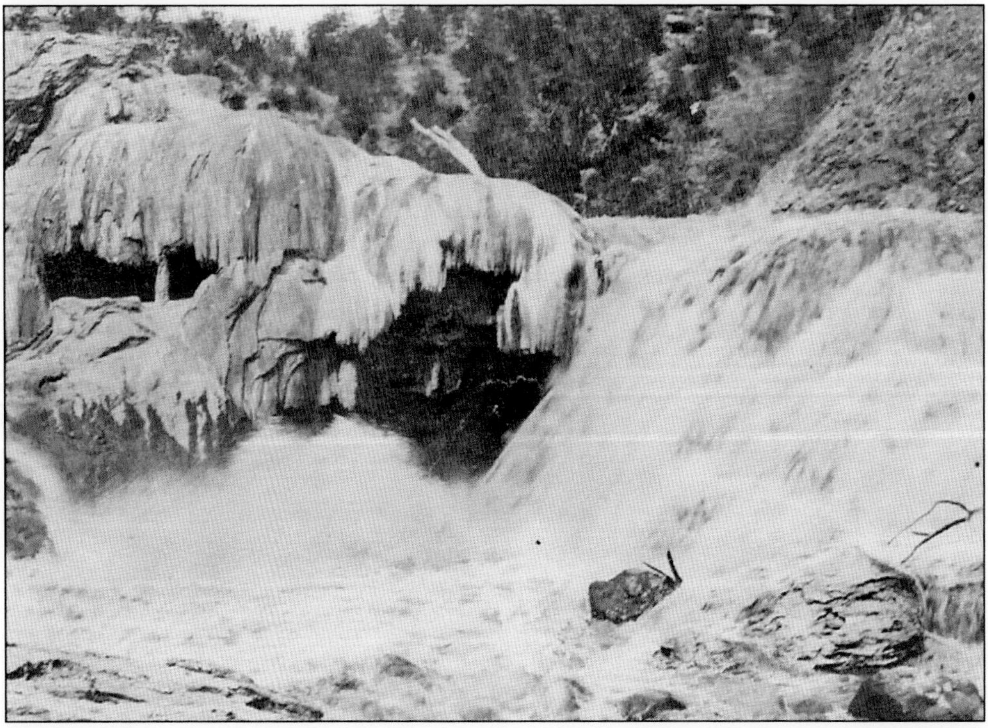

The Jemez River roared over the Soda Dam during the flood of 1941. The flood devastated Jemez Springs and the surrounding countryside. Bridges and buildings were destroyed because of the melting of a heavy snow pack farther north. There was a big flood in 1958 but none since then. (Courtesy Paul Adams.)

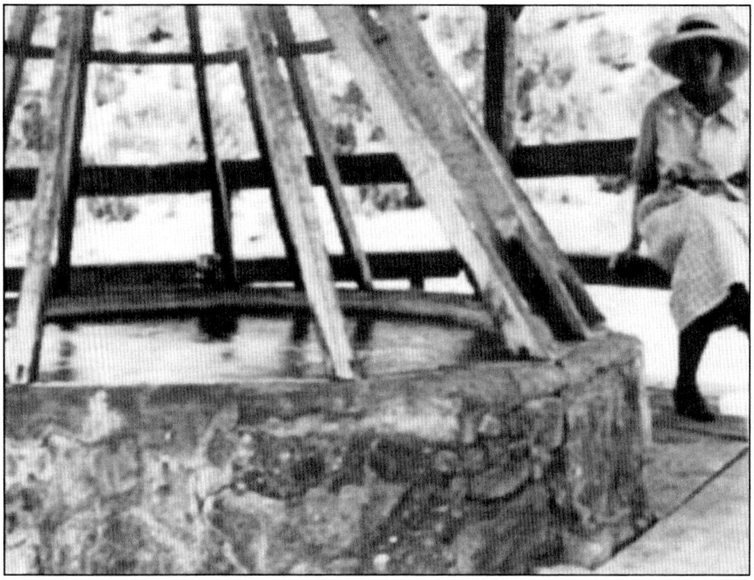

The spring that feeds the Jemez Springs Bath House is just behind the bathhouse, and the water is piped into the bathhouse tubs. This picture, taken in 1924, shows the spring edge as fairly free of travertine. Today the spring is encrusted with travertine just like Soda Dam. (Courtesy 2005 July 4 Committee.)

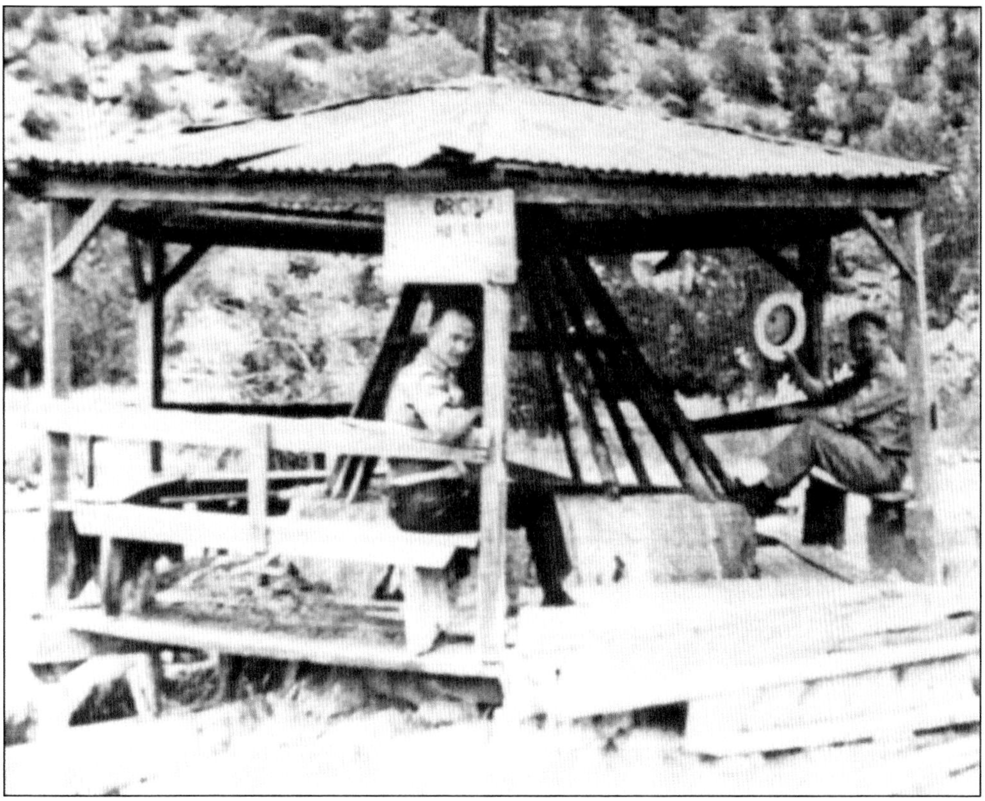

The gazebo over the hot spring in 1945 is little changed from the above photograph. (Courtesy Julie Crook.)

This is an old photograph of the hot spring gazebo in the center of the village. (Courtesy 2005 July 4 Committee.)

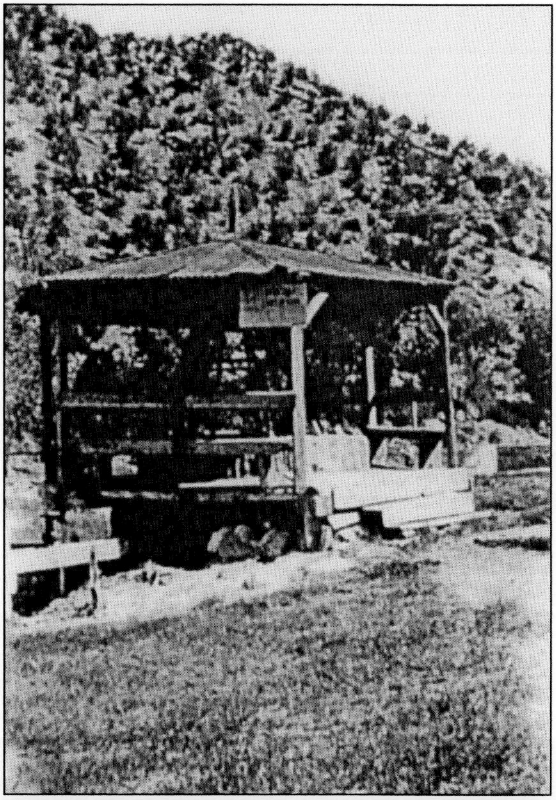

The covering for the hot spring that feeds water to the bathhouse was repaired in 2004. There is a roof over the spring to prevent extraneous material from dropping into the spring. (Courtesy Robert Borden.)

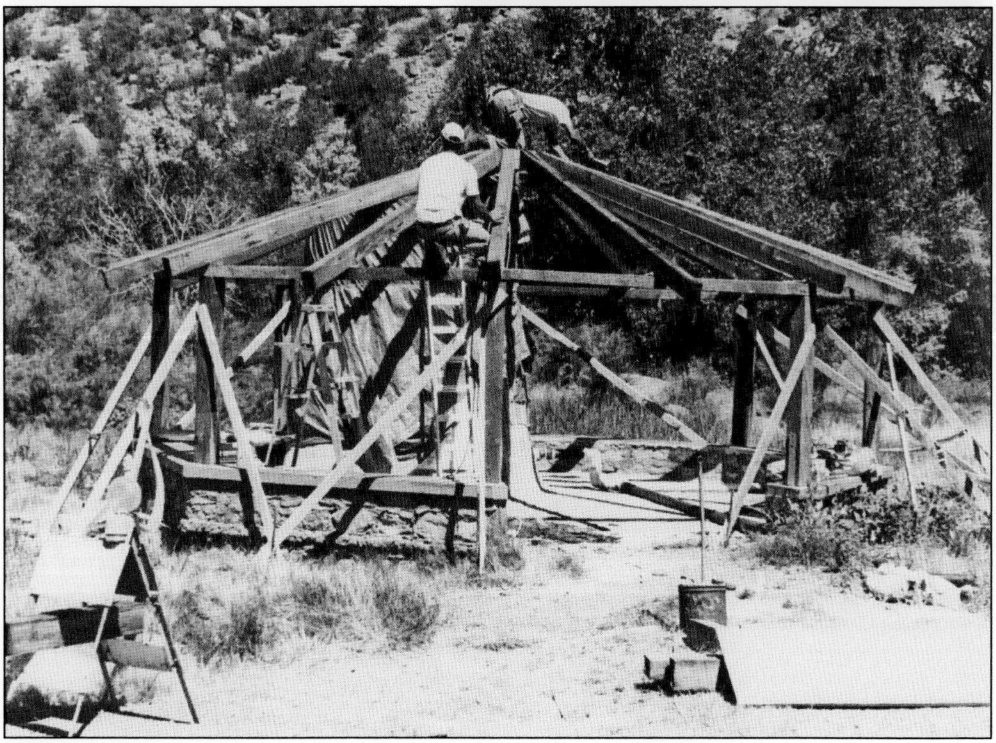

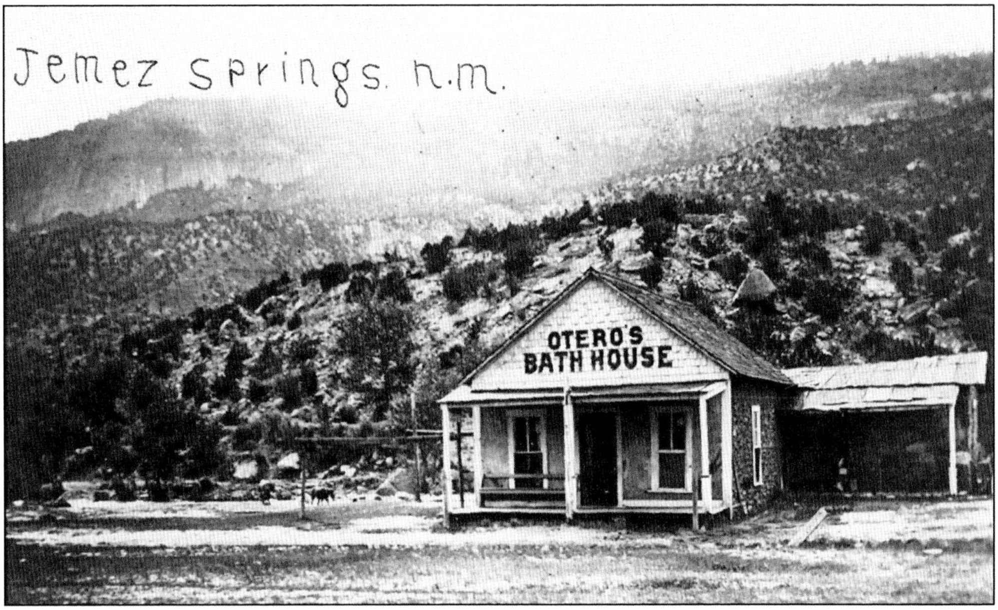

Otero family members were important cattlemen. One Otero sold the Valle Grande to an Eastern development company in 1909. People say they remember one of the Oteros riding down the street lighting his cigars with $5 bills. (Courtesy Richard Sanchez.)

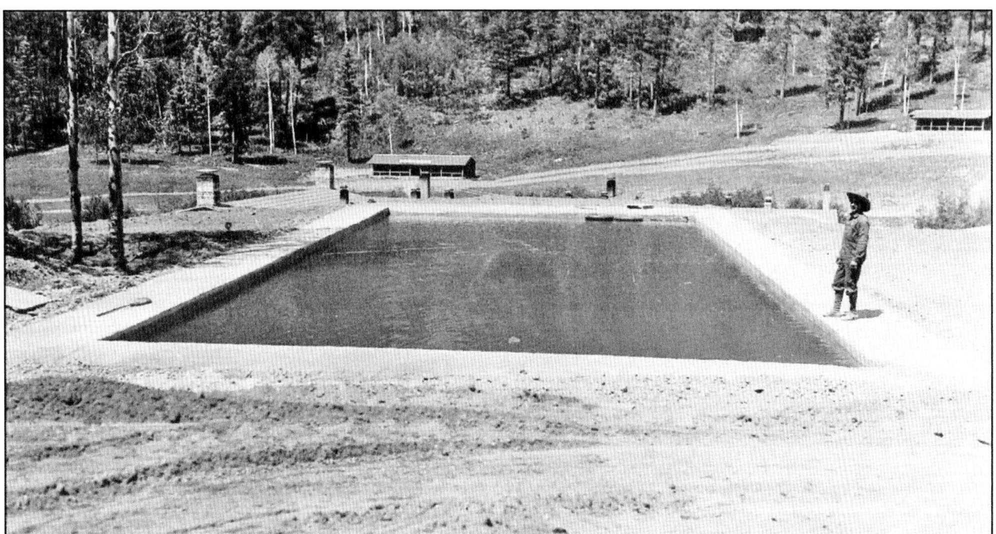

The Jemez Springs Bath House used to have a bathing pool of hot mineral-rich water on the premises, but it was covered over at some point. (Courtesy 2005 July 4 Committee.)

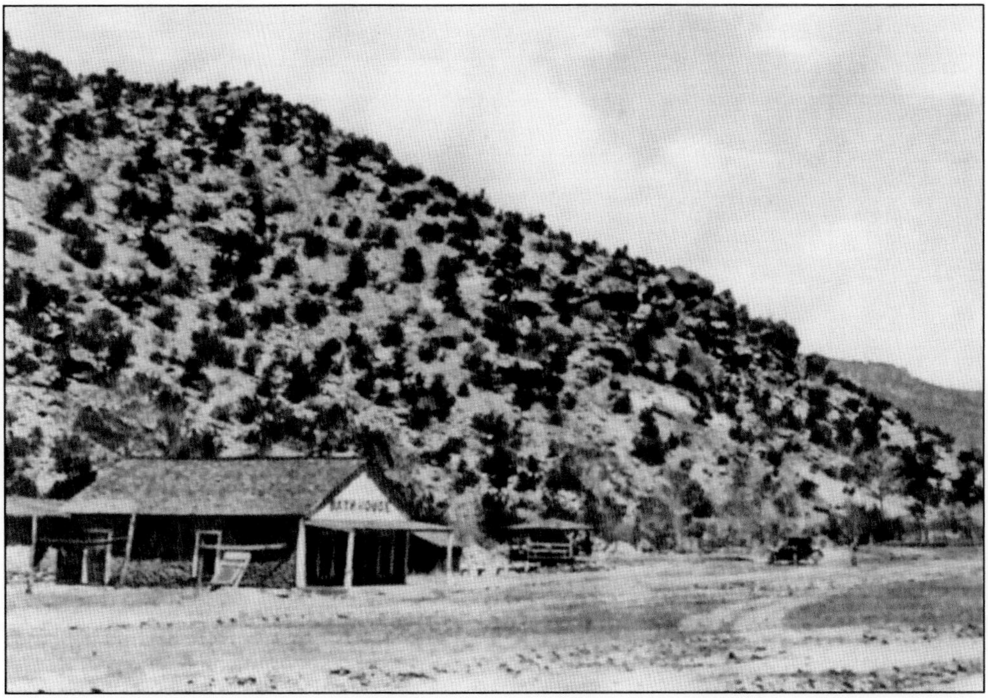

Various people ran the bathhouse until 1961, when the Village of Jemez Springs acquired it and then leased it out. Today the village itself runs the bathhouse. (Courtesy 2005 July 4 Committee.)

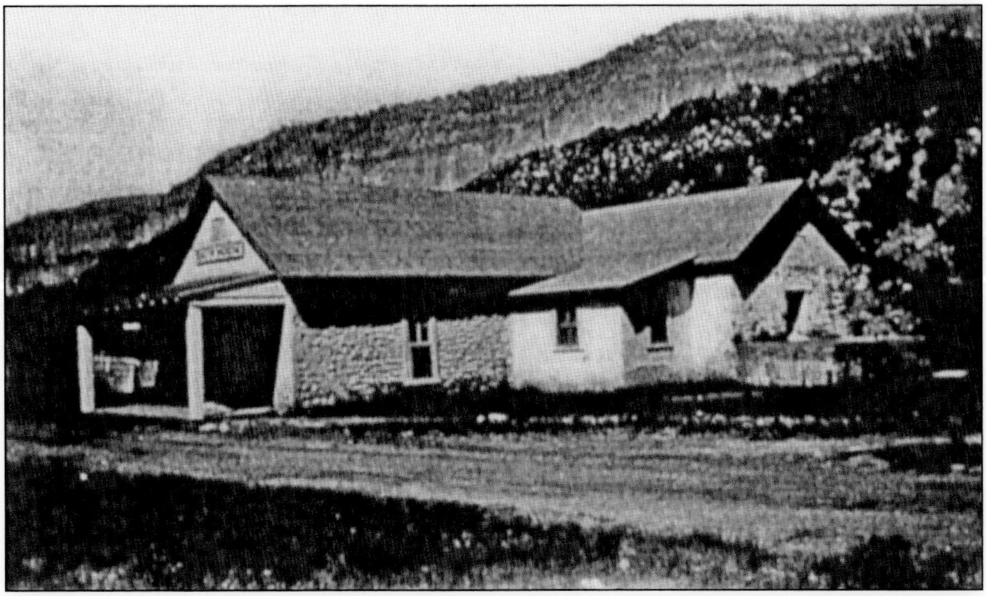

Because the water in the hot spring is around 150 degrees, it must be mixed with cold water. This photograph shows the holding tank for the Jemez Springs bathhouse on the north side of the building. (Courtesy Richard Sanchez.)

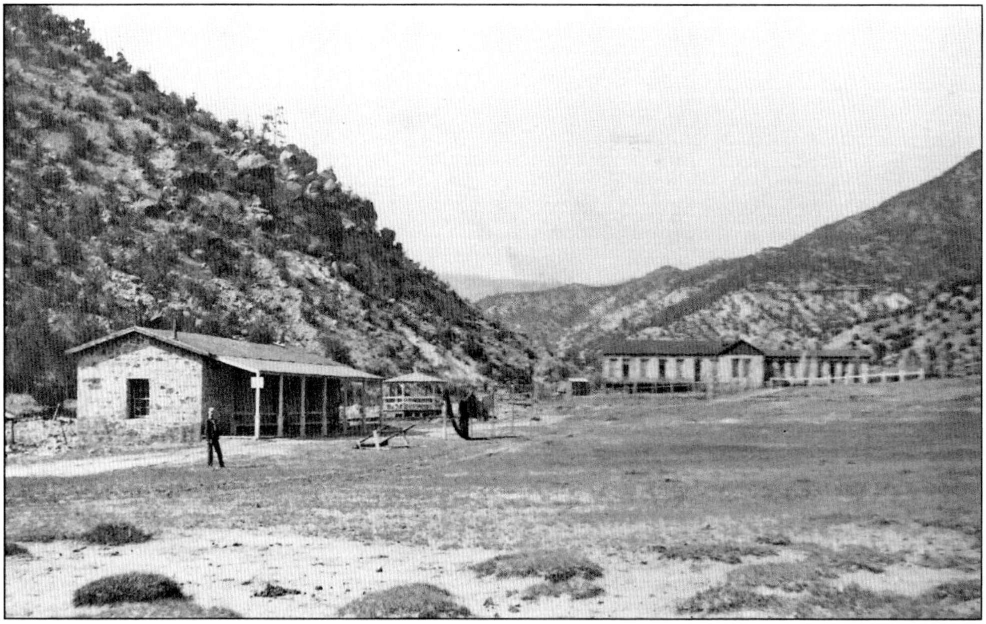

The bathhouse is to the left of the Jemez Springs village center. (Courtesy Richard Sanchez.)

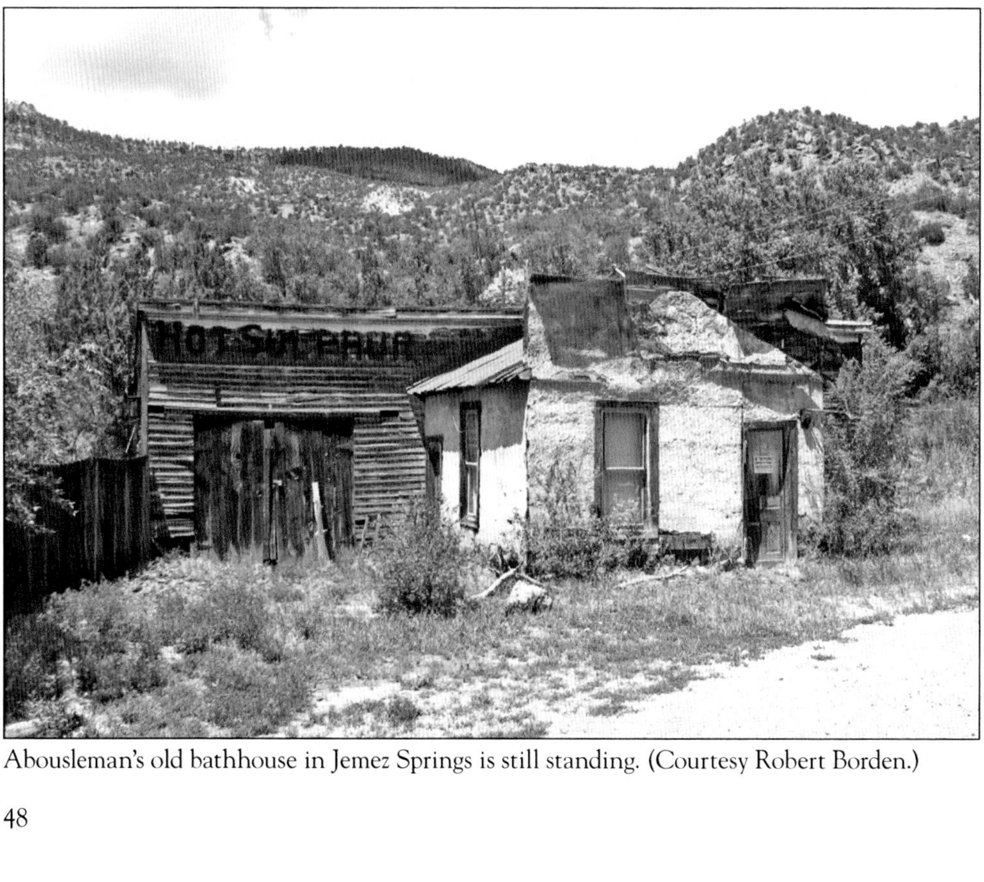

Abousleman's old bathhouse in Jemez Springs is still standing. (Courtesy Robert Borden.)

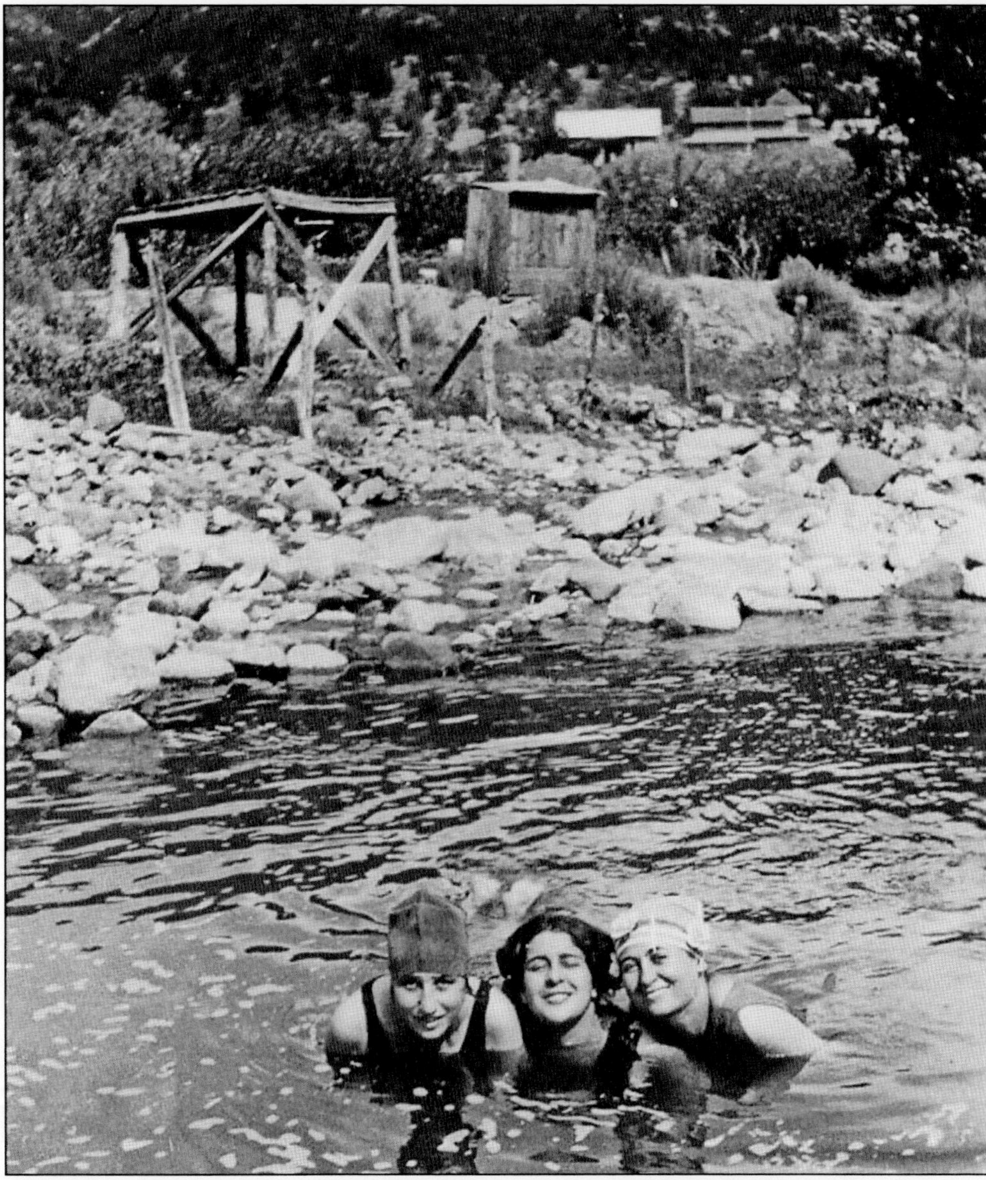

These three women in what may be Abousleman's old hot spring would not have even considered bathing nude. It was definitely bathing suits for them. (Courtesy 2005 July 4 Committee.)

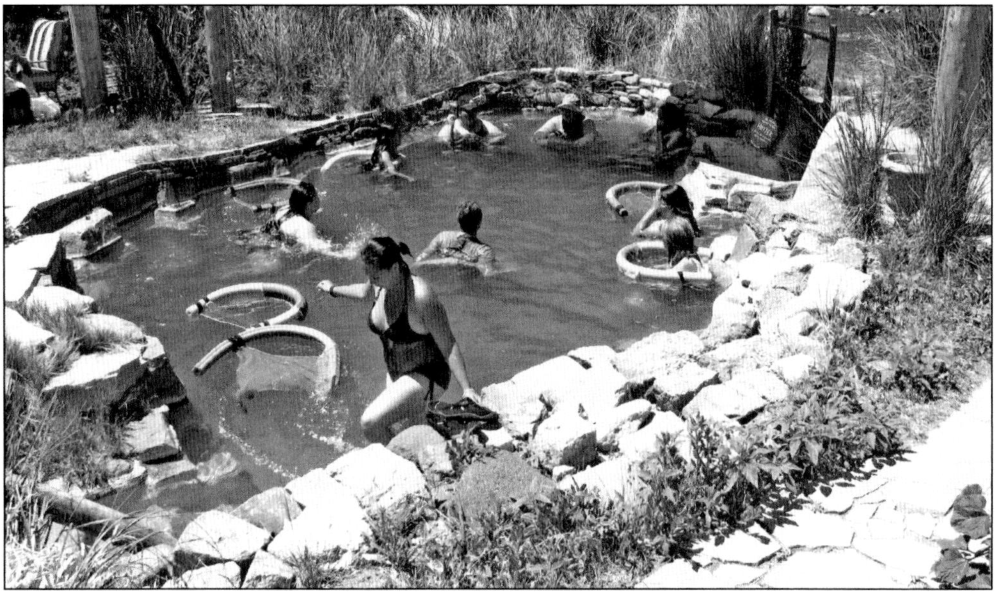

Giggling Springs is on the site of Abousleman's old bathhouse. The big flood of 1941 caused such damage to the spring that it was eventually shut down. The current owners dug out the hot spring and rent it out to hot spring lovers. (Courtesy Robert Borden.)

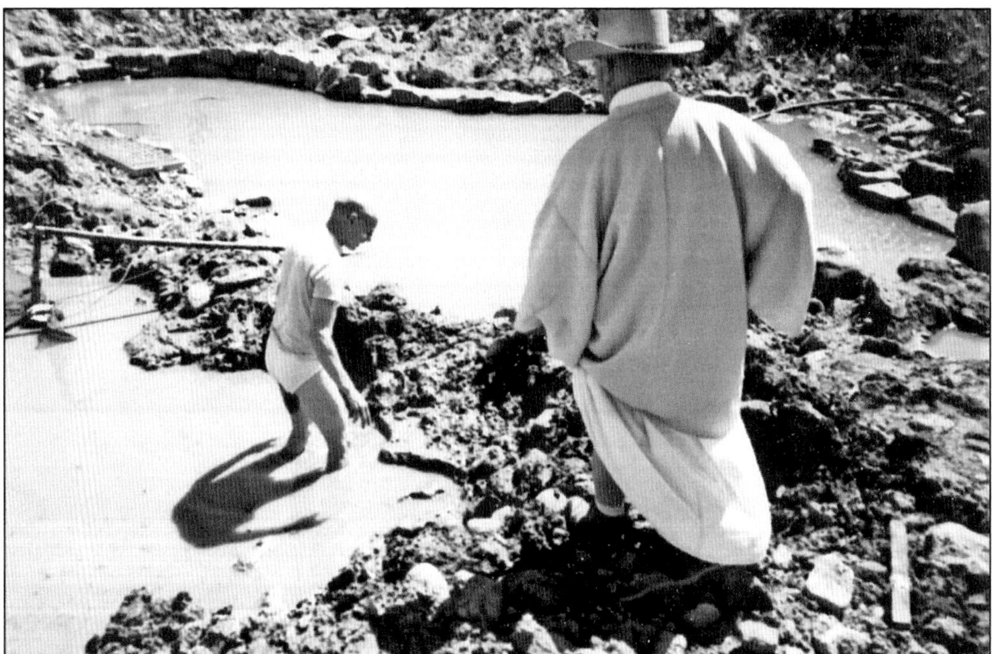

The Bodhi Manda Zen Center has several hot pools and also uses the hot spring to provide geothermal energy. (Courtesy Bodhi Manda Zen Center.)

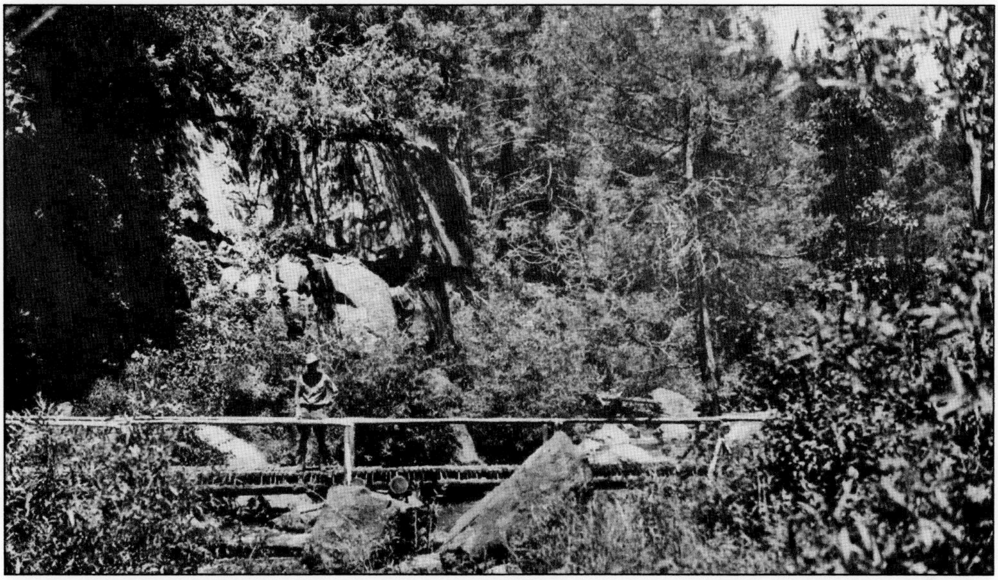

Spence Hot Springs, which is managed by the forest service, is a very popular spot. It can become very crowded, however, and the nudity of some of the people soaking is always a subject of controversy. (Courtesy U.S. Forest Service.)

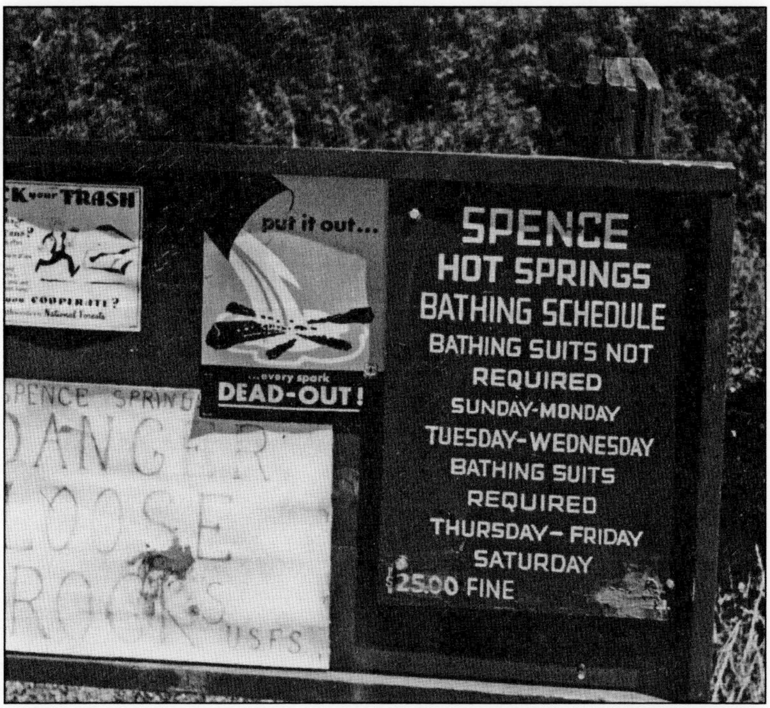

In earlier times, the forest service solved the nudity problem by scheduling clothed days and nude days. (Courtesy Joann Dolk.)

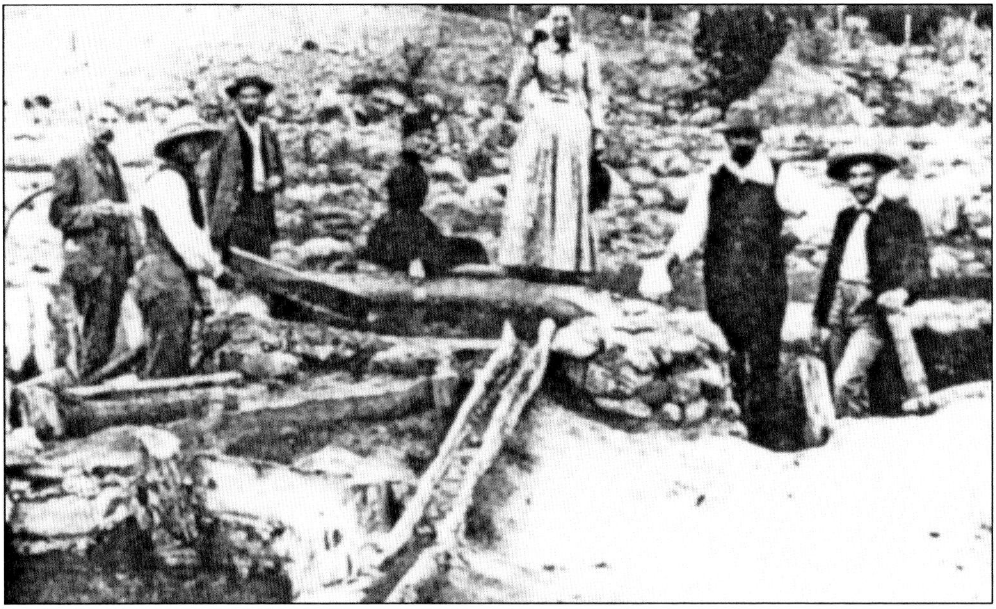

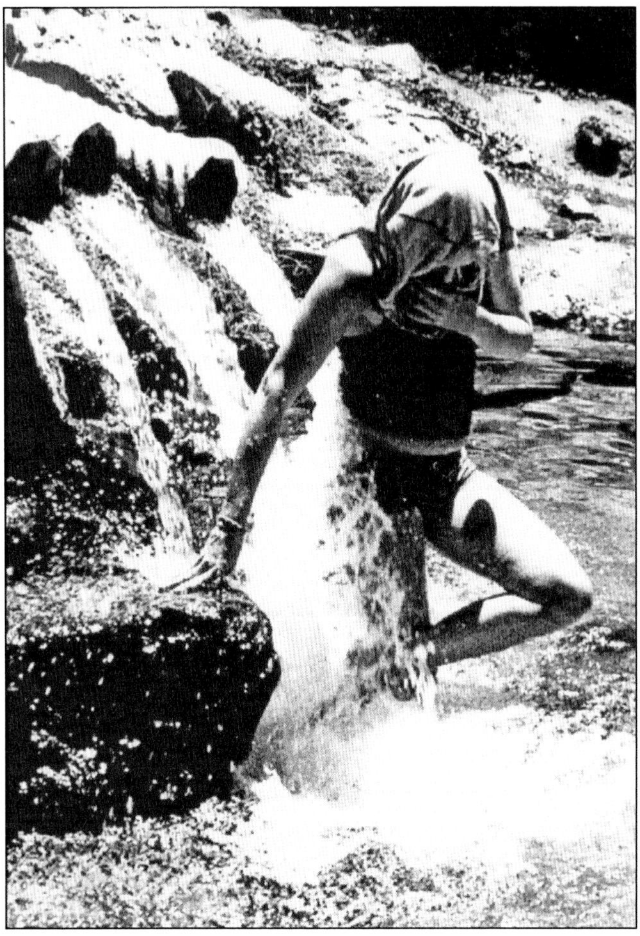

The springs in the Jemez have been a mecca for health seekers since the beginning of the Spanish occupation. This group gathered around a spring and was photographed in 1890. They did not soak in the water but drank it. (Courtesy *Desert Magazine*.)

San Antonio Hot Spring is perhaps the favorite of the hot spring crowd. (Courtesy Robert Borden.)

Four

Green Gold

Unlike many Western towns, it was timber—not gold or silver—that created wealth in the Jemez. But if valuable minerals were not common, there were trees in abundance, tall ponderosa pines perfect for making lumber. The supply lay in the hands of the U.S. Forest Service and private owners.

One such private tract was the Cañon de San Diego, a Spanish land grant that was deeded on March 6, 1798. The grant contained 116,000 acres. Congress confirmed the heirs of the original deed holders in their ownership in 1861.

The land grant was sold several times. Then in 1920, a venture called the Santa Fe Northwestern Railway was incorporated with the express purpose of the development of the coal, copper, timber, and sulfur resources of the Jemez Mountains. At the time the railroad was incorporated, it was estimated that 425 million board feet of ponderosa pine was standing on the land grant, with an additional 2 billion board feet in the adjacent Santa Fe National Forest.

Little immediate progress was made until the land grant, now owned by the Jemez Land Company, sold the timber on the Cañon de San Diego to Guy Porter and his wife, Mary C. Porter.

Porter incorporated the White Pine Lumber Company with himself as president. The WPL began purchasing heavy equipment for logging, and a sawmill was completed in nearby Bernalillo in 1924 with the capacity to cut 120,000 board feet of timber a day.

A railroad was built, but not before two tunnels had to be blasted through a sheer rock wall known as the Guadalupe Box.

The great flood of 1941 largely put an end to the railroad operations. The rail bed was washed out in innumerable places, and bridges were damaged. Big trucks operating off the rail bed replaced locomotives. The truck haul continued until 1973, when logging in the national forest ended. When logging on the San Diego grant came to an end, consideration was given to selling the property. Efforts were made to develop vacation properties, but eventually the land was deeded to the Santa Fe National Forest.

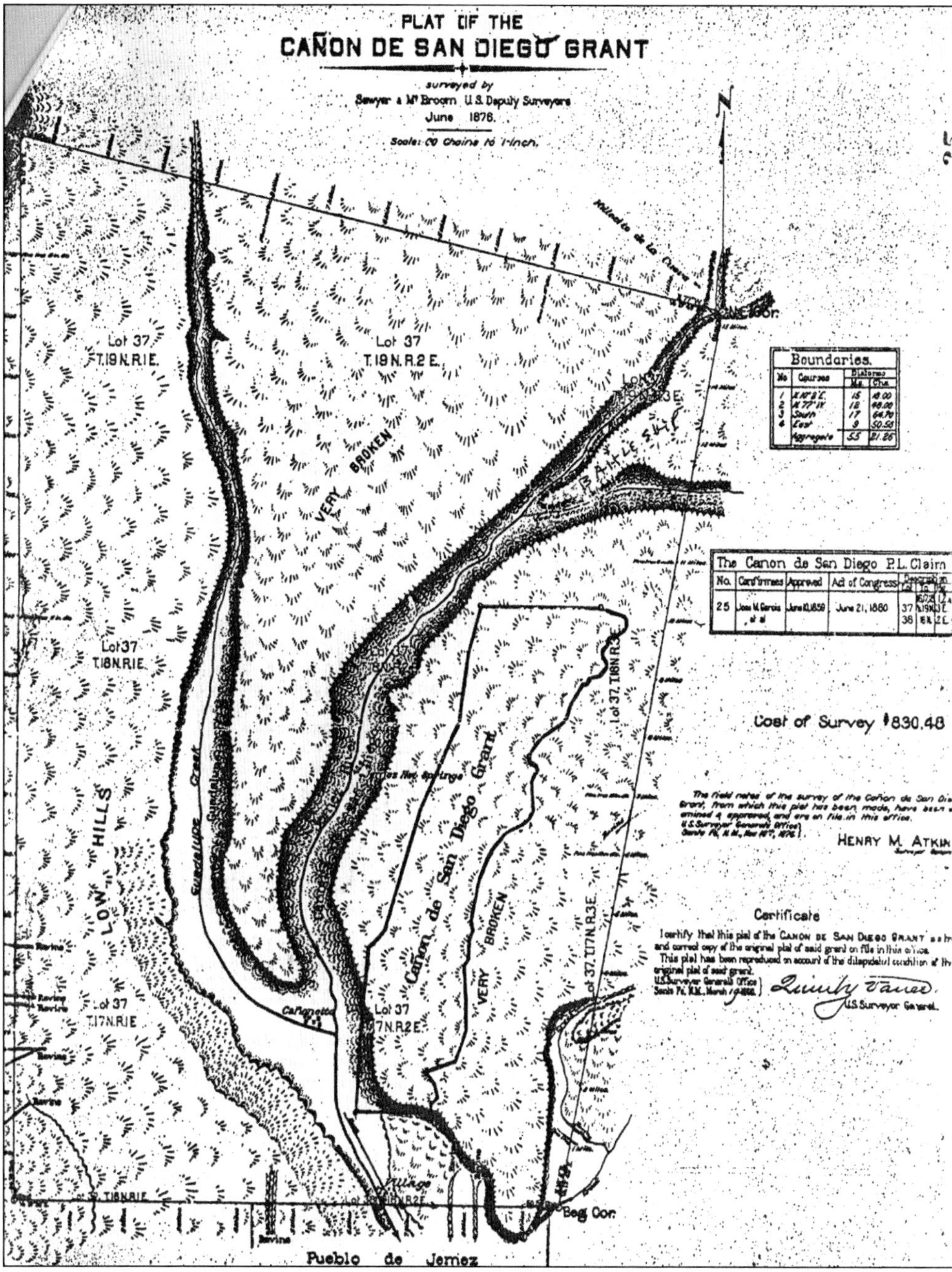

This is the plat for the Canyon de San Diego land grant. (Courtesy U.S. Forest Service.)

The Dye Timber Sale landing was at the foot of the mesa on the Jemez Division of the Santa Fe National Forest. (Courtesy U.S. Forest Service.)

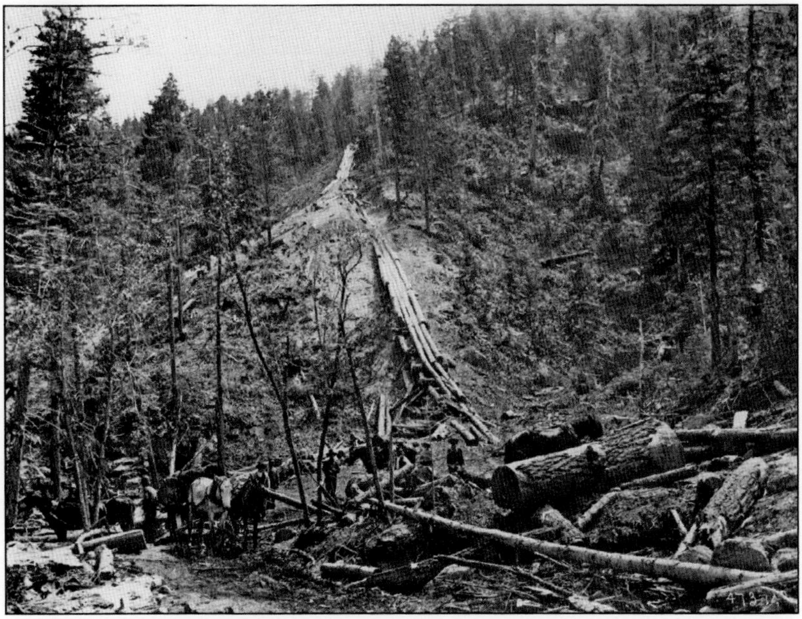

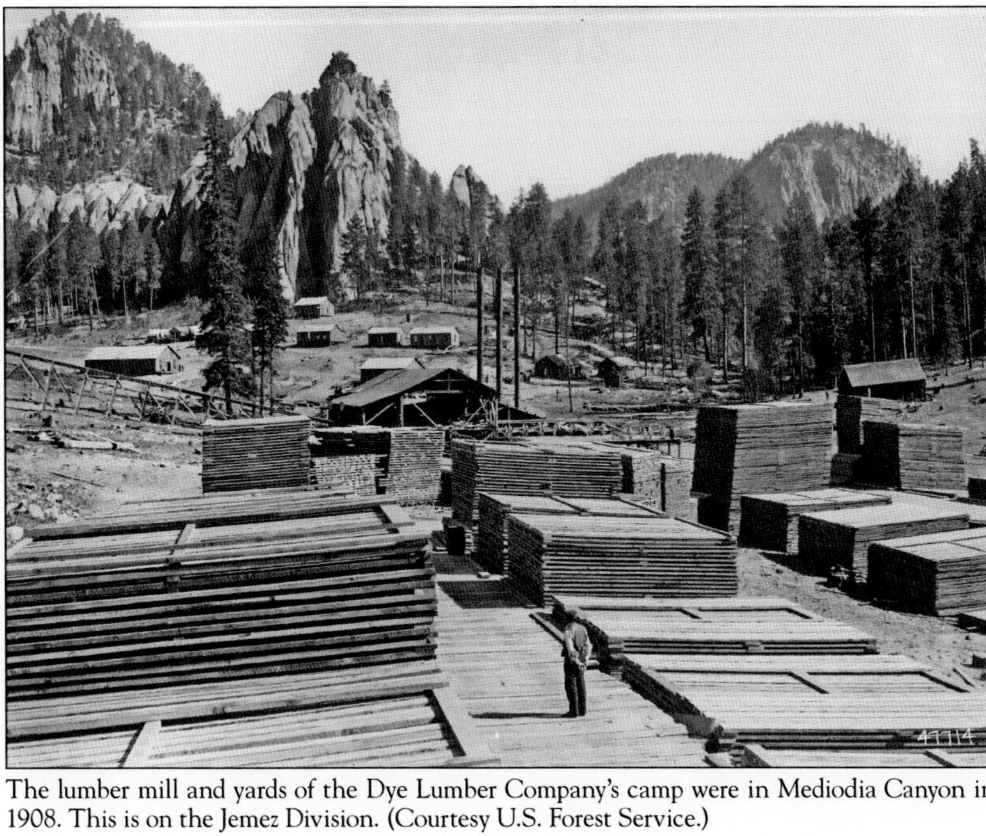

The lumber mill and yards of the Dye Lumber Company's camp were in Mediodia Canyon in 1908. This is on the Jemez Division. (Courtesy U.S. Forest Service.)

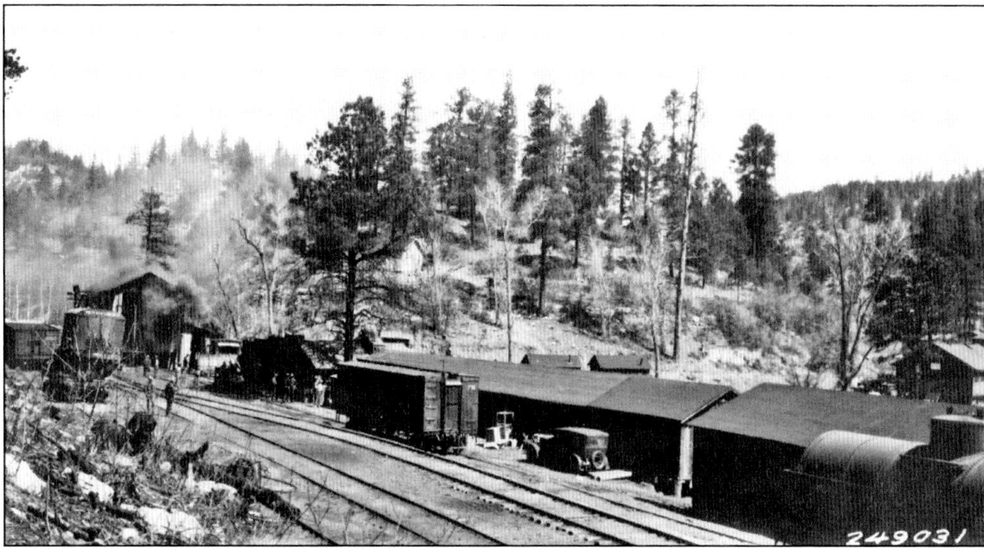

In 1930, the White Pine Lumber Company camp in Porter included railroad and shop facilities. Railroad rolling stock showed here are a boxcar (No. 701), a gondola (probably full of coal), and a log loader. (Courtesy U.S. Forest Service.)

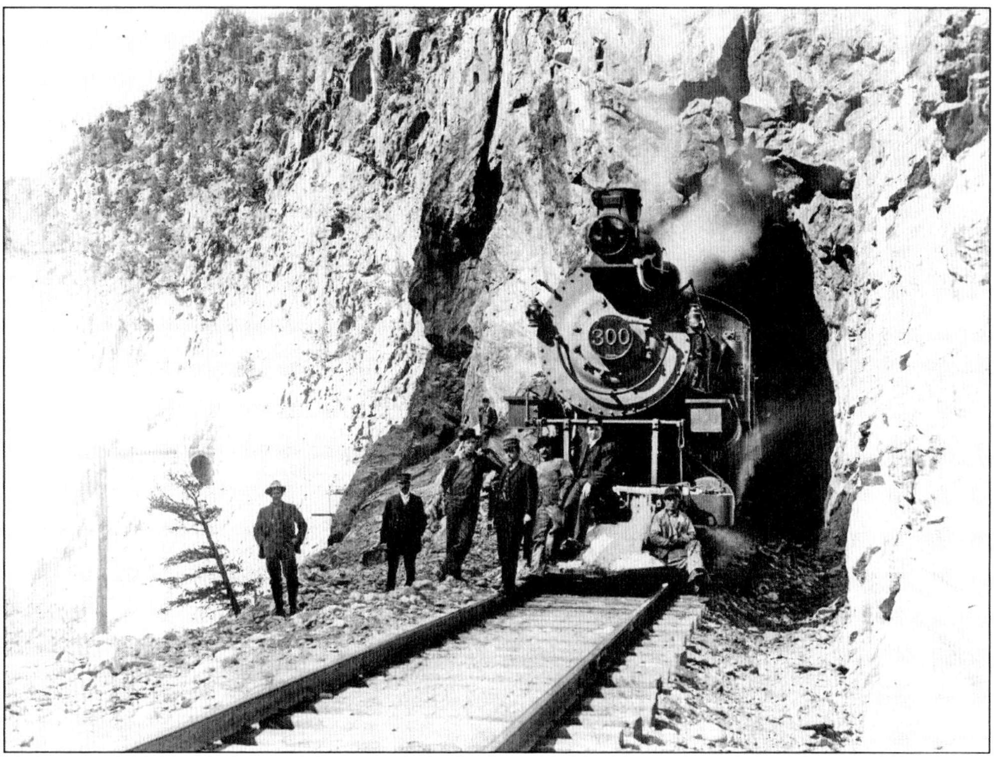

The dress of the men waiting for the train coming through the Gilman tunnels suggests that this may have been an inaugural run or at least an important one. Or, since it is a passenger train, they may just be waiting for the train. Today the tunnels are a favorite tourist destination. The road that comes after is a forest road that roughly follows the bed of the railroad. (Courtesy 2005 July 4 Committee.)

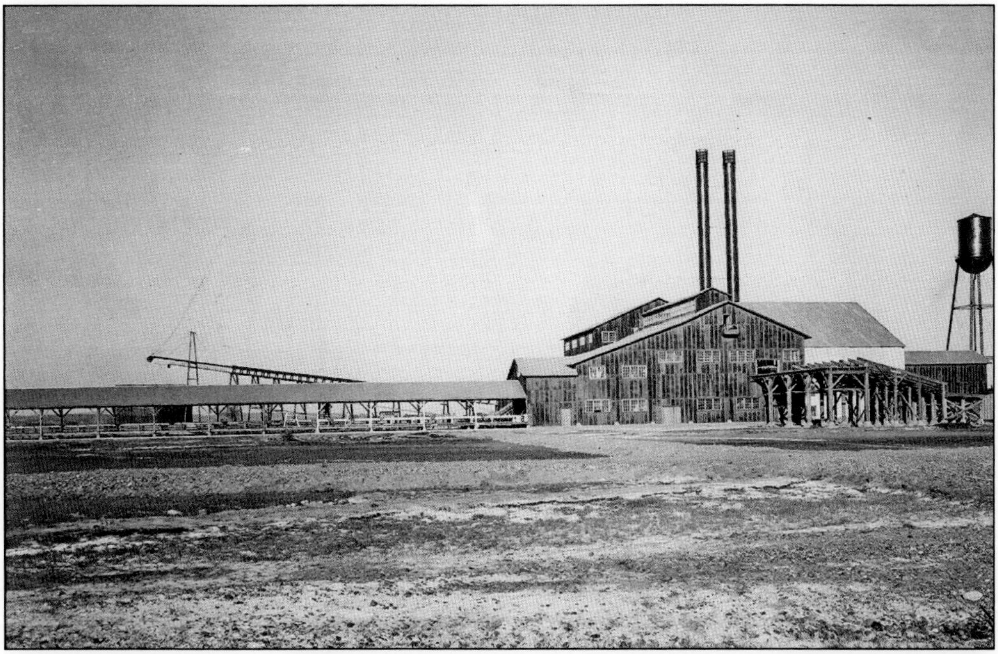

Logs would have been sent by rail or truck to White Pine sawmill in Bernalillo to be turned into lumber. This photograph shows the sawmill under construction. (Courtesy Sandoval County Historical Society.)

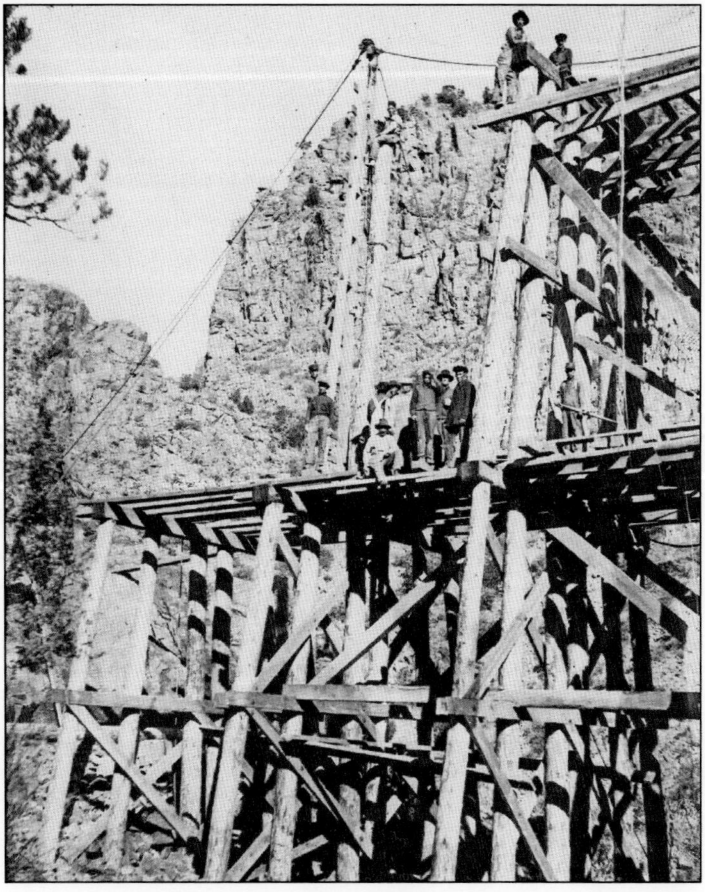

A high trestle was required to meet the Guadalupe Box. The roadbed was climbing steadily through this section. It was not until 1924 that tracks were laid through the tunnel. (Courtesy Sandoval County Historical Society.)

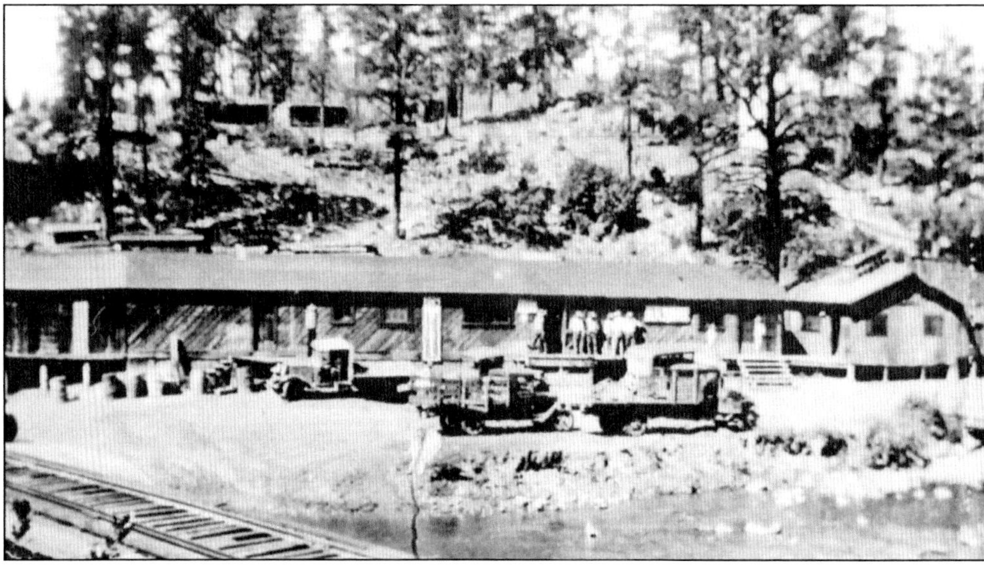

Porter became the center of logging activities. There was a store operated by Porter Mercantile. Like any company store, it offered loggers credit and company tokens as well as cash. Some 200 to 300 people eventually lived in cabins on the grounds. (Courtesy Sandoval Historical Society.)

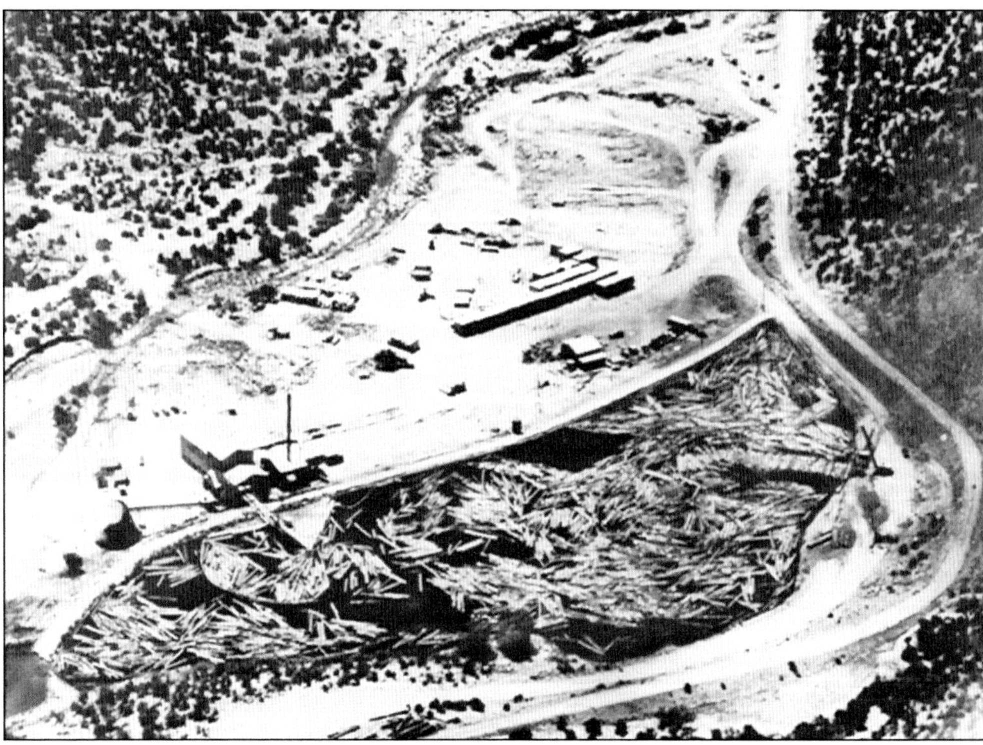

The millpond in Gilman would have contained several groups of logs separated by booms. (Courtesy Sandoval County Historical Society.)

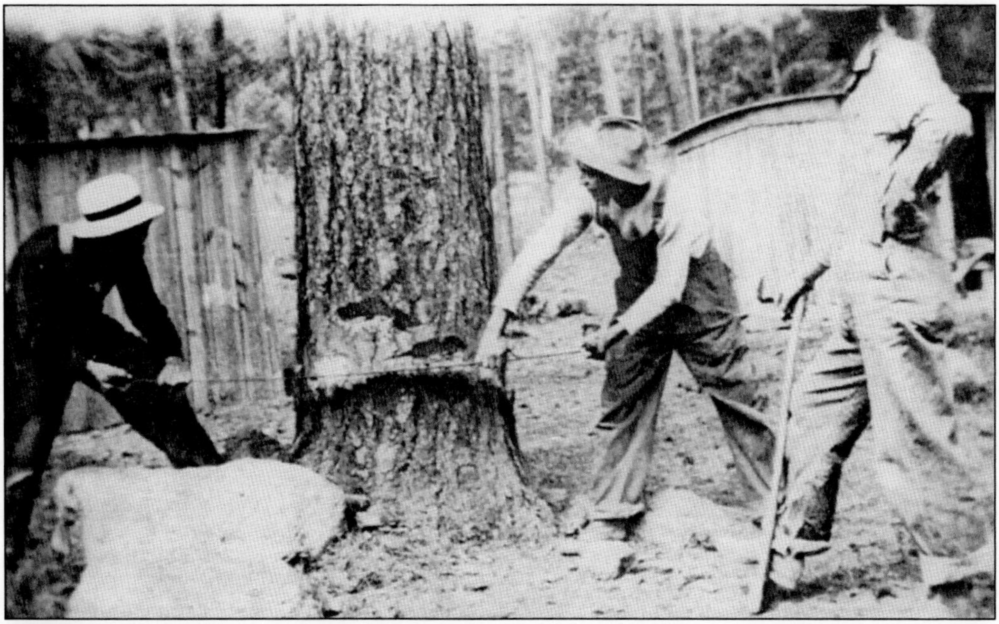

The chainsaw had yet to make an appearance, so trees were felled and logs cut with a cross saw. The logging techniques were typical of the period, cutting and skidding logs with a minimum of machinery and only horses used for skidding. (Courtesy Sandoval County Historical Society.)

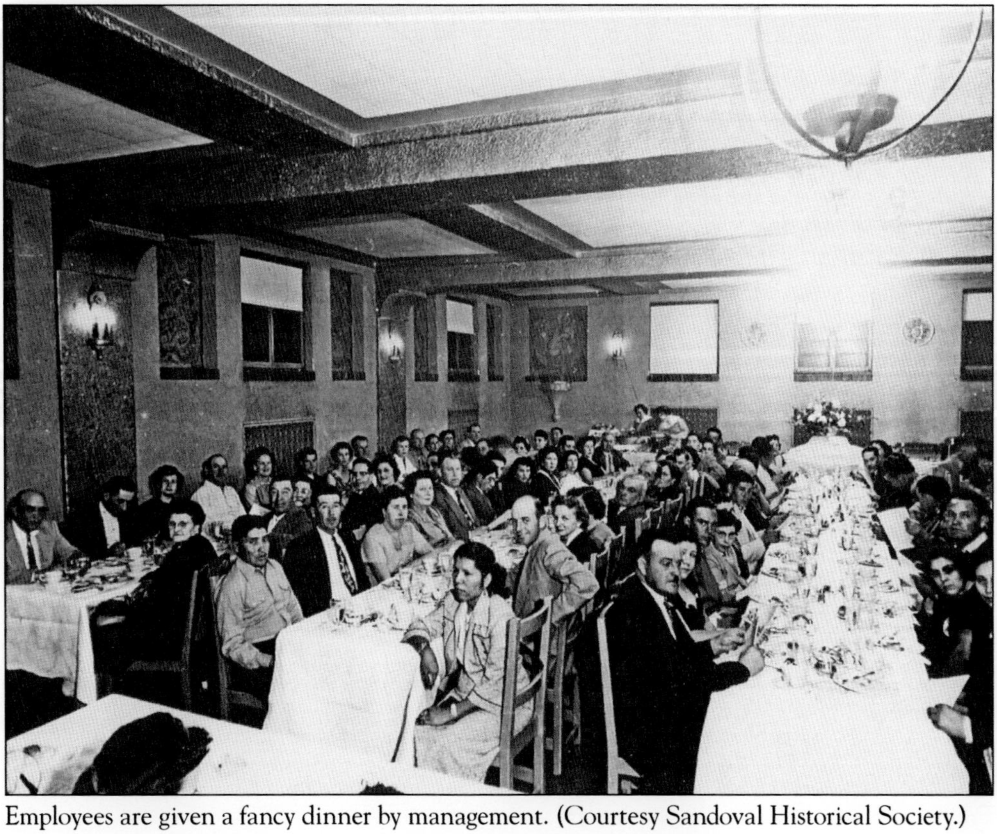

Employees are given a fancy dinner by management. (Courtesy Sandoval Historical Society.)

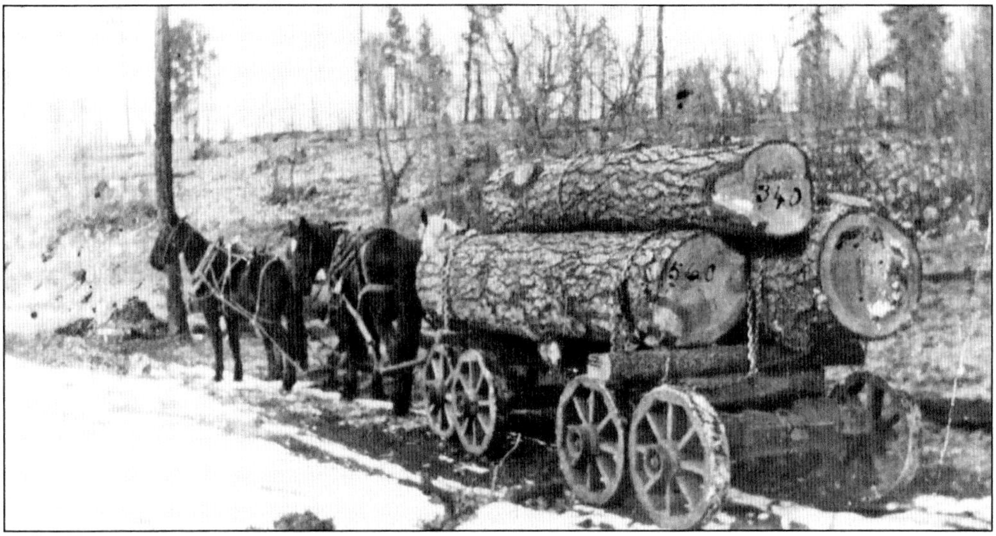

When the White Pine Lumber Company went into receivership in 1931, George Breece and T. P. Gallagher, who had formed the New Mexico Lumber and Timber Company, purchased the assets and obligations of the company. Breece was an expert in marketing lumber. (Courtesy Sandoval Historical Society.)

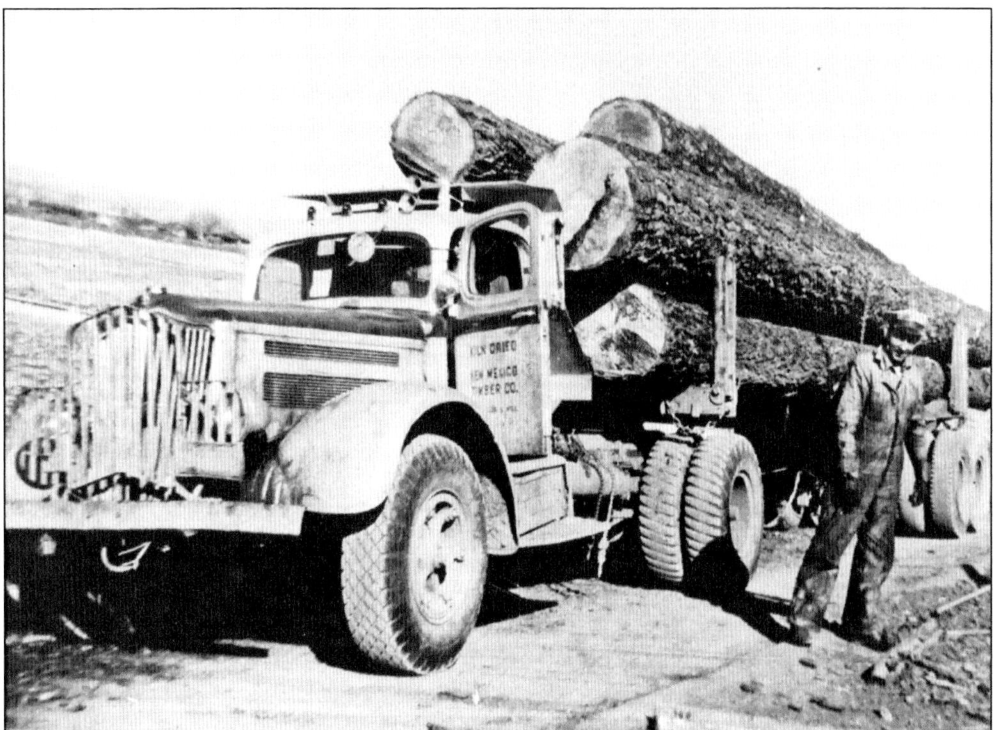

John Schorr worked for the New Mexico Lumber and Timber Company in the 1930s. (Courtesy Sandoval County Historical Society.)

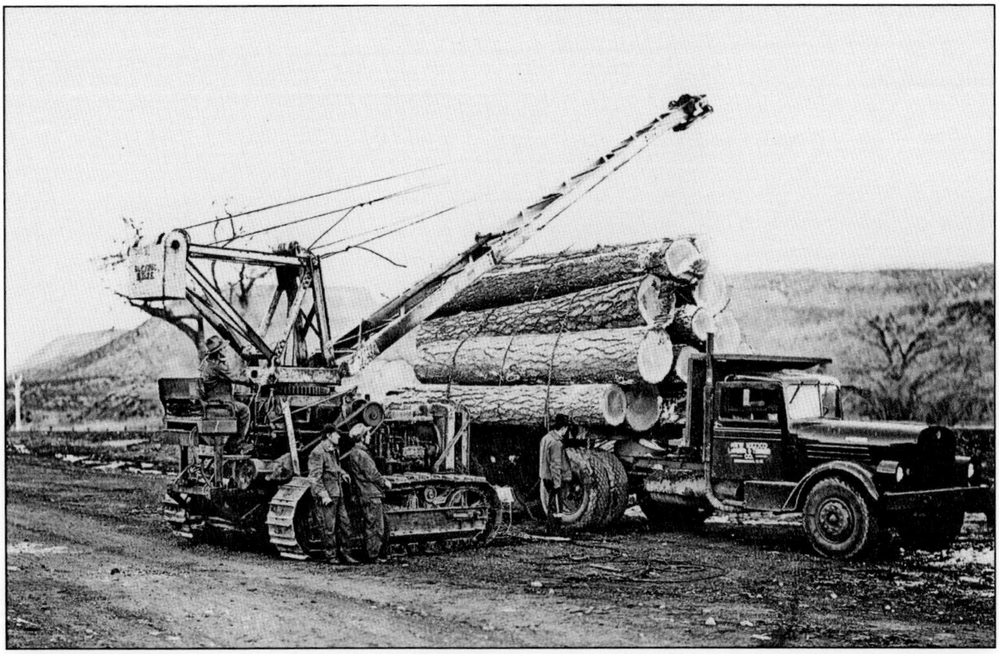

Henry Darnell is operating the first Load Master in a Jemez operation. J. L. Chesshire is standing by the truck. (Courtesy Sandoval Historical Society.)

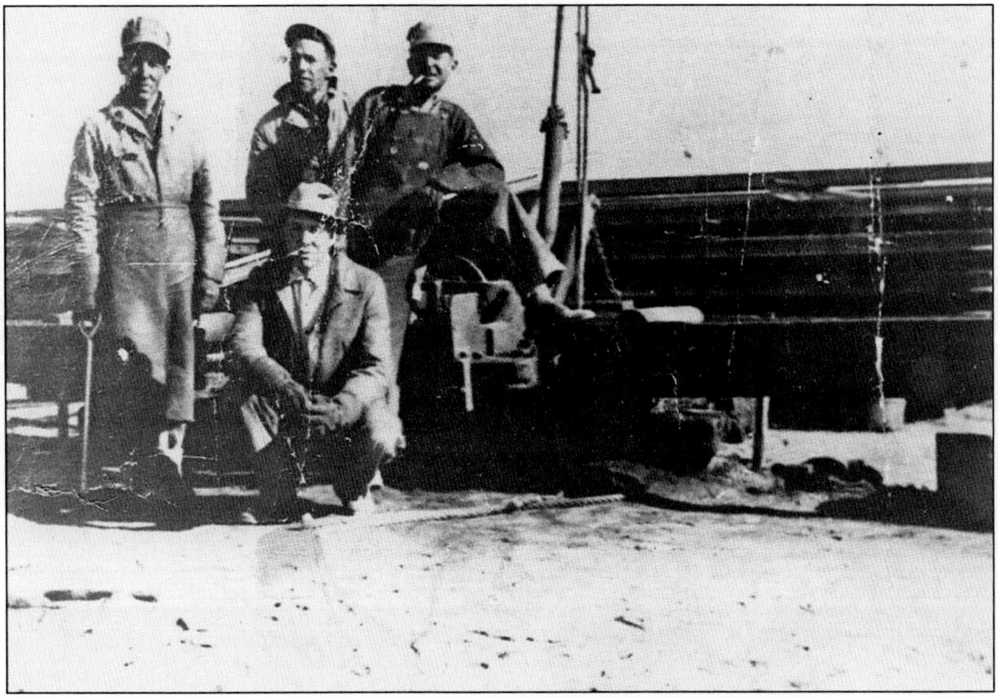

When the railroad became unfeasible, rails were pulled and sold to the war effort or to China. This picture was taken in 1941. (Courtesy Sandoval County Historical Society.)

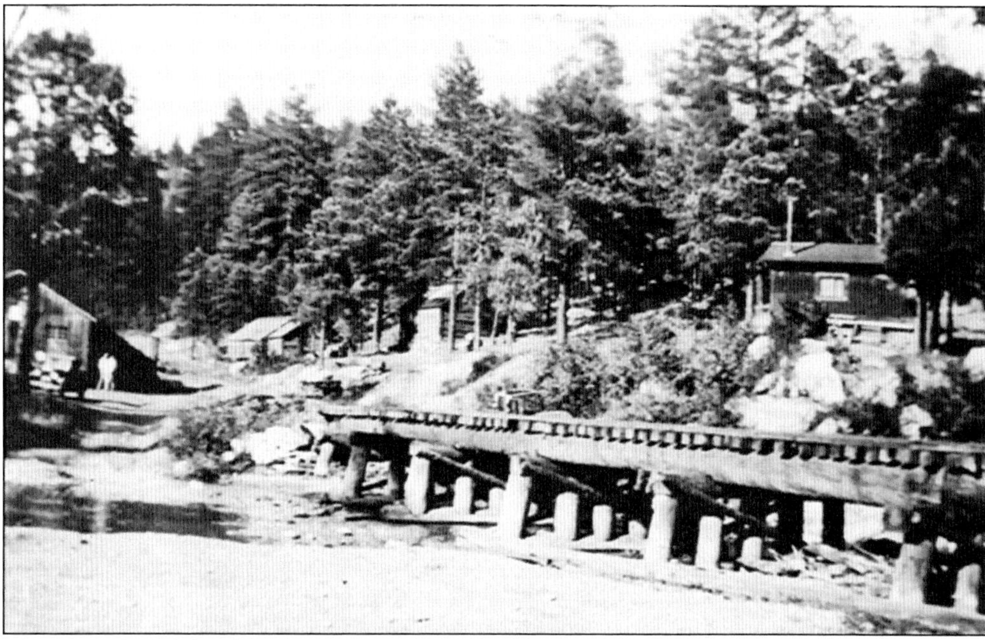

The cabins back behind the trestle are probably those of the workers in the Porter logging operation. The trestle brought railcars to the site. (Courtesy Sandoval County Historical Society.)

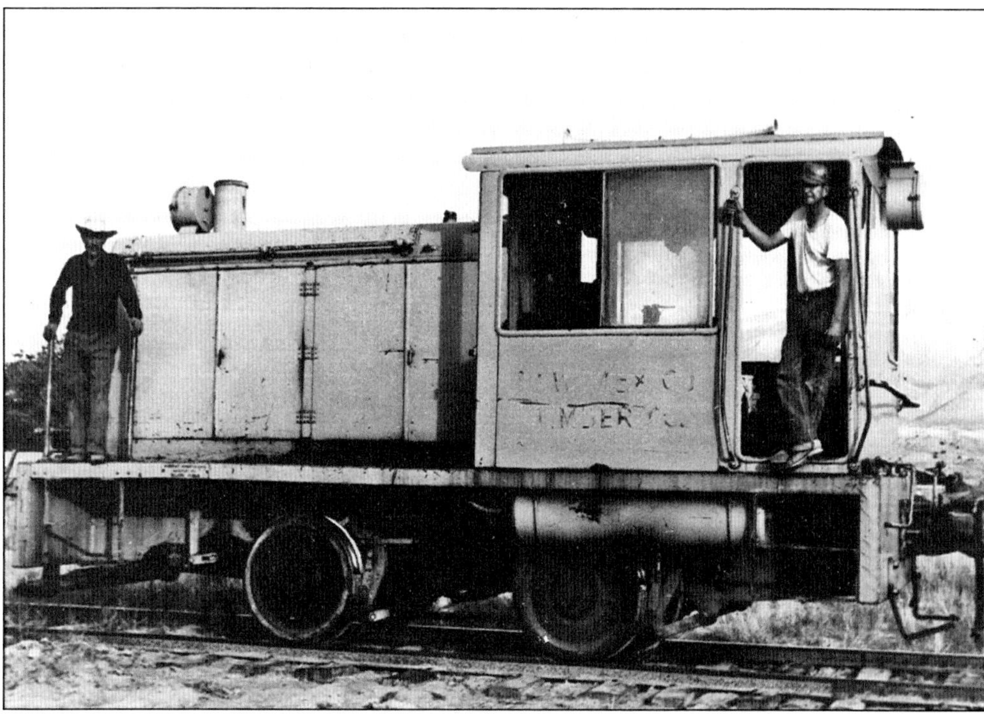

This was the New Mexico Timber Company's last railroad locomotive at Bernalillo in 1964. The 20-ton unit was used to switch cars of lumber from the mill to the Atchison, Topeka and Santa Fe connection. (Courtesy Sandoval County Historical Society.)

Harry Henry Koppel worked for White Pine Lumber Company. This picture was taken in 1937. (Courtesy Sandoval County Historical Society.)

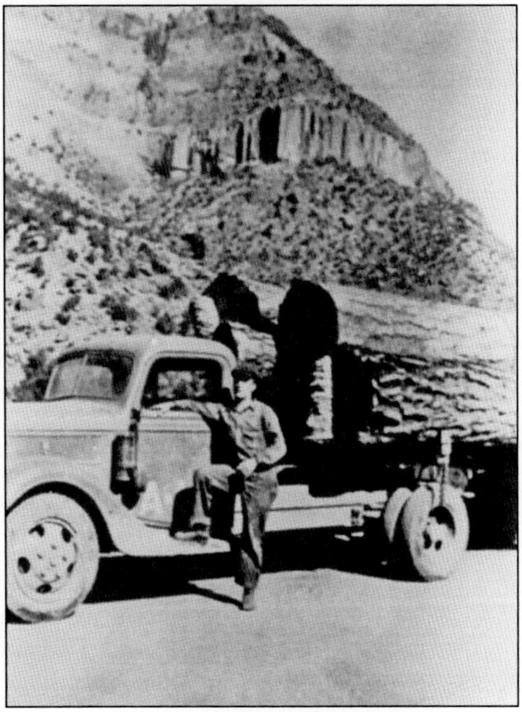

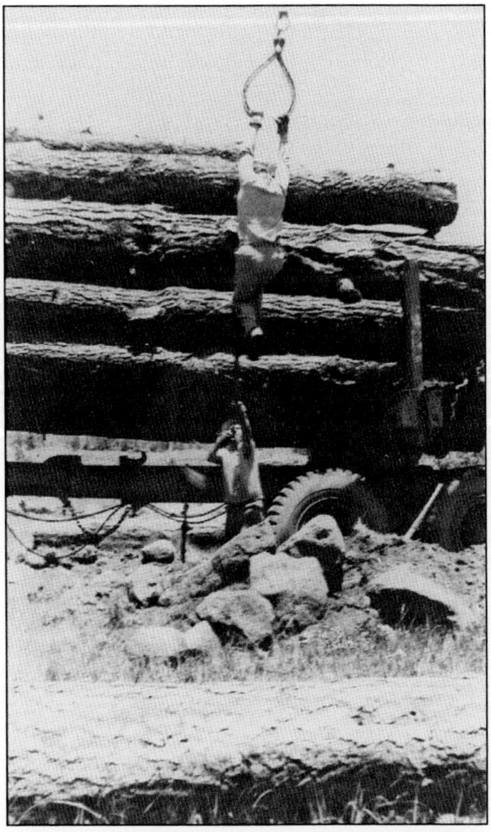

Working for the New Mexico Timber Company in the Jemez Mountains are Bill Aldridge on tongs and Bruce Stewart on the ground. (Courtesy Sandoval County Historical Society.)

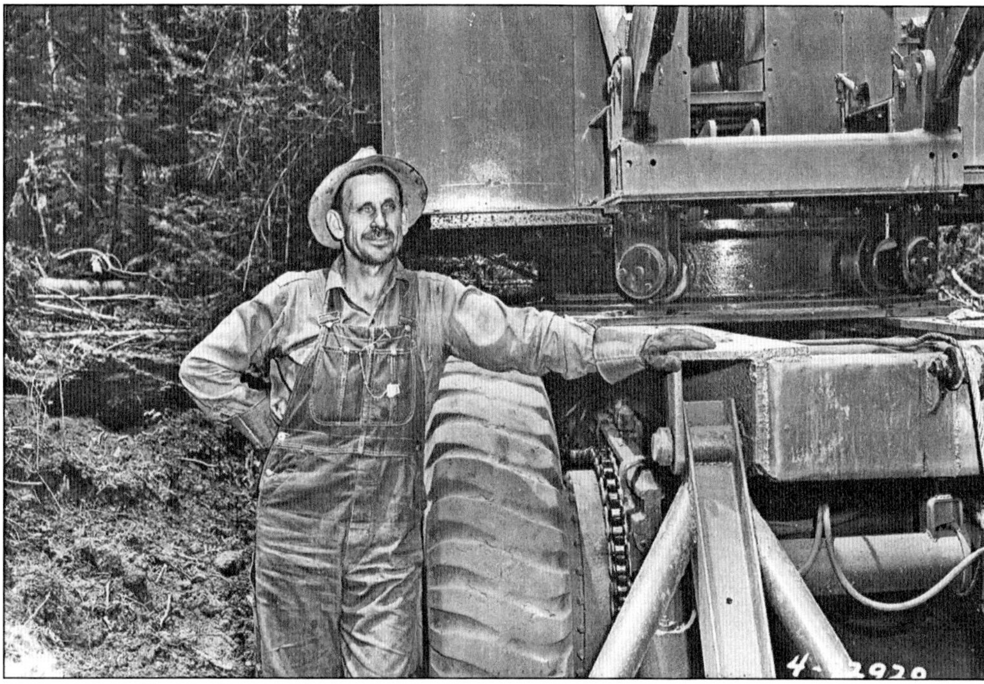

Henry Darnell was the woods foreman and operator of the link belt-logging crane. (Courtesy Sandoval County Historical Society.)

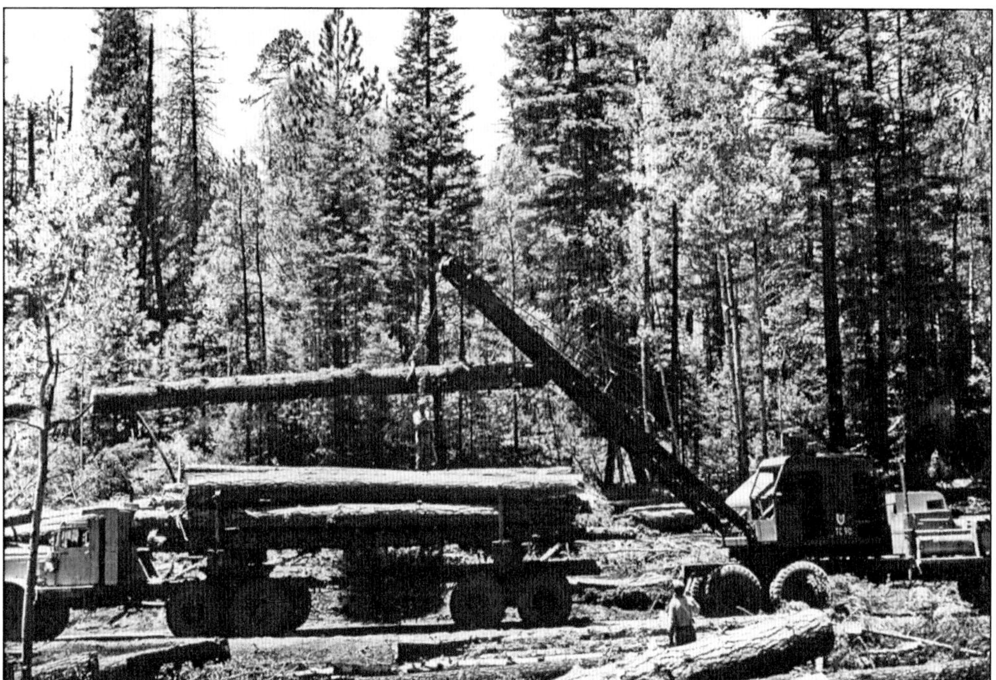

Henry Darnell (on top of truck) and Ford Ralston are top loading a timber truck in 1953. The new American log loader hoisted one log at a time onto a truck or rail car. (Courtesy Sandoval County Historical Society.)

Five

Smokeys

The Santa Fe National Forest plays a major role in the life of Jemez Springs. It surrounds the village and extends far north of Jemez Springs and south until it runs into the Pueblo of Jemez. It contains 2.8 million acres and became a national forest in 1915. Most visitors must go through Jemez Springs to reach hiking, camping, or fishing sites, so in the summer season, there is a line of cars driving through the village, sometimes stopping for lunch or dinner, picnic supplies, or gifts and souvenirs from one of the gift shops. When the U.S. Forest Service closes the forest because of a drought, all of the businesses in Jemez Springs suffer.

The forest service acts as the fire department for any fires that occur on its land, much to the relief of the local citizenry. It manages controlled burns to clear the forest of dead trees and overgrown areas to lessen the fire danger. It maintains forest service roads, which are often the only way to get from point A to point B. And some of the more popular tourist attractions such as Soda Dam, Battleship Rock, and Jemez Falls are on forest service land. The national forest grew largely by taking over land deeded to the service.

The village itself is a narrow strip of developed land surrounded by high mesas. Like the high mesas, the forest service land protects Jemez Springs from overdevelopment. There are not enough people or land for a McDonald's or Burger King, a movie theater, a drugstore, a hardware store, or anything but a convenience store and a Subway. Still people worry.

As an April Fool's joke a few years ago, some wag put up a sign in a vacant lot that read, "Coming Soon: McDonald's," complete with the golden arches logo. Several people forgot what day it was and went storming to the mayor to protest.

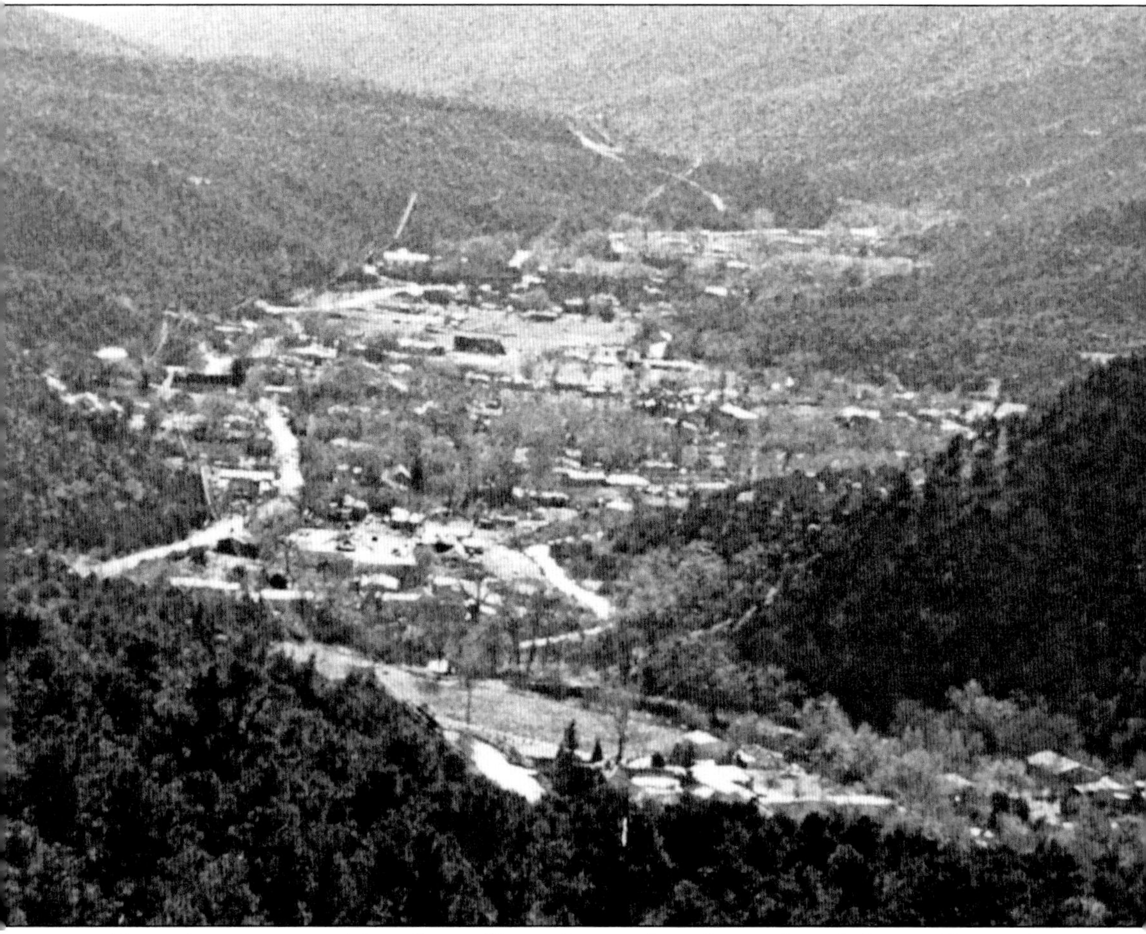

Shown here is a view of the village of Jemez Springs from the north end of town. Notice the way the forest encircles the village. (Courtesy Robert Borden.)

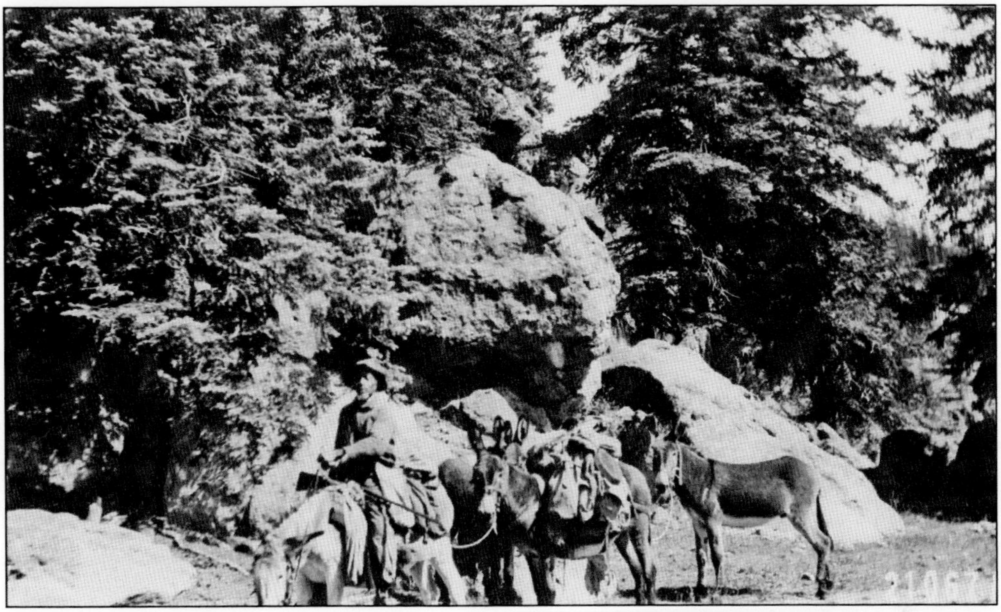

"Uncle" Reed, an old character of Bland, is on his way to Sulphur Springs to bring back a passenger. (Courtesy U.S. Forest Service.)

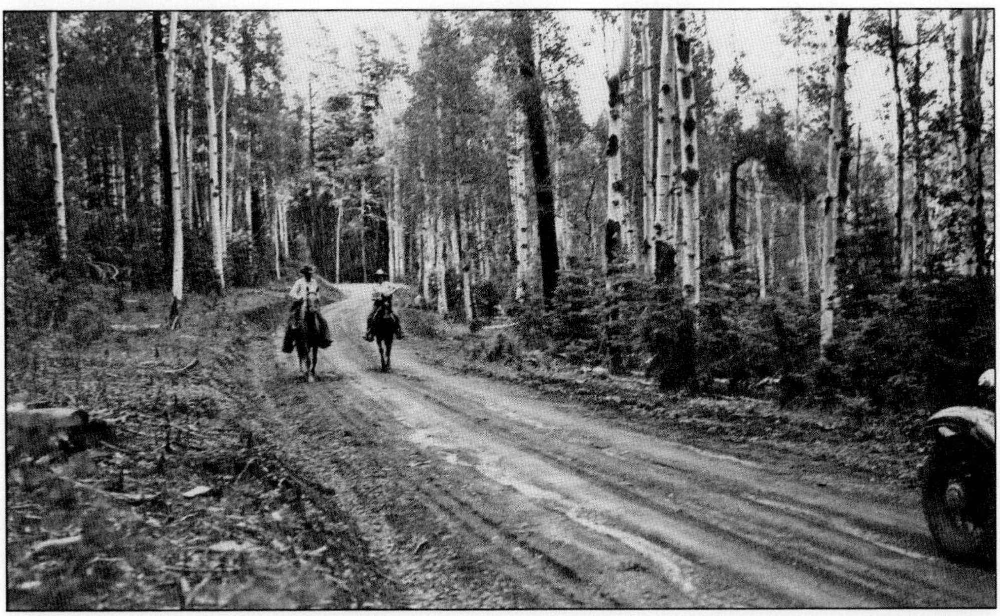

Even today, many of the forest roads remain unpaved, which probably makes traveling by horse easier than traveling by car. (Courtesy U.S. Forest Service.)

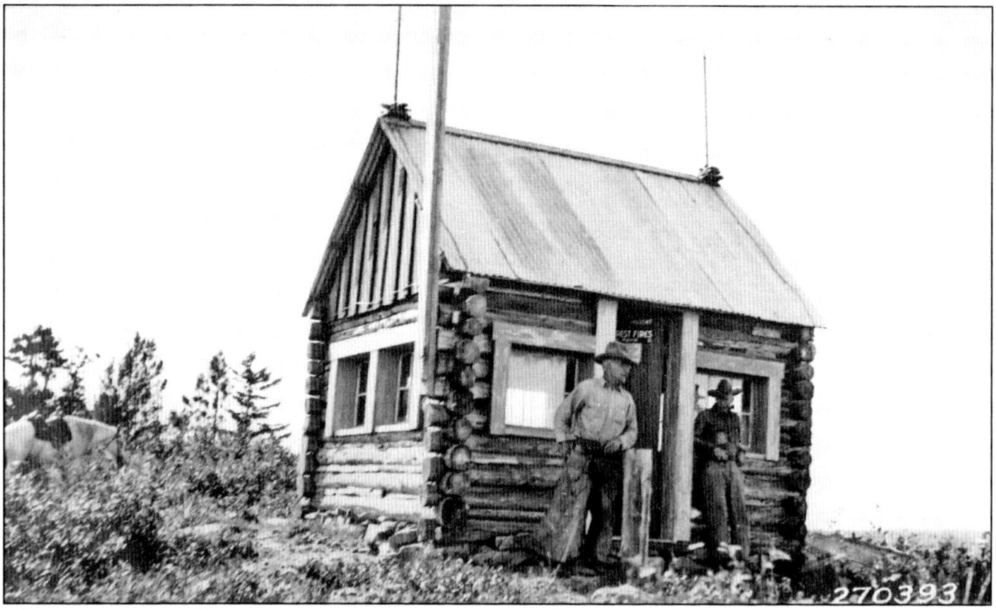

This was a fire lookout. It was replaced in 1933. Note the lightning protection. (Courtesy U.S. Forest Service.)

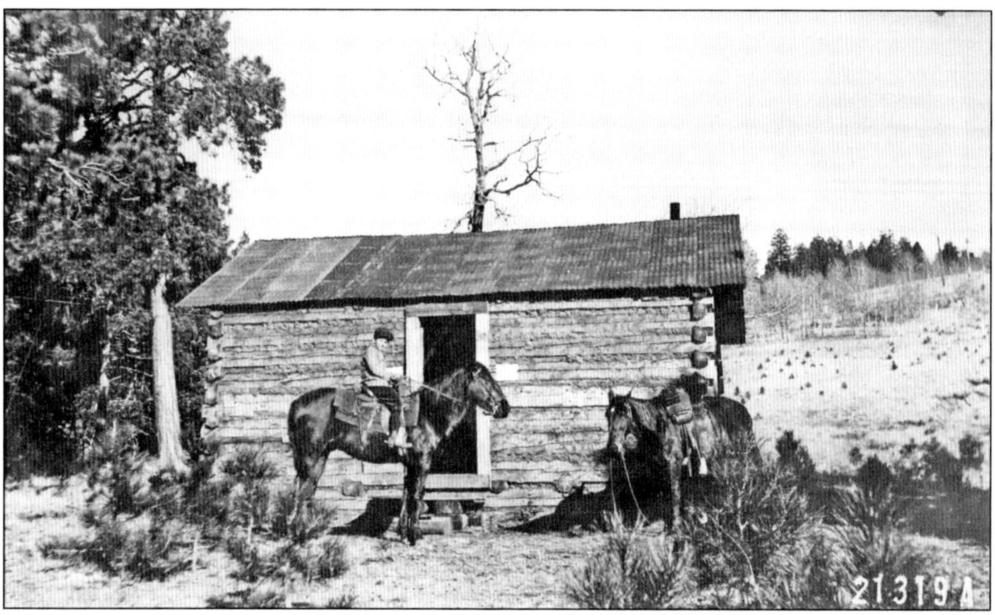

This is the barn at Gallinas Ranger Station in 1938. The horses, Traveler and Pardner, had personalized stall doors. (Courtesy U.S. Forest Service.)

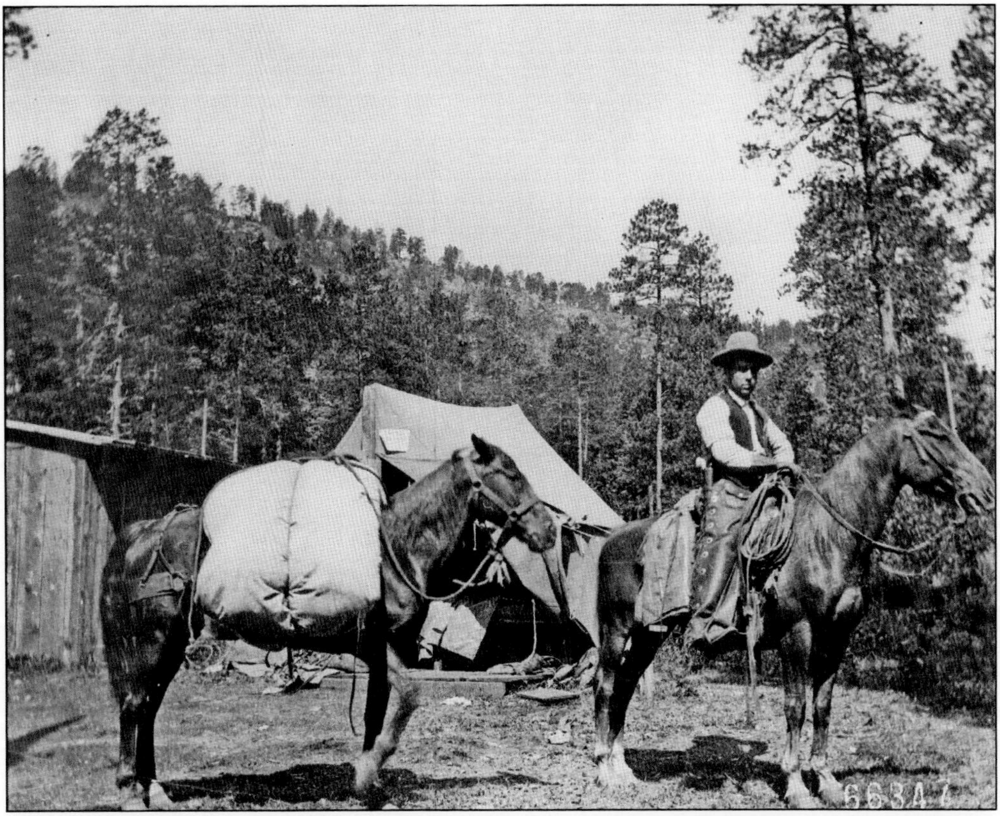

This is one of the rare photographs of an armed forest officer. Some districts and some forests were rougher than others. This ranger was in Horse Canyon in Sandoval County. (Courtesy U.S. Forest Service.)

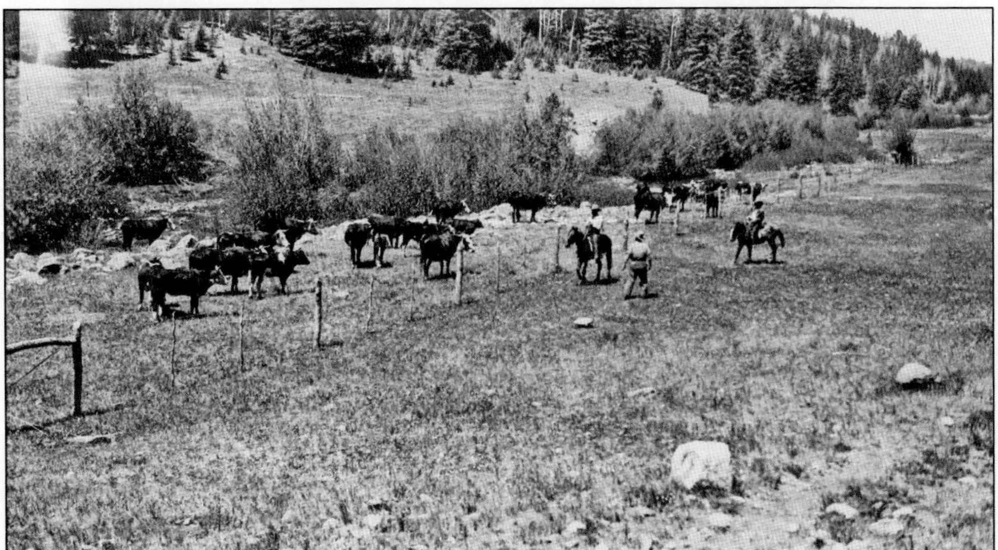

Some cattle graze in a Rio de las Vacas (river of the cows) pasture in 1936. Cattle grazing, lumbering, and mining are allowed in national forests. (Courtesy U.S. Forest Service.)

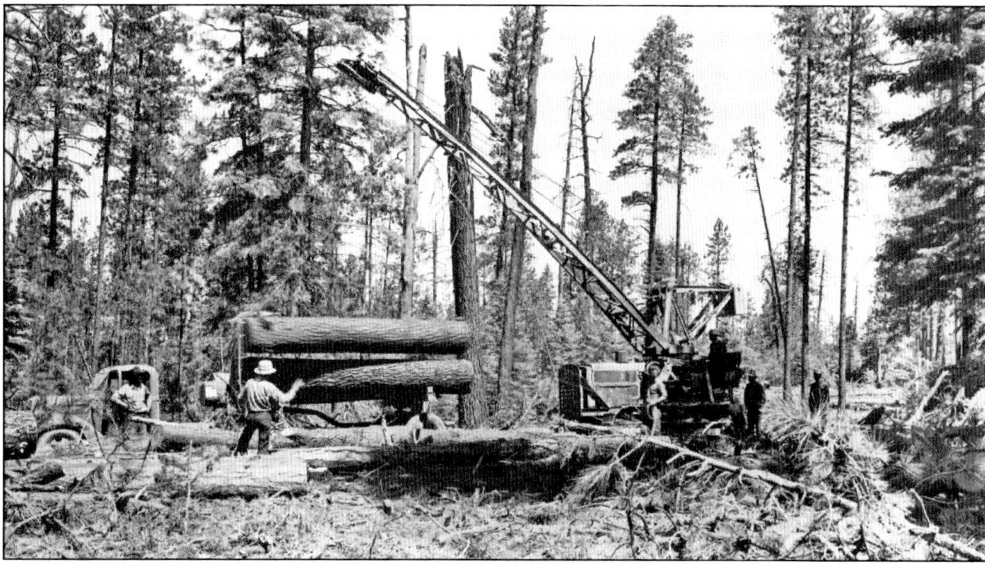

Laborers load large Douglas fir logs in 1937. This is part of a New Mexico Lumber and Timber Company timber sale. (Courtesy U.S. Forest Service.)

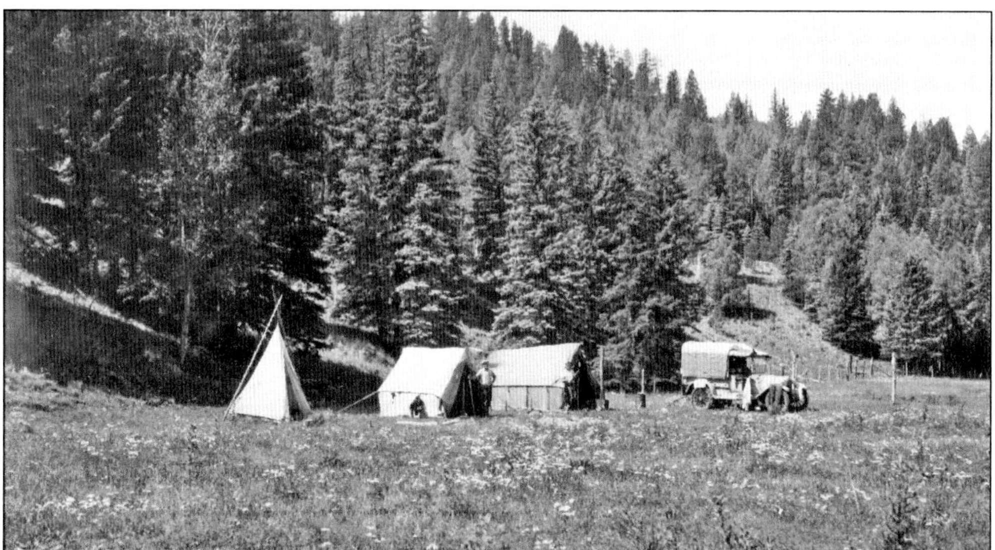

The value of the trees for lumber had to be appraised by the forest service before they could be put up for sale. This is a timber appraisal camp. (Courtesy U.S. Forest Service.)

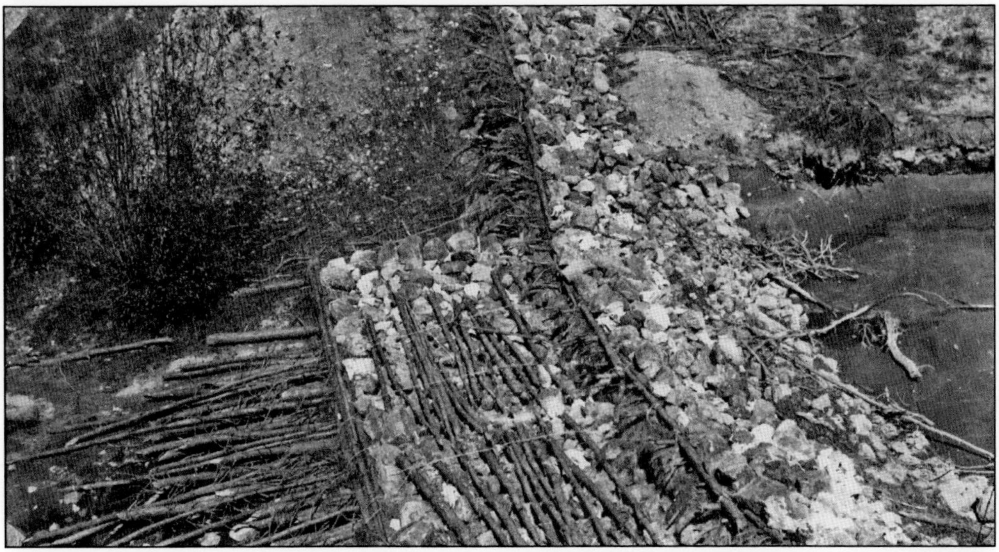

A forest service dam on Sulphur Creek shows a particular type of construction. It was done by the La Cueva Civilian Conservation Corps camp in 1933. The CCC was very active in the Jemez area. (Courtesy U.S. Forest Service.)

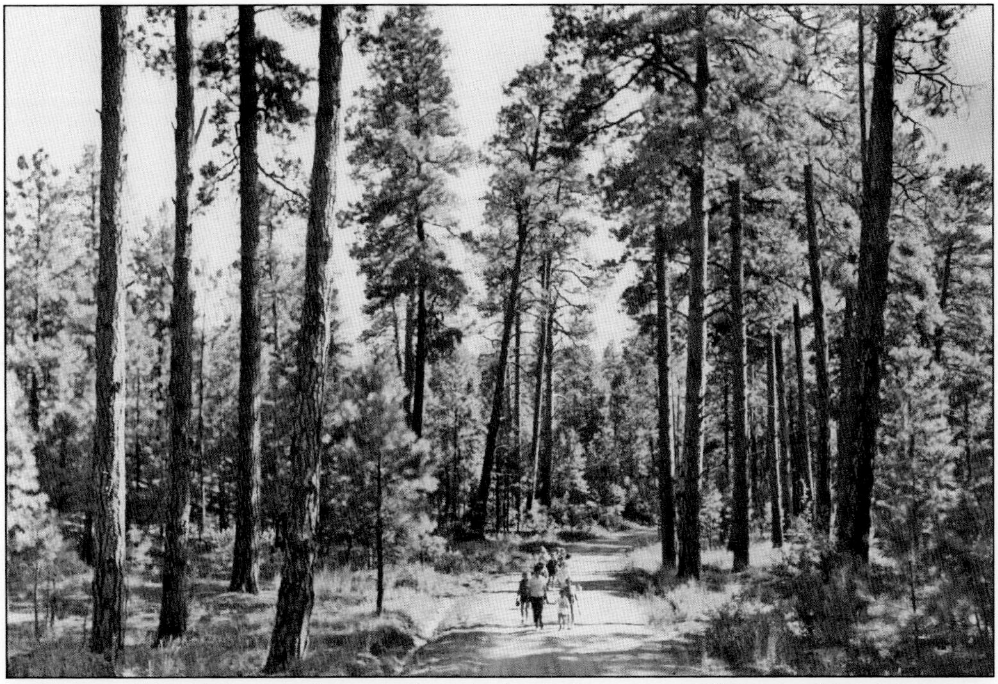

Girl Scouts take a hike on a forest road on the Jemez District in 1957. Camp Eliza Seligman is nearby on a small tract of private land. Most of the Scouts' recreational activity takes place on the national forest surrounding the camp. The camp, and the area, had a capacity of 66 girls, ages 9 through 11, every two weeks. (Courtesy U.S. Forest Service.)

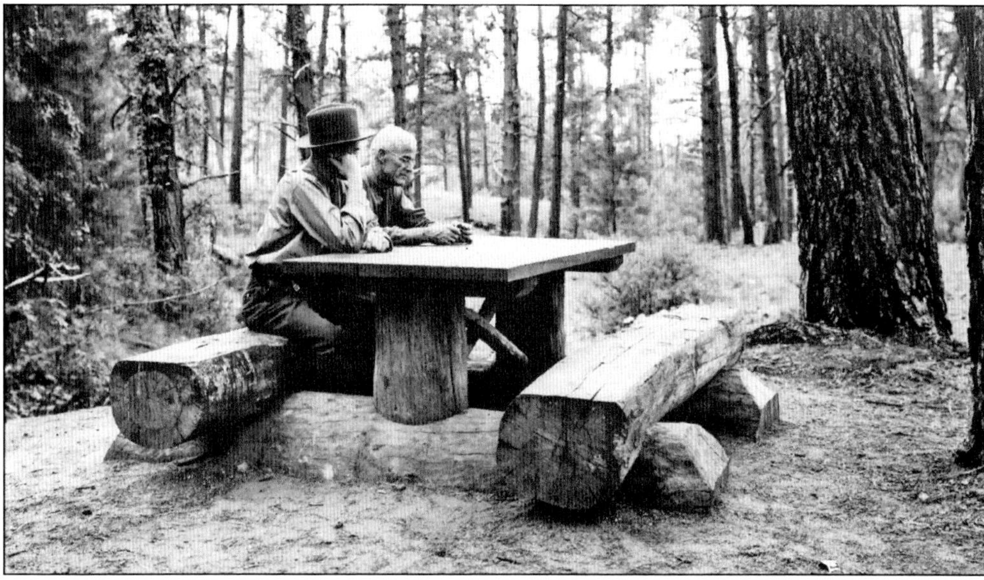

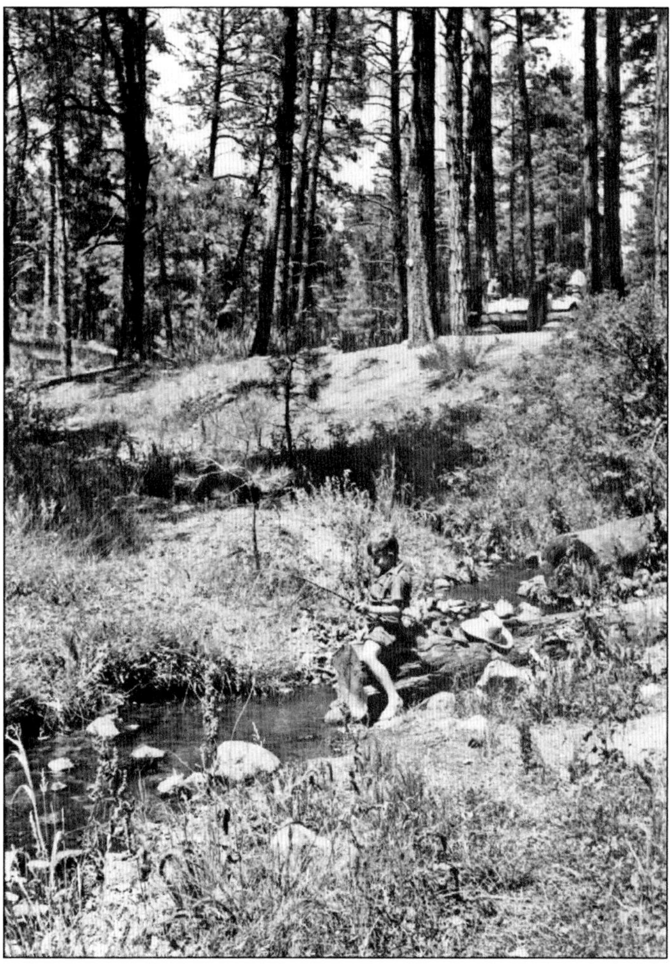

This photograph shows a typical picnic table in Paliza Campground and Picnic Area in 1936. The picture was taken by a Washington office inspector who commented that the large cross logs on which the table and seats rest do not seem necessary. They were a considerable expense, he said, that might be saved by supporting the log seats on individual posts under each end of the seat. (Courtesy U.S. Forest Service.)

A young fisherman at the Paliza Forest Campground in 1939 is almost hidden by the woodland scene. Paliza was a project of the Civilian Conservation Corps in the 1930s. (Courtesy U.S. Forest Service.)

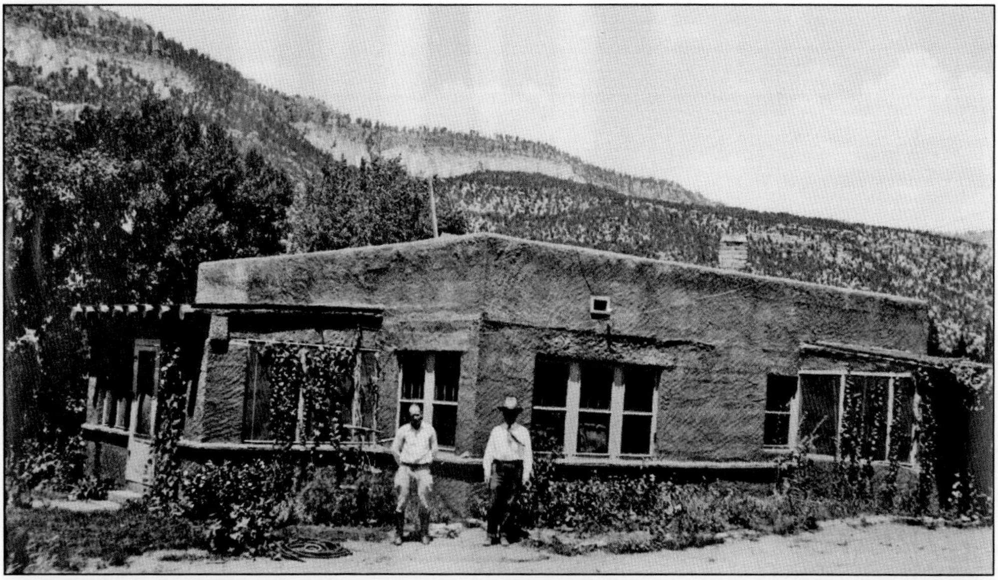

Shown here is the forest service ranger station in Jemez Springs. (Courtesy U.S. Forest Service.)

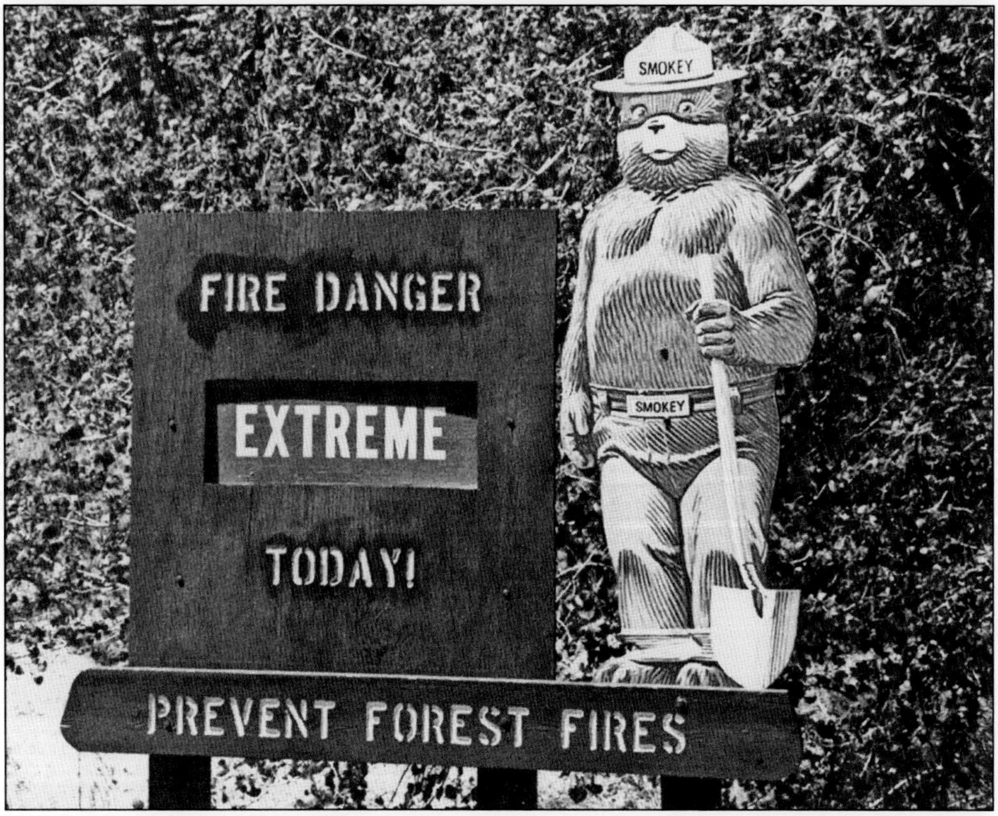

Smokey the Bear is still the symbol for warning people about forest danger. In the summer, lightning-caused fires require constant vigilance on the part of the national forest personnel. Signs like these tell people what the fire conditions are so they can take precautions. If the fire danger is too high, the forest service will close the forests to all uses. (Courtesy Robert Borden.)

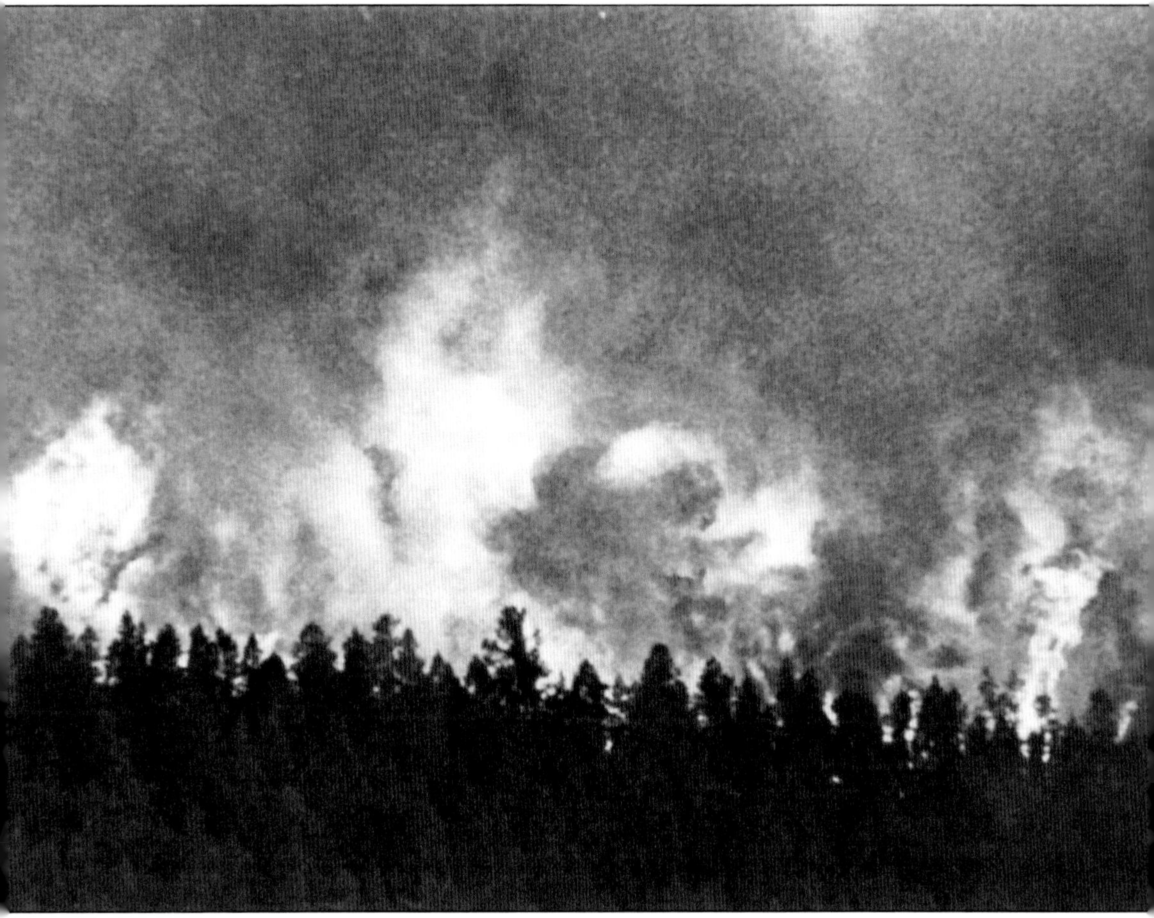

Fires like the Lakes Fire some 20 miles from Jemez Springs are a reminder that forests surround the people of Jemez Springs. The 2002 fire destroyed four summer homes, caused the evacuation of three communities, burned around 4,000 acres, and was the first time a Type 1 incident team had been dispatched to the Jemez in August. (Courtesy Robert Borden.)

Six

Jemez Country

Attempts were made to turn the Jemez's scenic beauty into a business opportunity. One such endeavor was Rancho Rea, an upscale ranch built in 1926. Seth Seiders, who owned Rancho Rea (named for his wife, Rhea), was a shady character said to have connections with the Chicago underworld. Seiders built a house, an exclusive and technically illegal bar, a little store, and various outbuildings. Rumors spread that Rancho Rea was really a hideout for Chicago mobsters. Strangers were seen on the road driven in Deusenbergs, Stutzes, Cadillacs, and Pierce Arrows. It was said guards at the gate carried machine guns. When Seiders's wife got tired of Rancho Rea, he built Rancho Chico on the north edge of Jemez Springs. He also built a hotel in Jemez Springs that was locally called "the old stone hotel."

The IRS forced the sale of Rancho Rea. The second owner died of a gunshot wound, and the ranch was idle until sold again. The next owners changed the name to Rancho Real (someone mistakenly told them that "Rea" meant "witch" in Spanish). World War II closed it down, and health problems caused another sale. The new owners changed the name to the Lazy Ray (their cattle brand).

Eventually the Lazy Ray was sold to an Albuquerque corporation, which attempted to turn it into a viable dude ranch. The new owners published a newspaper called the *Lazy Ray Ranch News*, whose purpose was to promote the ranch as a vacationer's paradise. Guests could watch rodeos at the ranch, fish and hunt on a private reserve, take early morning breakfast rides, and visit nearby towns. There was also a page soliciting buyers for 200 "plush" half-acre lots. All this promotion was in vain. In 1970, the forest service acquired the land and the buildings were torn down.

Today there are no dude ranches or private hideaways in the Jemez Mountains. What the Jemez had to sell—aside from the hot springs—was its scenery.

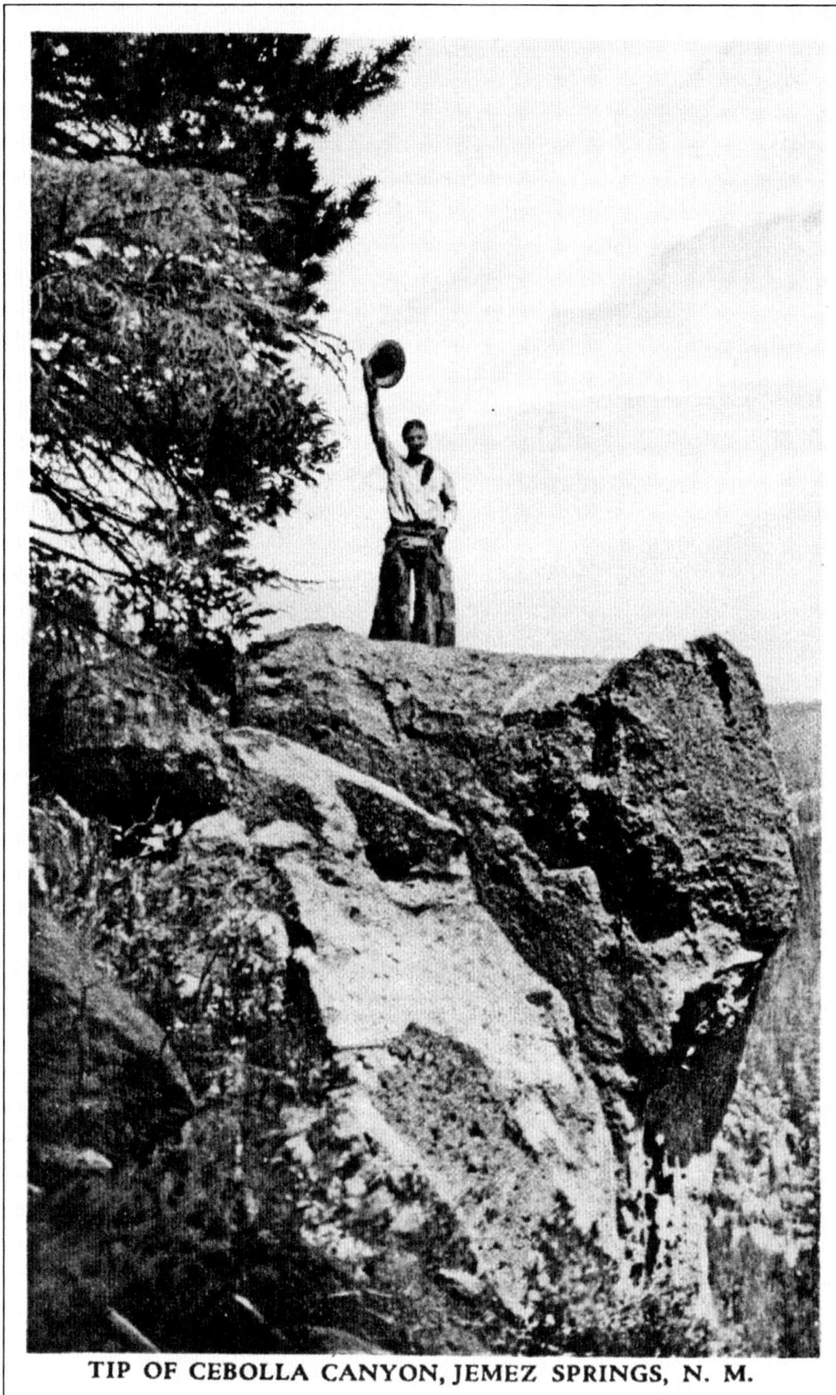

The scene of a lone man atop a high rock was a standard Western image. It was supposed to suggest the grandeur of the Western landscape as well as the independent, rugged nature of the men who inhabited the place. Cebolla Canyon is about 25 miles northeast of Jemez Springs. (Courtesy Nancy Tucker.)

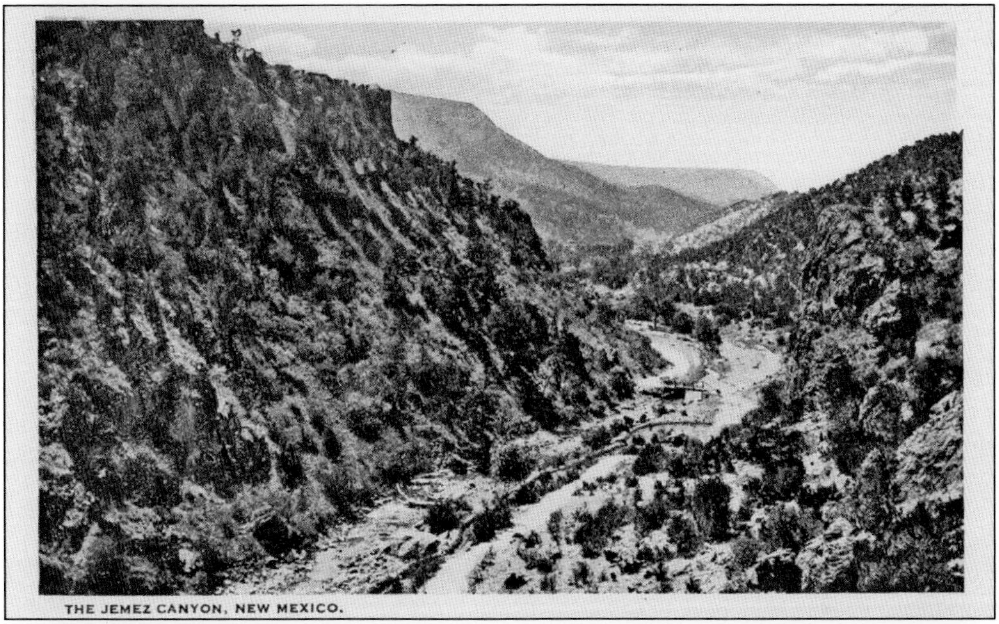

The back of this postcard reads, "This canyon is located about fifty miles northwest of Albuquerque, and is one of rare scenic beauty: it contains many wonders in mineral springs that effect miraculous cures, historic ruins and the famous Soda Dam." (Courtesy Nancy Tucker.)

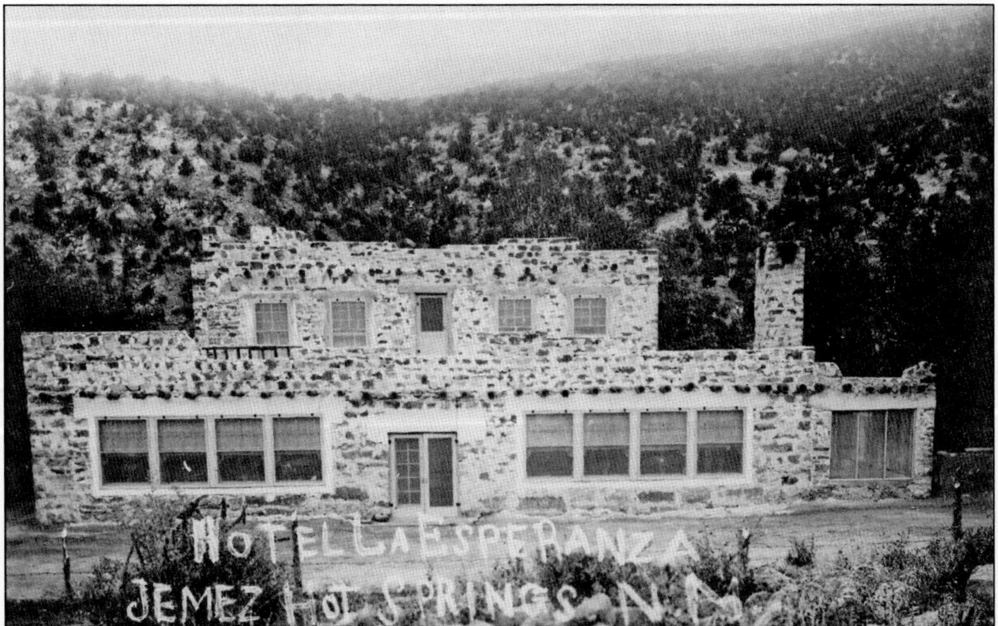

The back of the postcard from Esperanza Hotel in Jemez Springs reads, "Here's the Hotel where we spent the 4th of July. It's 65 miles from Albuquerque and called 'Hay-mez'. The eats are fine and it's up in the big pines. Fine drives take you to the soda and sulphur springs up at an elevation of 10,000 ft. The streams are full of water and trout as well as fishermen. Most people go up here to spend their vacation, as it's so restful and pretty up here. The guests dress up in their best in the evening and play cards or dance and have a good time generally." (Courtesy Jim Coad.)

Rancho Rea

In the Cool, Green Jemez Mountains, Most Beautiful in America

LOCATION—Eighty-five miles northwest of Albuquerque, N. M., in the green, picturesque Jemez Mountains, southern end of the Colorado Rockies. In the center of a quarter-million acres of forest preserve.

ALTITUDE—9,000 feet.

CLIMATE—Floods of sunshine! Cool in summer. Mild in winter. Rain a rarity and fogs unknown.

SEASONS—Summer, May first to Thanksgiving. Winter, December fifteenth to February fifteenth.

RECREATIONS—Hunting, fishing, hiking, trail riding, pack trips, motor tours, weekly rodeo, polo, horse games, swimming and aquatic sports, tennis, archery, trap shooting and target practice, horseshoe pitching. In winter, skiing, skating, tobogganing, sleighing, bobsledding, trapping.

ACCOMMODATIONS—Limited to thirty guests at a time. No tourists or transients. Just your own little party—plus true Western hospitality!

RANCH-HOUSE—Brand-new. Built for its owner's private use. Living and lounge room like your city club. Specially designed, hand-wrought fixtures. Tile floors—Navajo rugs—big, comfortable chairs and couches—Indian and Old Mexican pottery—animal heads and skins—reproducing piano—Orthophonic Victrola—eight-tube Radiola.

SLEEPING SUITES—In varying color schemes. Hardwood floors, electric lights, steam heat, private baths, fireplaces.

FOOD—Fit for a king! Prepared by a French chef. Everything raised on the place.

TRADING POST—Carries everything you'll need. Western clothing—cowboy hats—cameras and camera supplies—drugs and cosmetics—guns, ammunition and fishing equipment—Indian and Mexican pottery, rugs, silver, jewelry—cowboy souvenirs and far western novelties.

TRANSPORTATION—Fast, luxurious Santa Fe train service to Albuquerque or Bernalillo, N. M. Thence by Packard or Pierce-Arrow through the most colorful country in the Southwest.

Far away from the crowds, off all the traveled trails, Rancho Rea is ideal for small house parties by the month or season—for a quiet, exclusive place of rest and recreation for wives and children accustomed to every convenience—and for business and professional men who like to rough it during the day but come in at night to all the comforts they have at home. Rancho Rea will be good for your body and good for your soul.

For beautiful portfolio of photographs, complete information and rates, address the

RANCHO REA COMPANY

155 East Superior St., CHICAGO, ILL. JEMEZ SPRINGS, NEW MEXICO

Chicago Telephone: Superior 0857

Seth Seiders built a rambling ranch (named after his wife, Rhea) that included a house, a dance hall, a small store, and extensive outbuildings. Seiders, who came from Chicago, was known in that city for producing and selling illegal liquor, cheating on his taxes, and engaging in questionable business deals. (At left, courtesy 2005 July 4 Committee; below, Nancy Tucker.)

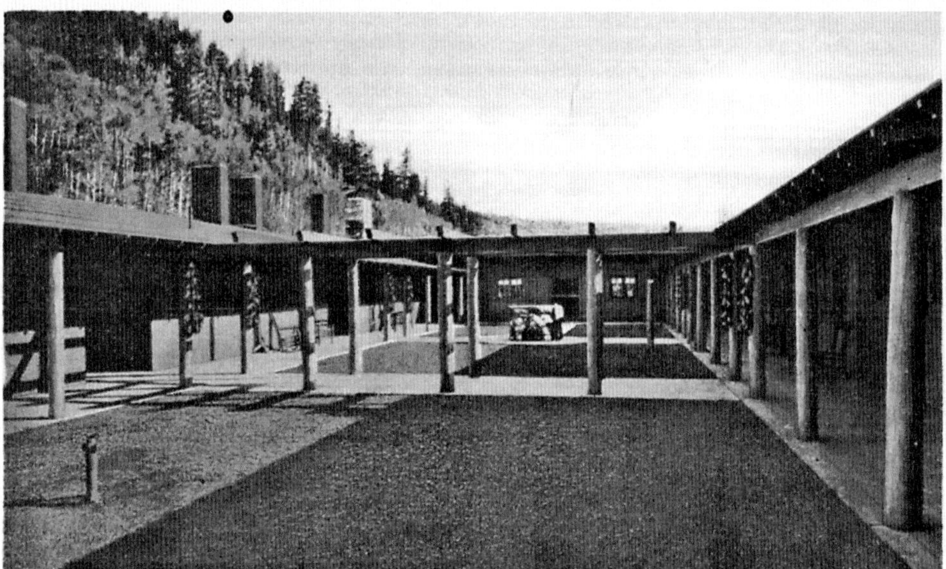

PATIO, RANCHO REA, JEMEZ SPRINGS, N. M.

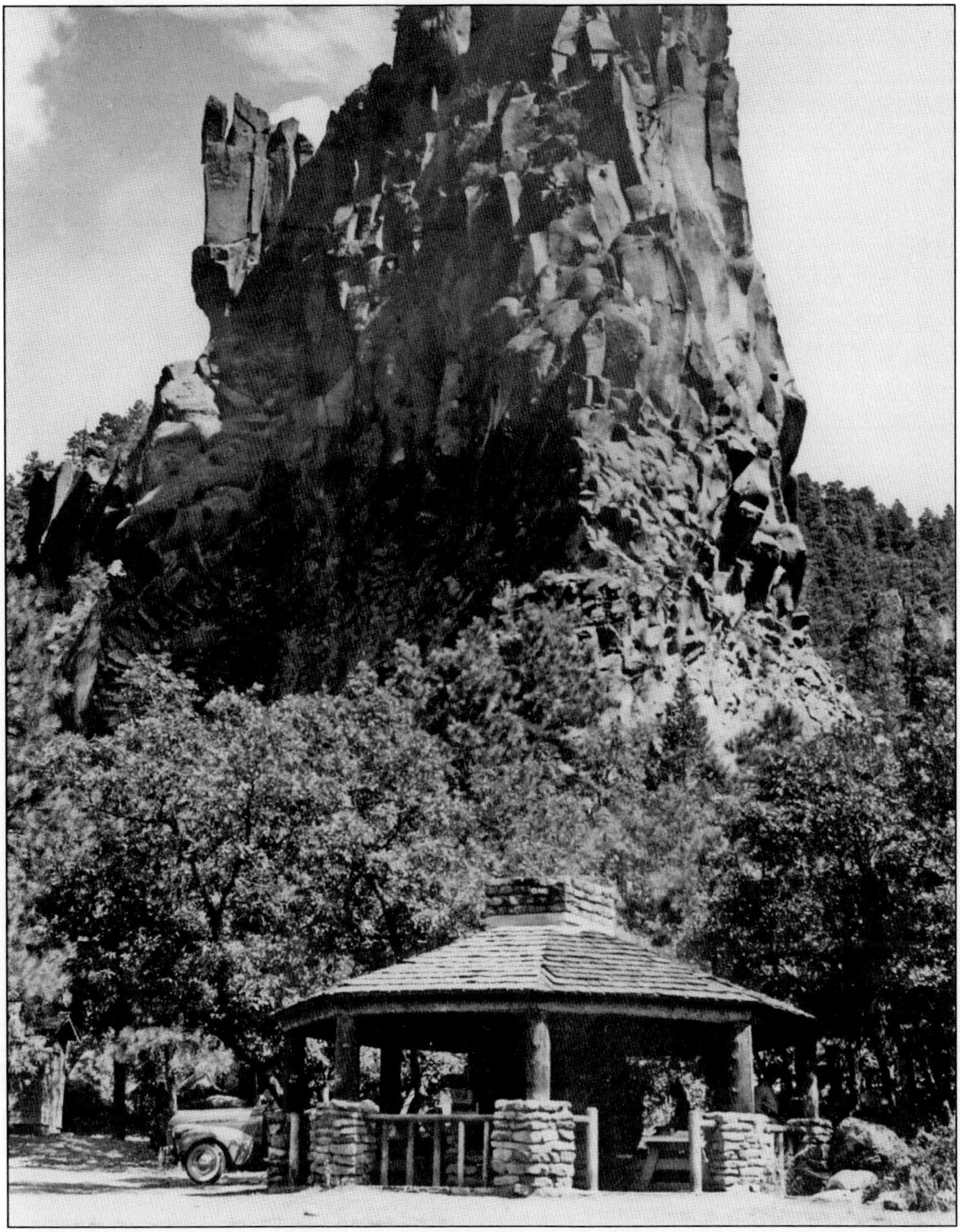

Another natural tourist stop is Battleship Rock, so named because it looks like the prow of a ship. YMCA Camp Shaver lies close to the rock. (Courtesy Jim Coad.)

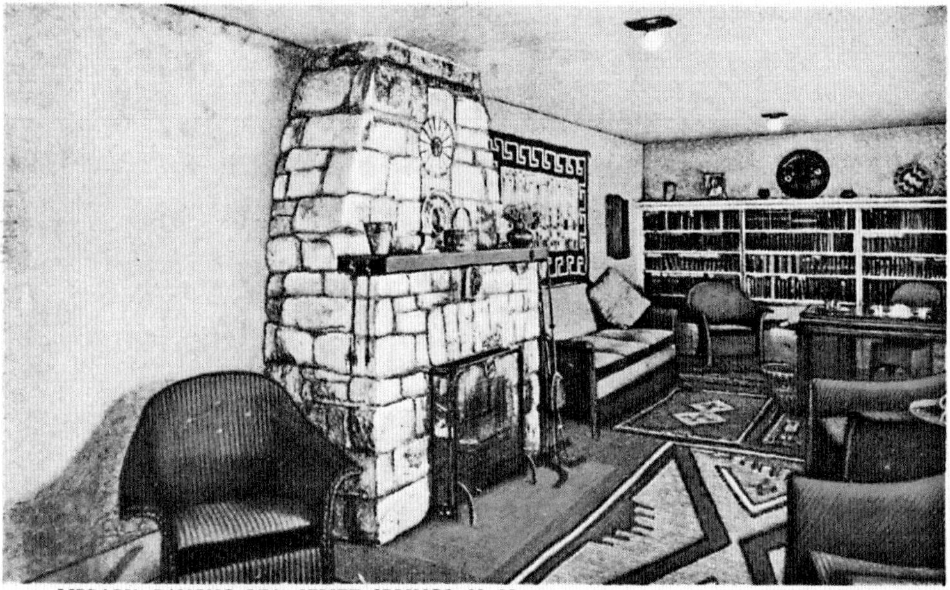

LIBRARY, RANCHO REA, JEMEZ SPRINGS, N. M.

Rancho Rea, limited to only 30 guests at a time—"no tourists or transients" welcome—offered a wide range of activities (including polo). The brochure bragged that the ranch library and lounge room was like a city club. Rough it by day, and then come back to all the comforts of home. It was widely speculated that those "30 guests" were actually gangsters or shady characters hiding out from the law. While no one can prove this, it is commonly believed by residents of the Jemez that Al Capone was one of the gangsters who chose Rancho Rea for a hideout. If so, he certainly had a plush hideout. Seth Seiders, the owner, did his best to make it feel like a Western experience, from the Navajo rugs to the animal heads mounted on the walls. (Both courtesy Jim Coad.)

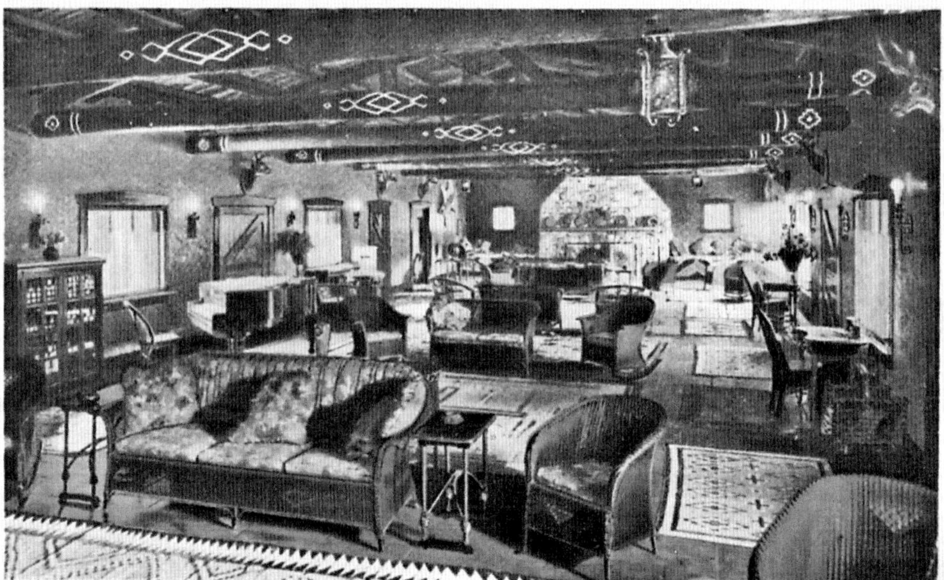

LIVING AND LOUNGE ROOM, RANCHO REA, JEMEZ SPRINGS, N. M.

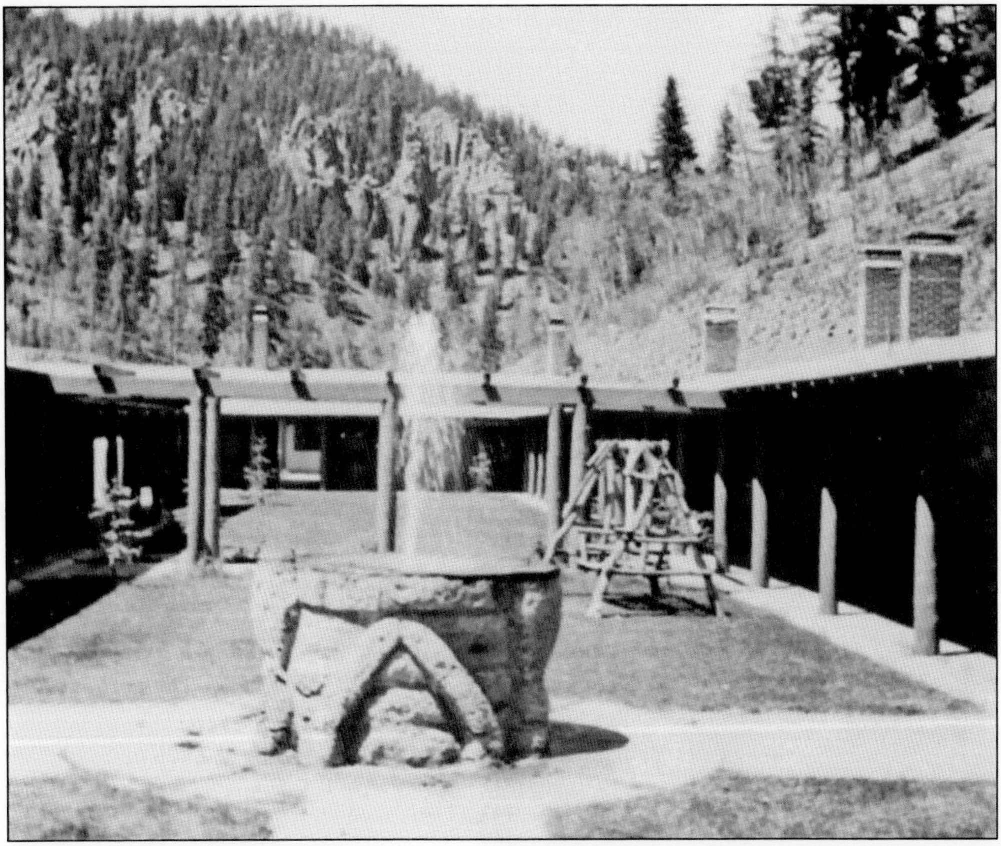

The sleeping suites at Rancho Rea bordered this beautiful patio. The suites had varying color schemes, and each had a hardwood floor, electric lights, steam heat, private bath, and fireplace. (Courtesy Jim Coad.)

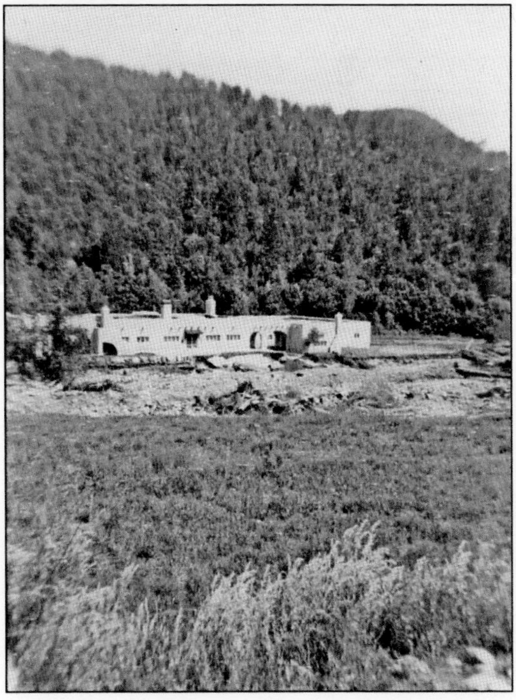

This photograph of Rancho Rea from a distance shows how it was backed by a huge pine forest but was high desert on the other side. (Courtesy Jim Coad.)

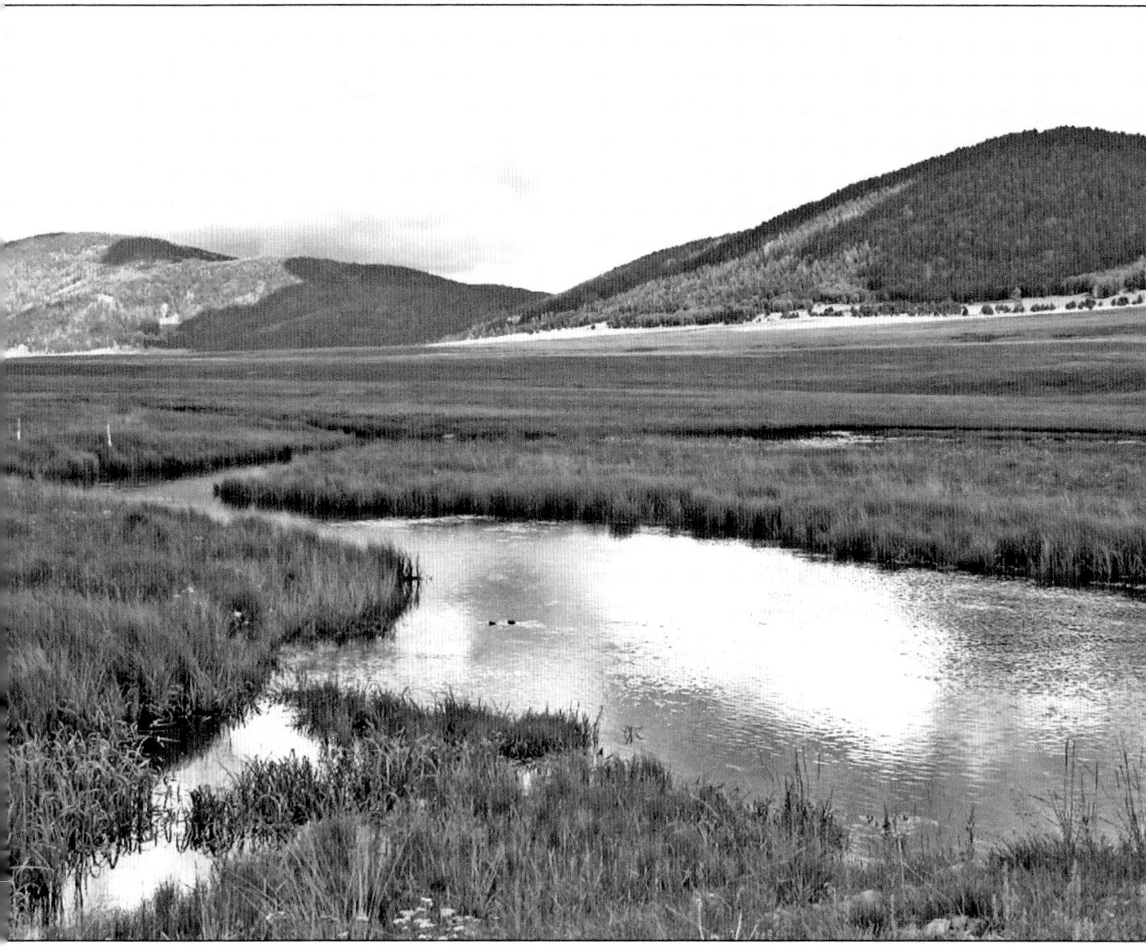

In July 2000, the federal government bought 88,900 acres of land, which has become the Valles Caldera National Preserve. At various times, the land, known as Baca Location No. 1, was used for sulfur mining, homesteading, a hot springs resort, and extensive livestock grazing. The land passed through several owners until it was sold to the federal government for $101 million. (Courtesy Robert Borden.)

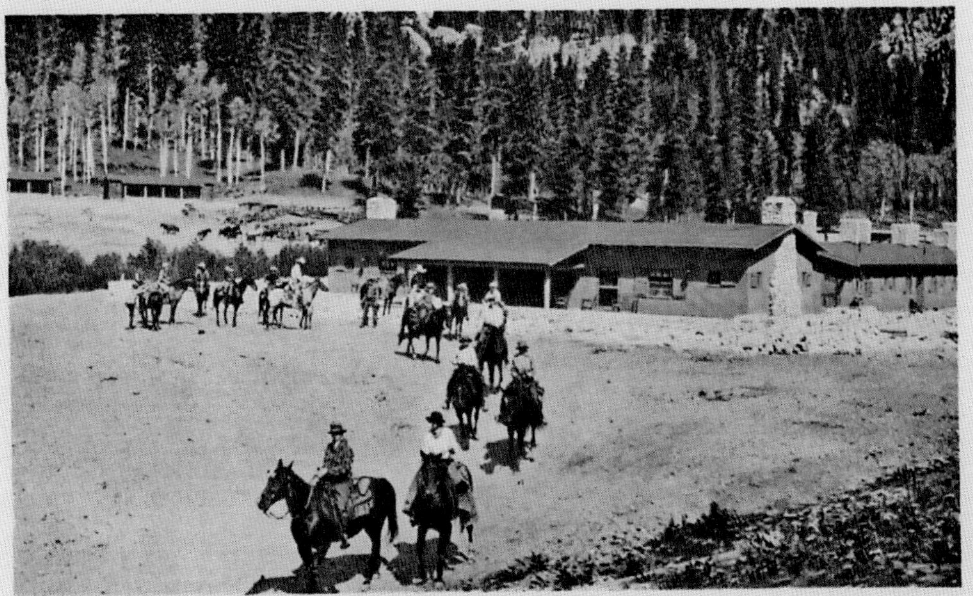

OFF FOR THE TRAILS, RANCHO REA, JEMEZ SPRINGS, N. M.

Trail riding was a popular activity at Rancho Rea. It gave the guests a chance to play cowboy as well as encounter some of the beautiful scenery, which lay at 9,000 feet above sea level. (Courtesy Jim Coad.)

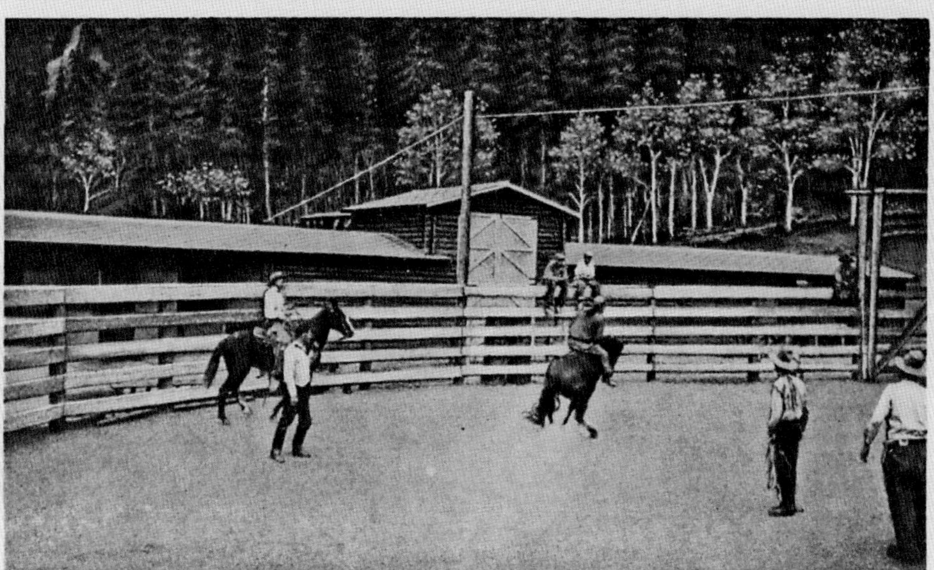

HIGH JINKS IN CORRAL, RANCHO REA, JEMEZ SPRINGS, N. M.

The hands at the ranch entertained guests with a rodeo complete with bucking broncos. Guests at the ranch were given a full menu of what life in the West was like—or what they thought it was like. (Courtesy Jim Coad.)

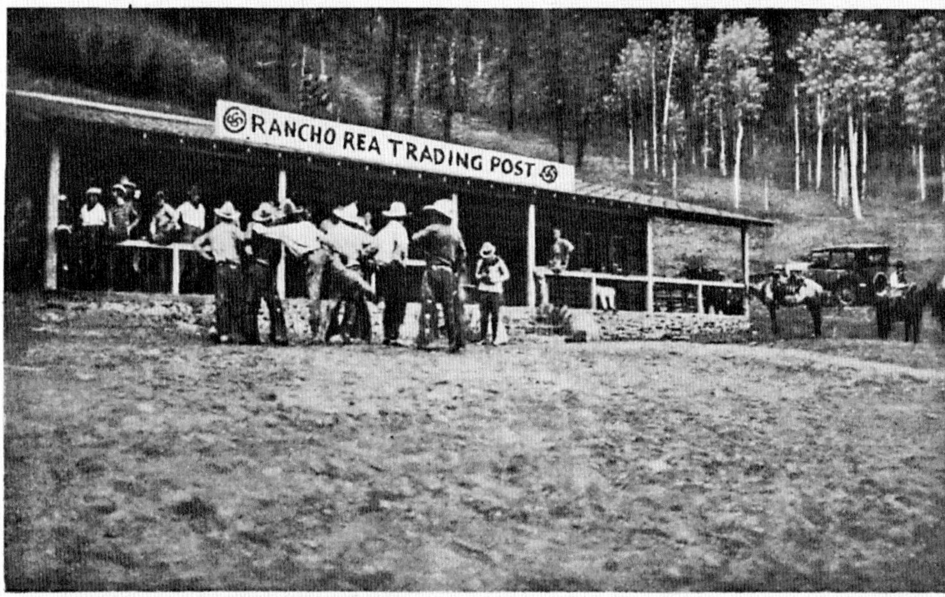

TRADING POST, RANCHO REA, JEMEZ SPRINGS, N. M.

The Trading Post at Rancho Rea had people in cowboy gear lounging on the trading post porch. This is another image of the Old West the ranch was trying to sell. (Courtesy Nancy Tucker.)

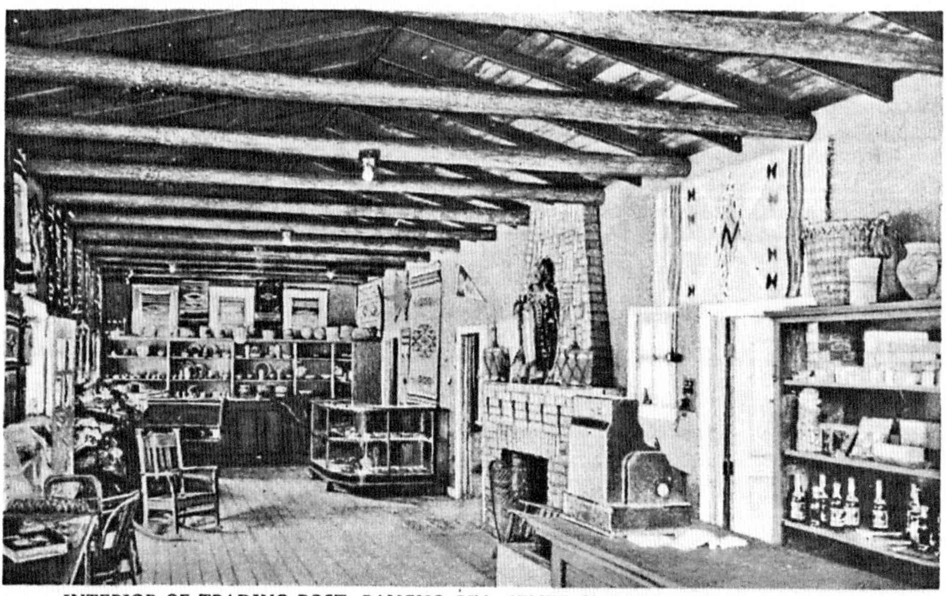
INTERIOR OF TRADING POST, RANCHO REA, JEMEZ SPRINGS, N. M.

The Trading Post sold Western and Native American goods as well as liquor (see far right-hand corner). (Courtesy Nancy Tucker.)

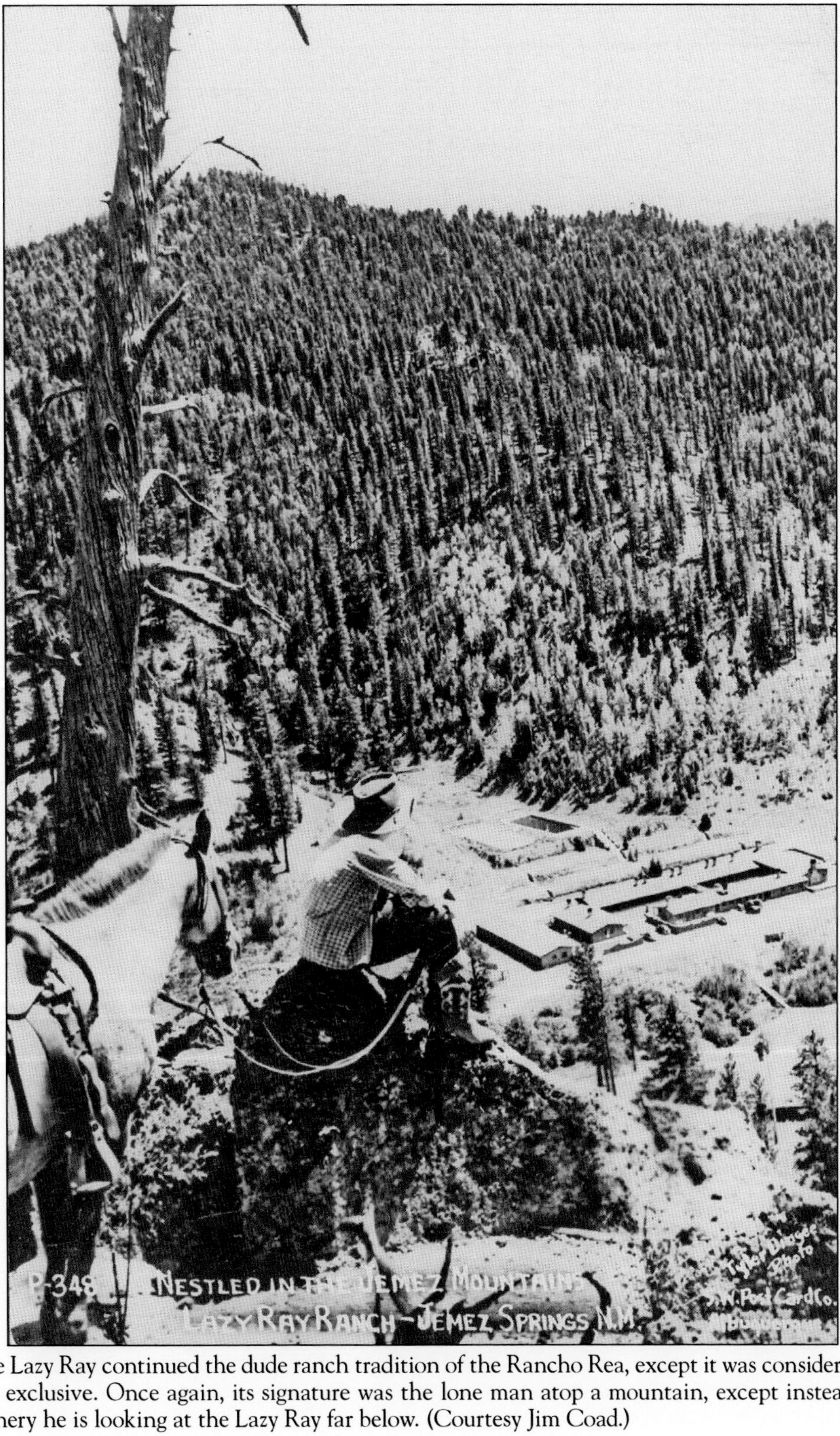

The Lazy Ray continued the dude ranch tradition of the Rancho Rea, except it was considerably less exclusive. Once again, its signature was the lone man atop a mountain, except instead of scenery he is looking at the Lazy Ray far below. (Courtesy Jim Coad.)

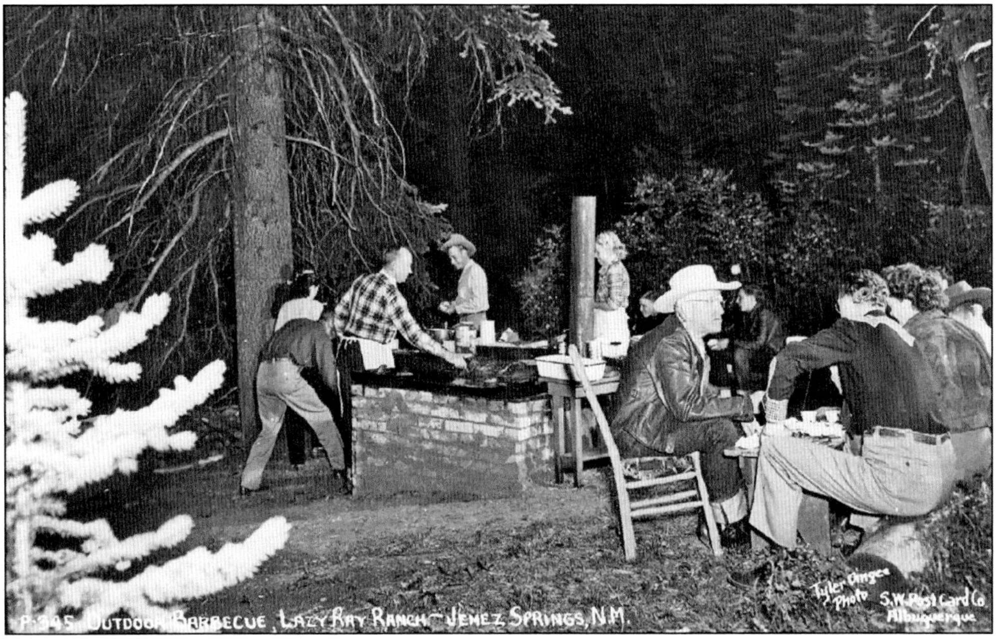

Trail rides and outdoor barbecues made guests feel as if they were in contact with the great outdoors. The Lazy Ray also offered fishing opportunities and Sunday Morning Breakfast Rides, which included a chapel service outdoors, and of course breakfast. The Lazy Ray offered swimming, lounging on the outdoor patio, or perhaps a bit of putting. There were rodeos, hayrides and square dancing, archery, and overnight pack trips. (Courtesy Jim Coad.)

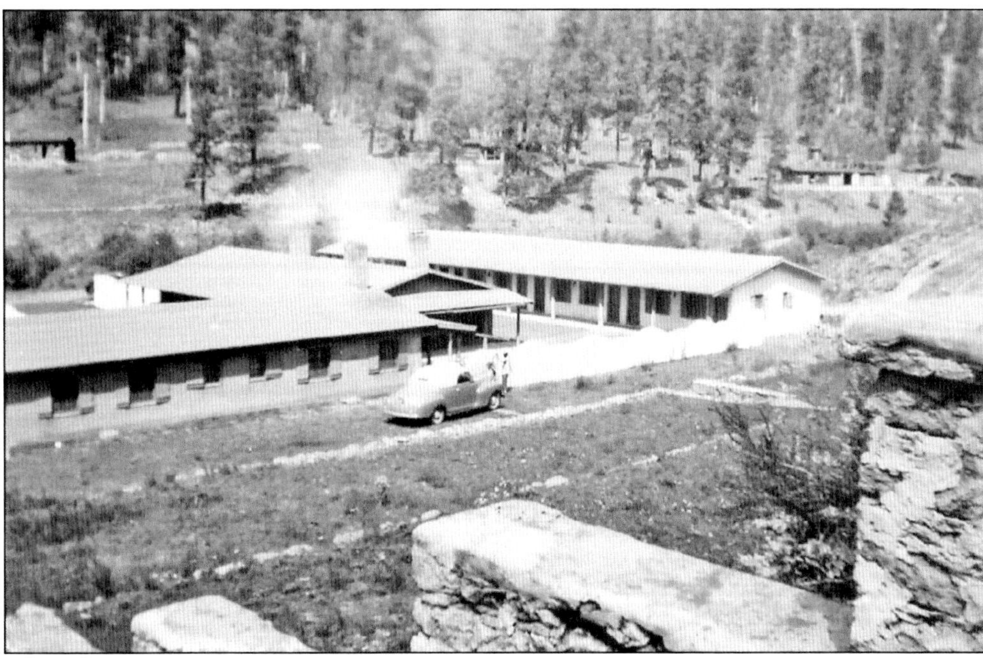

The Lazy Ray looks bleak and uninviting in the winter, but this photograph gives an idea of the T-shaped layout of the buildings. (Courtesy Jim Coad.)

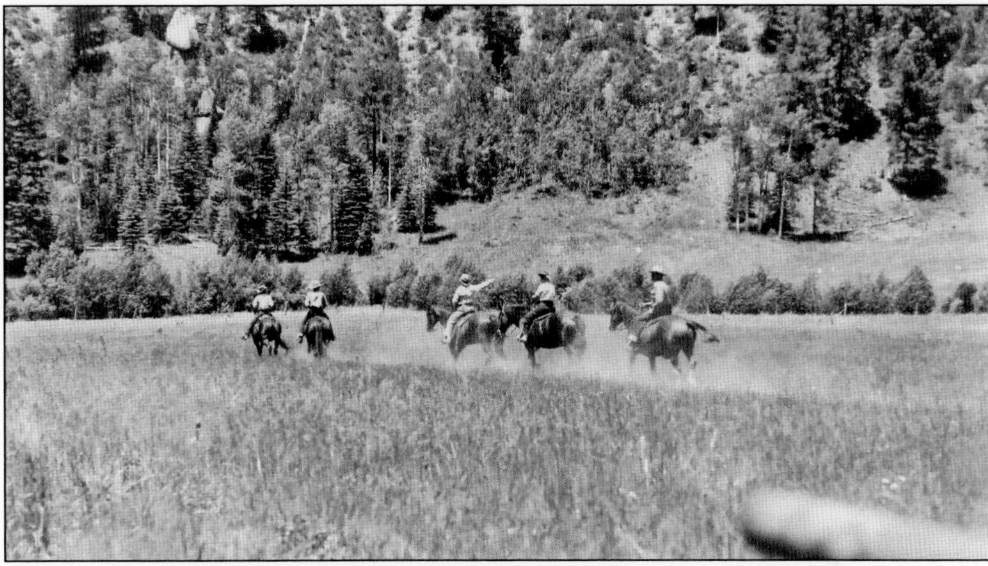

The Lazy Ray continued the tradition of trail rides. As one can see from this photograph, the high country of the Jemez is near the rider's path. (Courtesy 2005 July 4 Committee.)

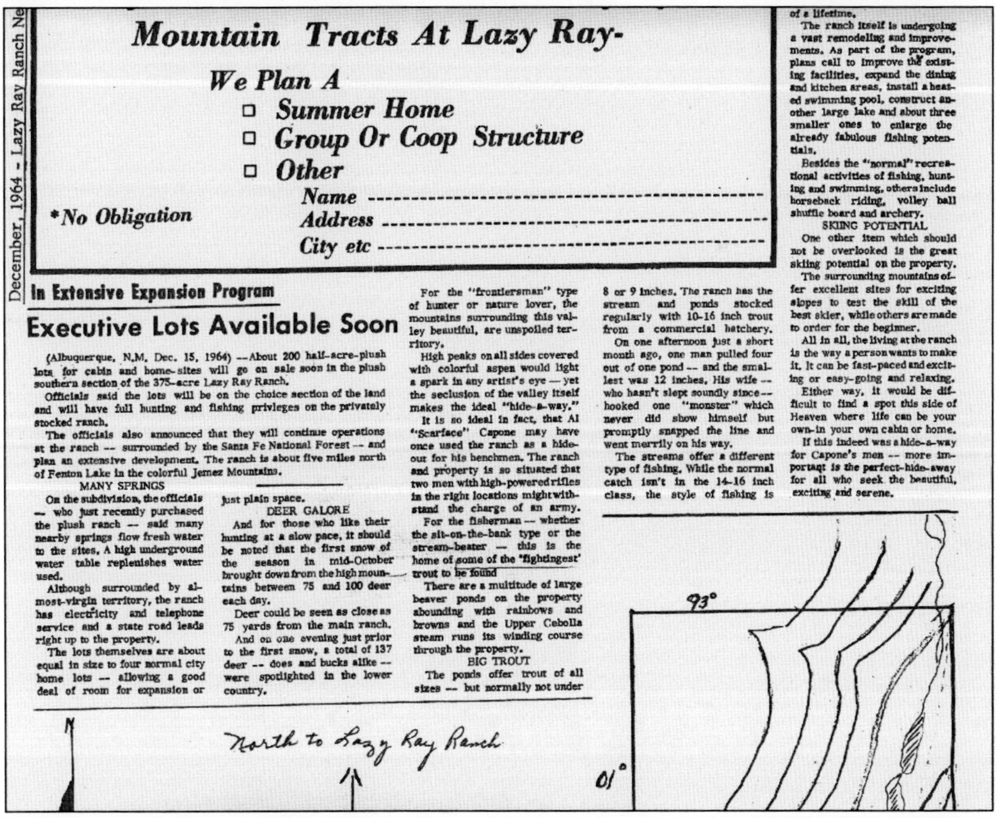

December, 1964 – Lazy Ray Ranch Ne

Mountain Tracts At Lazy Ray-

We Plan A

- ☐ *Summer Home*
- ☐ *Group Or Coop Structure*
- ☐ *Other*

Name ------------------------------------
Address ------------------------------------
City etc ------------------------------------

**No Obligation*

In Extensive Expansion Program

Executive Lots Available Soon

(Albuquerque, N.M. Dec. 15, 1964) —About 200 half-acre-plush lots for cabin and home-sites will go on sale soon in the plush southern section of the 375-acre Lazy Ray Ranch.

Officials said the lots will be on the choice section of the land and will have full hunting and fishing privleges on the privately stocked ranch.

The officials also announced that they will continue operations at the ranch -- surrounded by the Santa Fe National Forest -- and plan an extensive development. The ranch is about five miles north of Fenton Lake in the colorful Jemez Mountains.

MANY SPRINGS

On the subdivision, the officials — who just recently purchased the plush ranch -- said many nearby springs flow fresh water to the sites. A high underground water table replenishes water used.

Although surrounded by almost-virgin territory, the ranch has electricity and telephone service and a state road leads right up to the property.

The lots themselves are about equal in size to four normal city home lots -- allowing a good deal of room for expansion or just plain space.

DEER GALORE

And for those who like their hunting at a slow pace, it should be noted that the first snow of the season in mid-October brought down from the high mountains between 75 and 100 deer each day.

Deer could be seen as close as 75 yards from the main ranch.

And on one evening just prior to the first snow, a total of 137 deer -- does and bucks alike -- were spotlighted in the lower country.

For the "frontiersman" type of hunter or nature lover, the mountains surrounding this valley beautiful, are unspoiled territory.

High peaks on all sides covered with colorful aspen would light a spark in any artist's eye — yet the seclusion of the valley itself makes the ideal "hide-a-way."

It is so ideal in fact, that Al "Scarface" Capone may have once used the ranch as a hideout for his benchmen. The ranch and property is so situated that two men with high-powered rifles in the right locations might withstand the charge of an army.

For the fisherman — whether the sit-on-the-bank type or the stream-beater — this is the home of some of the 'fightingest' trout to be found

There are a multitude of large beaver ponds on the property abounding with rainbows and browns and the Upper Cebolla steam runs its winding course through the property.

BIG TROUT

The ponds offer trout of all sizes — but normally not under 8 or 9 inches. The ranch has the stream and ponds stocked regularly with 10-16 inch trout from a commercial hatchery.

On one afternoon just a short month ago, one man pulled four out of one pond -- and the smallest was 12 inches. His wife -- who hasn't slept soundly since -- hooked one "monster" which never did show himself but promptly snapped the line and went merrily on his way.

The streams offer a different type of fishing. While the normal catch isn't in the 14-16 inch class, the style of fishing is of a lifetime.

The ranch itself is undergoing a vast remodeling and improvements. As part of the program, plans call to improve the existing facilities, expand the dining and kitchen areas, install a heated swimming pool, construct another large lake and about three smaller ones to enlarge the already fabulous fishing potentials.

Besides the "normal" recreational activities of fishing, hunting and swimming, others include horseback riding, volley ball shuffle board and archery.

SKIING POTENTIAL

One other item which should not be overlooked is the great skiing potential on the property.

The surrounding mountains offer excellent sites for exciting slopes to test the skill of the best skier, while others are made to order for the beginner.

All in all, the living at the ranch is the way a person wants to make it. It can be fast-paced and exciting or easy-going and relaxing.

Either way, it would be difficult to find a spot this side of Heaven where life can be your own-in your own cabin or home.

If this indeed was a hide-a-way for Capone's men -- more important is the perfect-hide-away for all who seek the beautiful, exciting and serene.

When a corporation in Albuquerque took over the Lazy Ray, it promoted it heavily. In addition, it began selling lots for vacation homes or group housing. But by 1970, the Lazy Ray was out of business. (Courtesy 2005 July 4 Committee.)

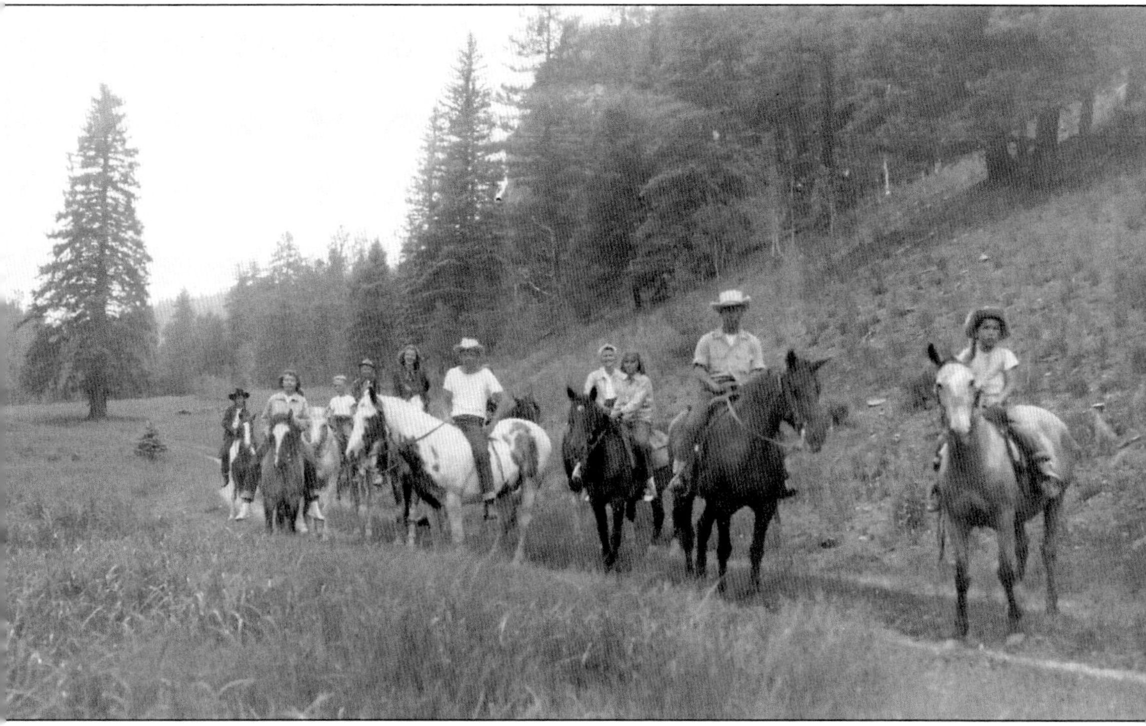

A happy group of ranch guests poses for their picture. (Courtesy 2005 July 4 Committee.)

Seven

Houses of Prayer

For many years, the two religions in Jemez Springs were Protestant (represented by the Presbyterian church) and Catholic. Because the Catholics had a history that dated back to the Spanish habitation, every small village had a Catholic church: Jemez Springs, Cañon, Ponderosa, the Pueblos of Jemez and Zia, and San Ysidro. All of these churches are still active today. The Catholics can also lay claim to the extensive land holdings north of town that house the Servants of the Paraclete and the Handmaids of the Precious Blood.

A Presbyterian missionary arrived at the Jemez Pueblo around 1877. John M. Shields, M.D., an elder in the Presbyterian Church of Mount Pleasant, Pennsylvania, came to Jemez Pueblo with the intent of establishing a mission there. He soon moved to Jemez Springs. Since then the church, its bell tower a landmark, has at various times housed elementary and high school classes, a public library, a medical clinic, and community gatherings, as well as Sunday services.

The Catholic church in Jemez Springs is Our Lady of the Assumption, just a little way south of the Presbyterian church. It was built in the 1890s. But the largest Catholic establishments, at least in terms of land size, are the Servants of the Paraclete, which owns 2,600 acres in Jemez Springs, and the Handmaids of the Precious Blood adjacent to the Servants. While they were involved in the village in the early days, the Handmaids are now a cloistered order. The Reverend Gerald Michael Cushing Fitzgerald, whose goal was to provide a home for troubled priests, started the Servants of the Paraclete in 1947 and the Handmaids the same year.

Some of the Paraclete land was sold to the Bodhi Manda Zen Center, which was established in 1972. The Zen Center now is quite extensive with its own hot springs, gardens, and lately a new building for religious services. One of its active members is poet and songwriter Leonard Cohen. The center opened in 1974.

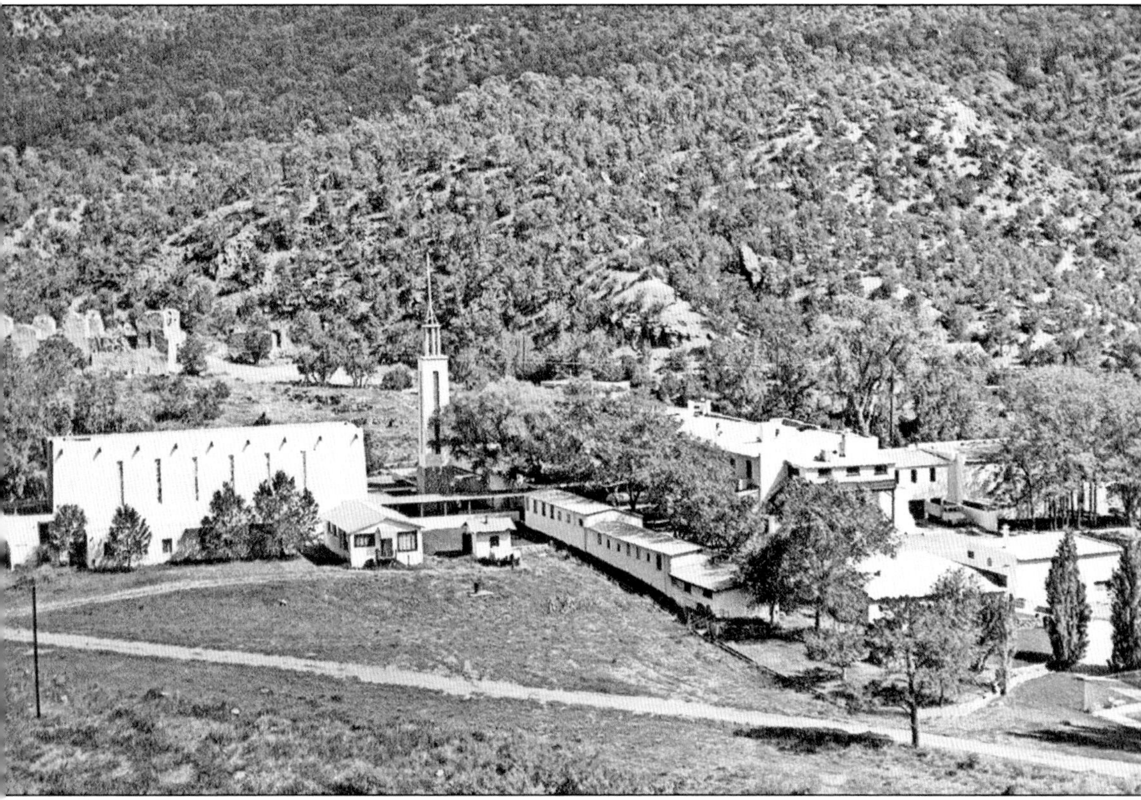

This complex, known as Via Coeli, was just a small part of the Servants of the Paraclete holdings. However it has been turned over to the Handmaids of the Precious Blood, whose cloister abuts on Via Coeli. (Courtesy Servants of the Paraclete.)

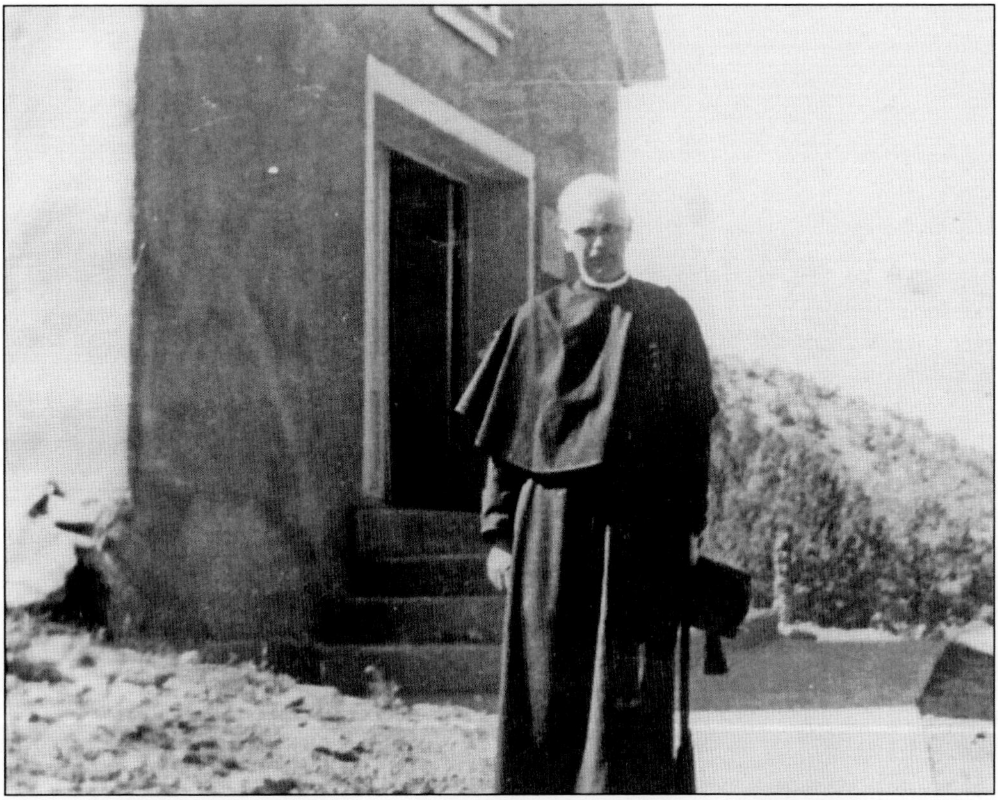

Father Fitzgerald saw his mission as one of "priests helping priests." But he also took an active role in the community. He was named an honorary fire chief in Jemez Springs. The Servants operated the telephone service in Jemez Springs, the only religious order in the United States to do so. Because one of the major problems with the priests at the Paraclete was alcoholism, Father Fitzgerald also tried to replace the local bar with a bowling alley, to no avail. The Servants of the Paraclete ran into trouble in the 1990s when it was discovered that a number of pedophile priests had been "treated" at the retreat. No longer able to get insurance, the retreat has been effectively closed down except for a few older priests. Efforts have been made to sell one of the buildings or a parcel of land, but to date nothing has come of these attempts. (Both courtesy Servants of the Paraclete.)

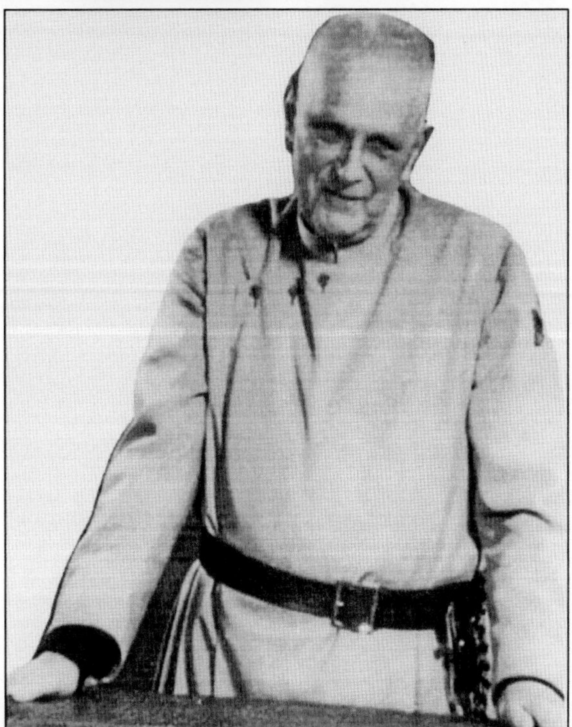

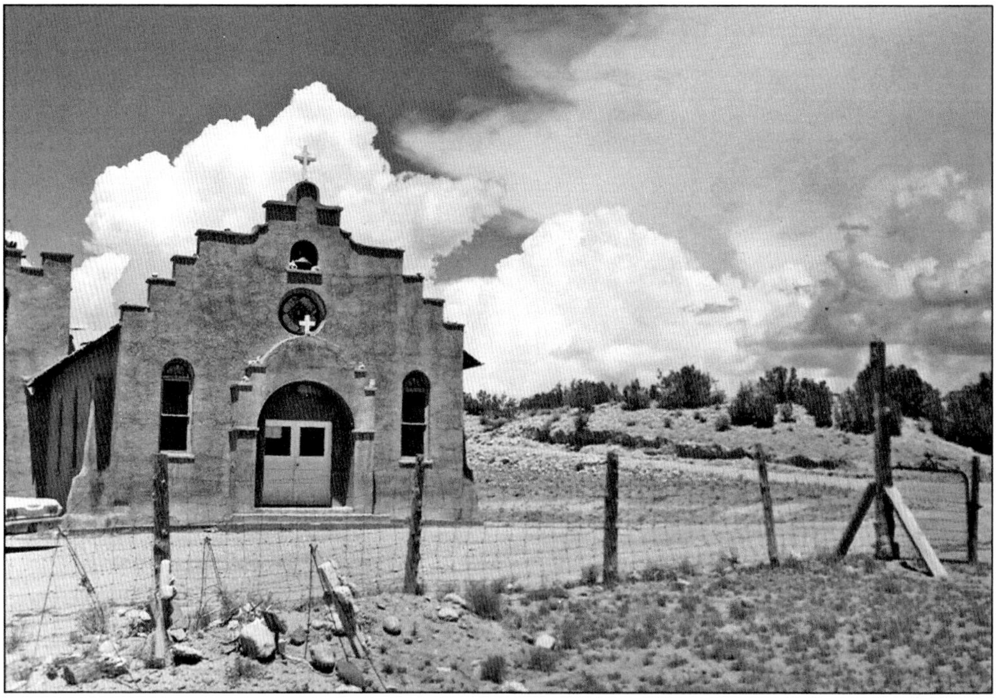

Our Lady of Guadalupe Catholic Church in Cañon is built in the mission style so prevalent across the Southwest. The facade of the church curves up to the single bell at the top. (Courtesy Sandoval County Historical Society.)

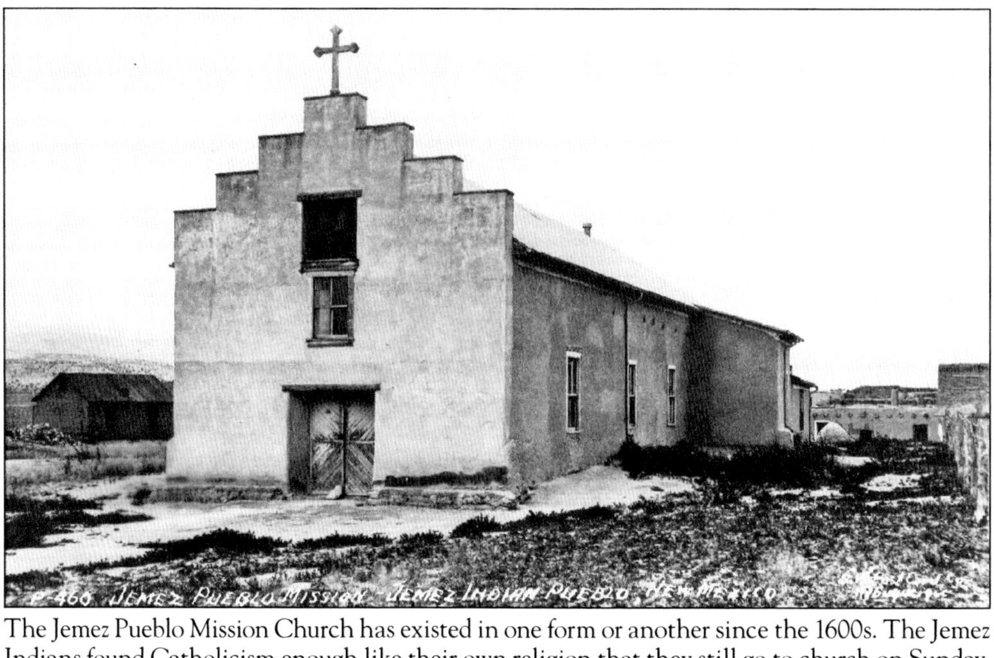

The Jemez Pueblo Mission Church has existed in one form or another since the 1600s. The Jemez Indians found Catholicism enough like their own religion that they still go to church on Sunday, for baptisms and other Catholic ceremonies. (Courtesy Jim Coad.)

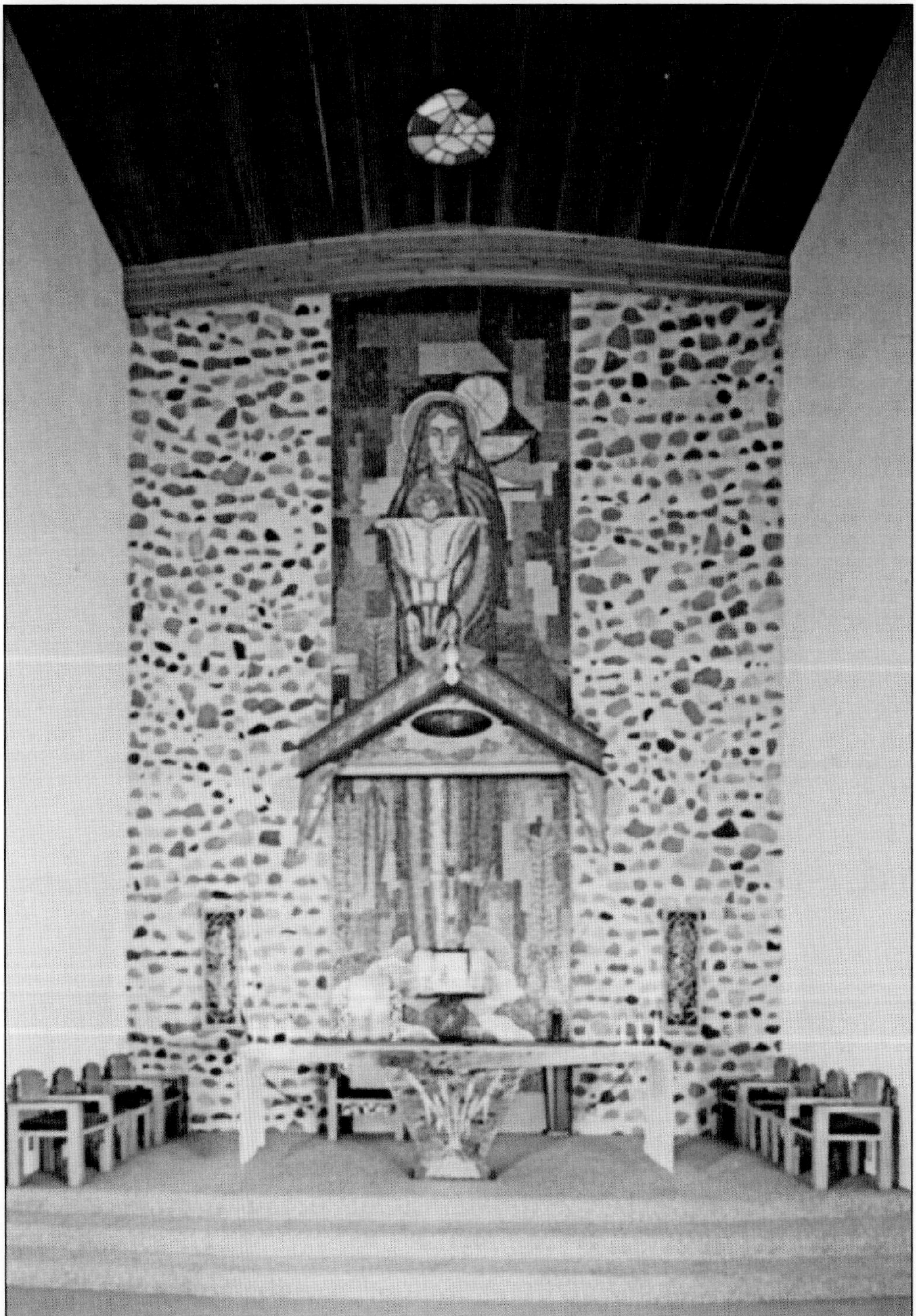

For years, this mosaic was covered over and only discovered when Mary Mother of Priests chapel was being remodeled. It was built in the early 1960s and is the tallest building in Jemez Springs (Courtesy Jim Coad.)

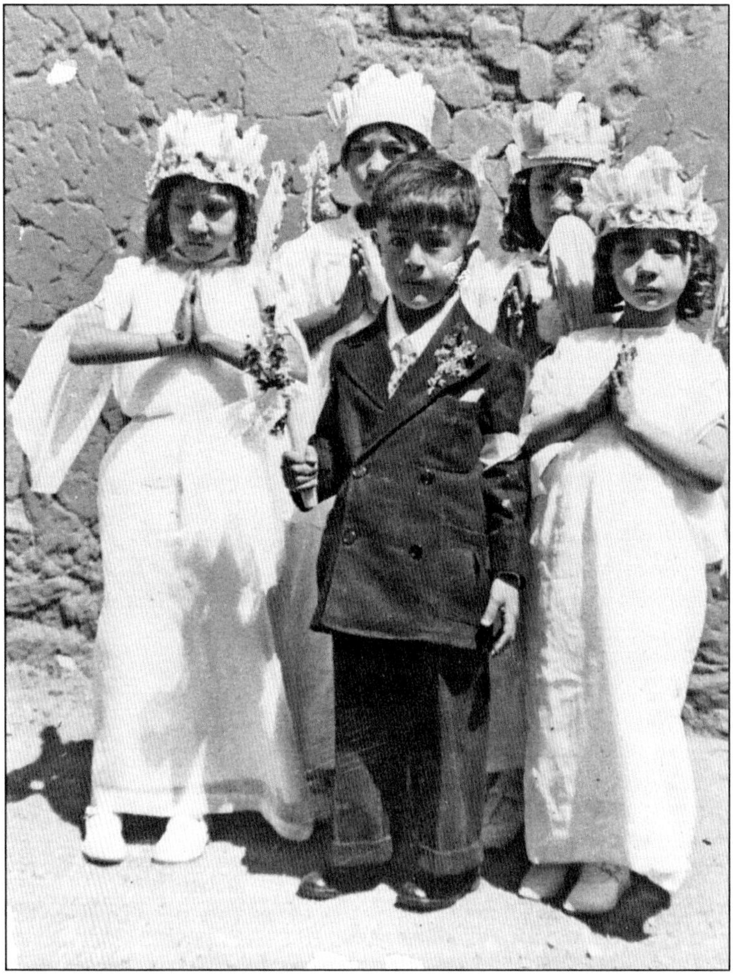

There are numerous photographs of children on the day of their First Holy Communion, the girls in white dresses and the boys in white shirts and perhaps jackets. This particular photograph, dating from the 1920s, shows children outside the church in Cañon serious in their angelic attire. (Courtesy Sandoval County Historical Society.)

Seen here in 1956, Our Lady of the Assumption Church is very bare compared to what it is today. There is a rich green lawn and statues of Christ and Our Lady of the Assumption. (Courtesy 2005 July 4 Committee.)

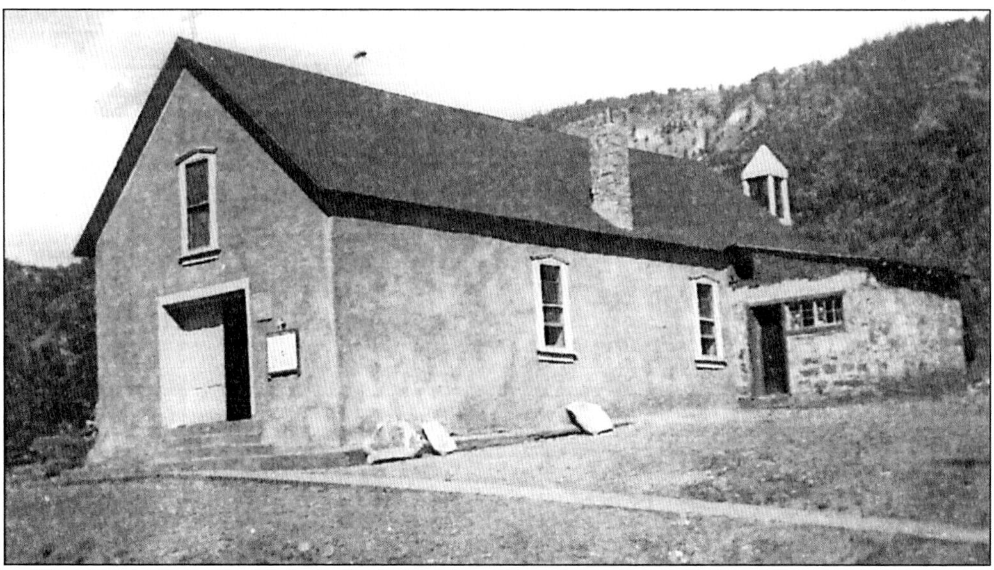

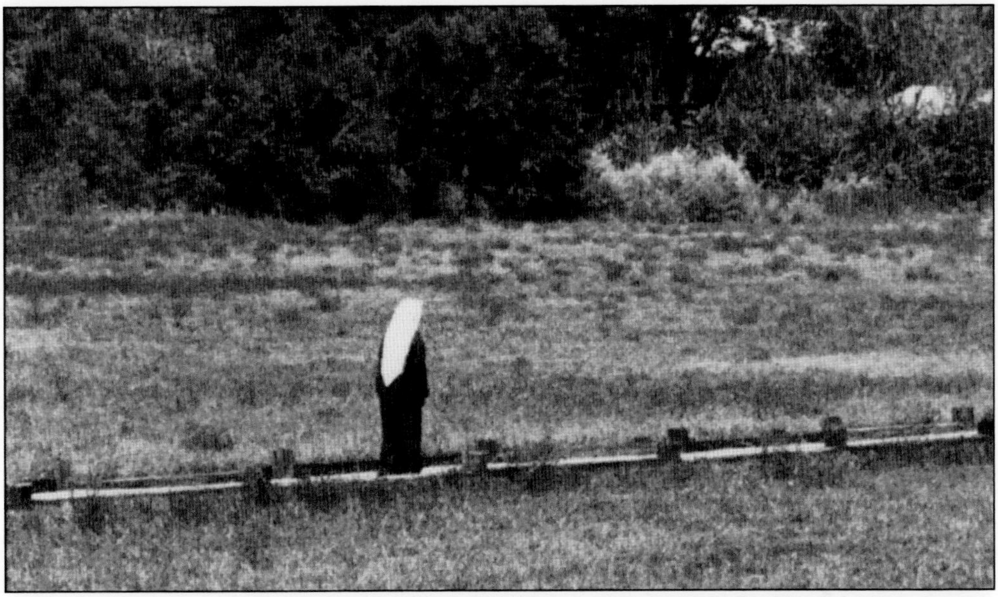

A lone Handmaid makes her way along the path that runs between the buildings of the convent. When the members of this cloistered order must leave to vote or to get medical assistance, they do not wear the full habit. (Courtesy Robert Borden.)

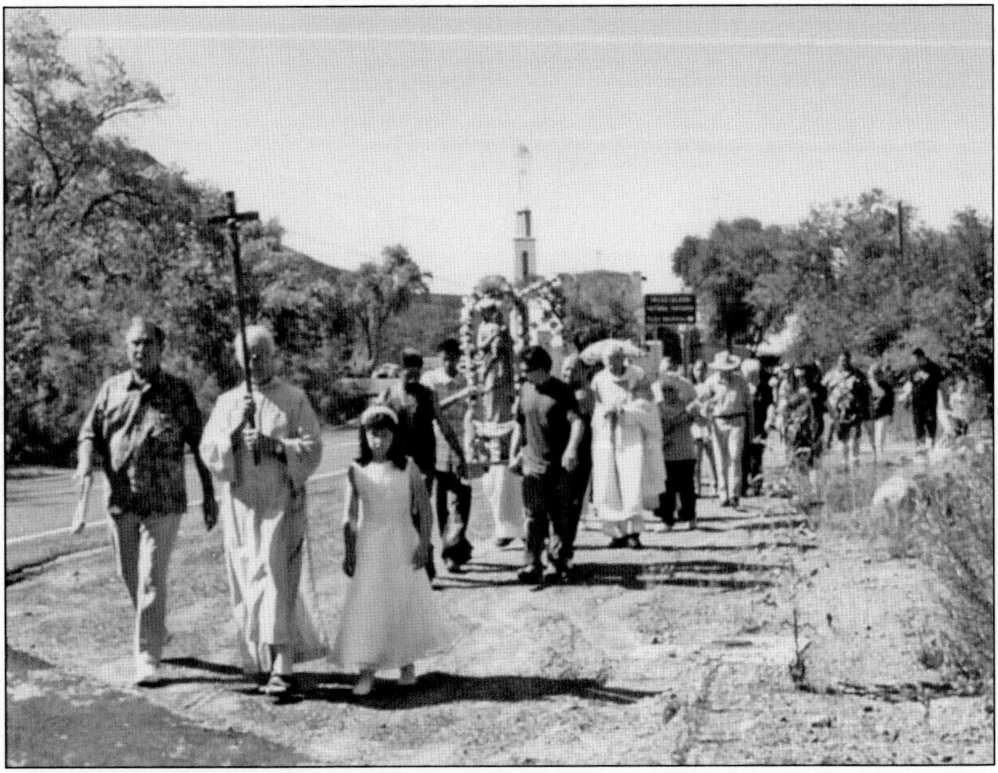

Even today, the faithful form a procession on the day of the Assumption and carry the statue of the Virgin through town. The man on the far left is the mayor of Jemez Springs, John Garcia. (Courtesy Jim Forcier-Call.)

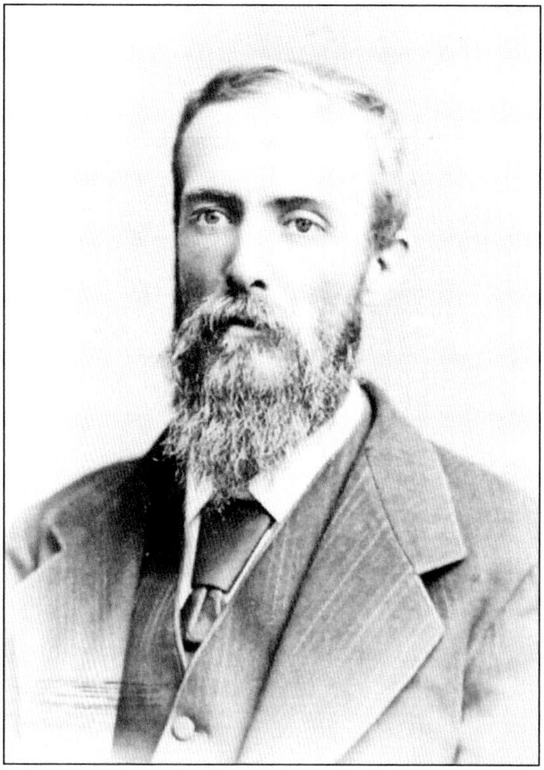

The beginning of the official Protestant activity in the Jemez area originated about October 1, 1877, when two ministers and their wives made a mission trip to the Jemez Pueblo with the idea of establishing a school. The following spring, on February 18, John Shields, M.D., an elder in the Presbyterian Church of Mount Pleasant, Pennsylvania, moved his family to New Mexico to establish a mission at the pueblo of Jemez. The trip from Pennsylvania involved a train ride, a two-day stage ride, and then the last two days of the trip in an ambulance. In 1881, Jose F. Archuleta deeded a tract of land in Jemez Springs for a school and church. A descendant of Dr. Shields currently lives in Jemez Springs. The Jemez Springs Community Presbyterian Church is still generous with its space, making rooms available for volunteer organizations with no space of their own and serving as a place to have a funeral service even if the deceased was not Presbyterian. (Both courtesy 2005 July 4 Committee.)

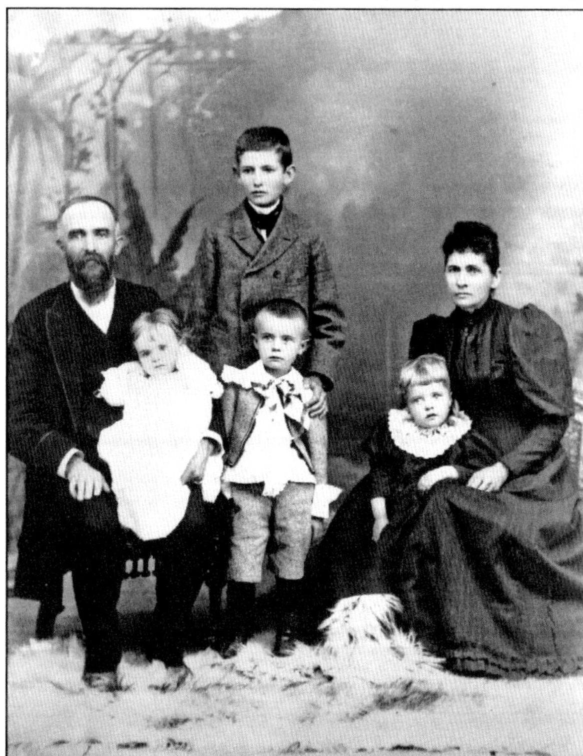

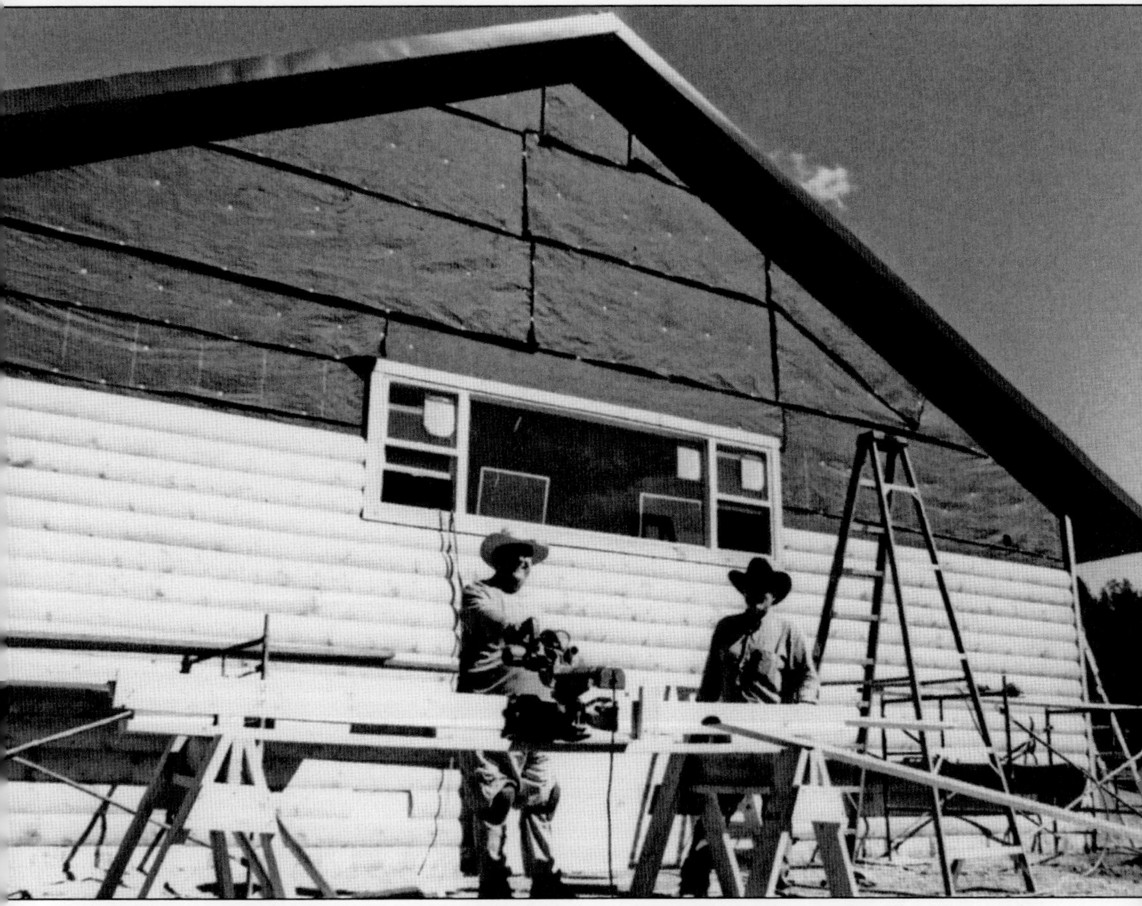

Other Protestant religions are making their presence felt in the Jemez. This church under construction is the Jemez Mountain Baptist Church in La Cueva, north of Jemez Springs. There are other Baptist churches in Cañon and San Ysidro. (Courtesy Robert Borden.)

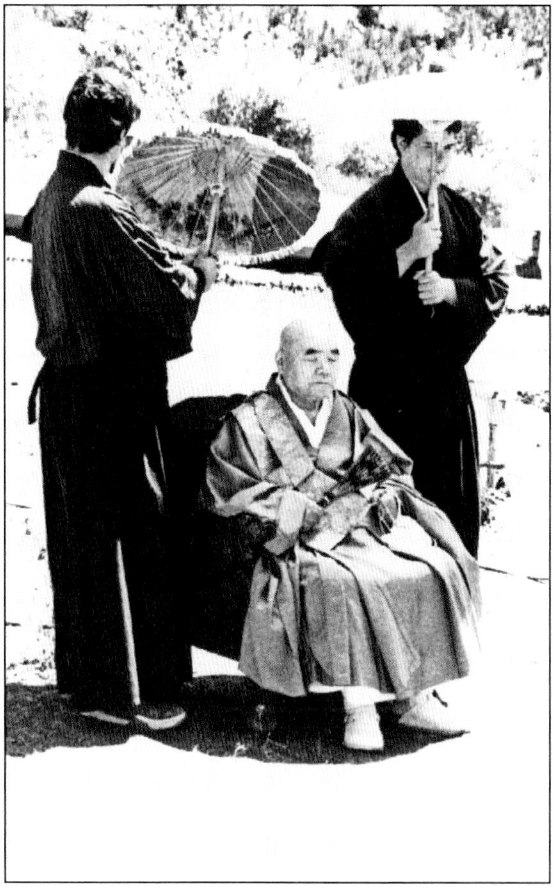

Joshu Sasaki Roshi, the spiritual leader of the Bodhi Manda Zen Center, is now 101 years old. In the early 1970s, when a student asked Roshi to come to New Mexico to conduct what is known as a Dai-sesshin, Roshi replied, "You find hot springs, I come." The student found an old Catholic monastery with a spring for sale. Roshi came and has been coming ever since. (Courtesy Robert Borden.)

Students come from all over to learn more about Zen practice and to participate in the services. These students are walking along the side of what is known as the long house where the kitchen and dining room are housed. (Courtesy Bodhi Manda Zen Center.)

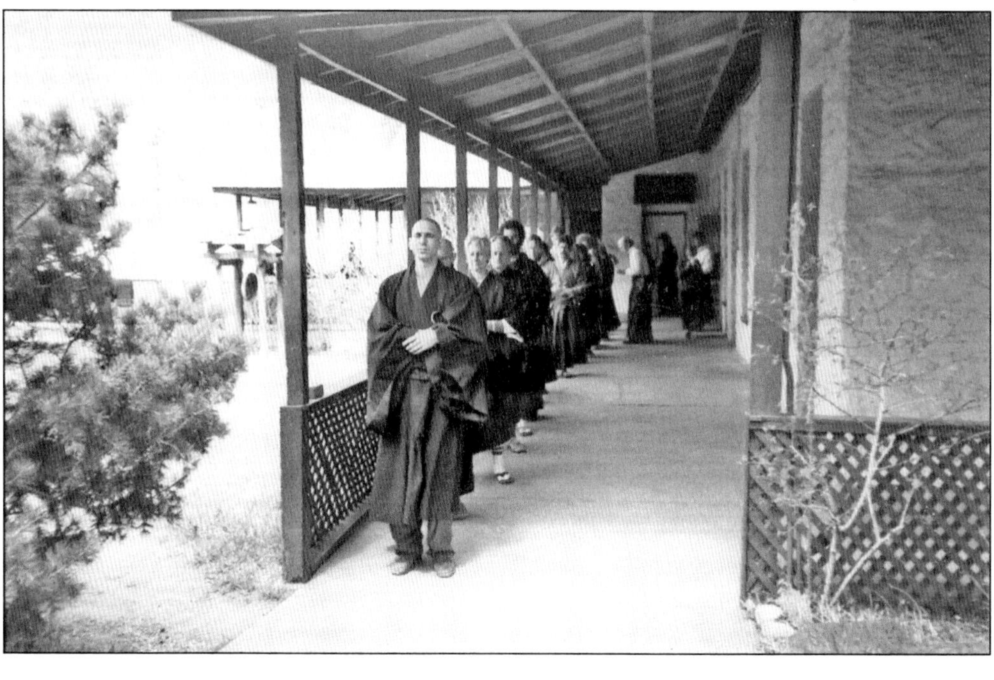

Eight

School Days

Until recently, education in the Jemez was highly fragmented. There had been Spanish mission schools teaching reading, writing, and music along with the catechism as far back as the 1600s. In the early part of the 18th century, Franciscan friars maintained schools on the pueblos, teaching reading and writing. Banished from the United States by the Mexican government, they did not return for 75 years. In 1905, the ground-breaking took place on a new mission school at Jemez Pueblo. The new school was opened in 1906 in a small room in the father's residence with 25 pupils. The Presbyterians already had a mission school at the pueblo, but a shortage of money forced them to close the school down. Elsewhere, children who did not live near a populated area were home-schooled. Jemez Springs, Cañon, Ponderosa, and San Ysidro had two- or three-room schools, and there were even some one-room schools. The Jemez Springs school first shared space with the electric cooperative and then the Presbyterian church. In 1929, the Bureau of Indian Affairs started the BIA Day School on the pueblo. In the 1930s, the WPA built three new schools for Ponderosa, Cañon, and San Ysidro. In the 1950s, students from Jemez Springs were being bussed on an 80-mile round-trip to Bernalillo. The story goes that Josephine Shepard saw the students standing in the dark waiting for the bus and decided Jemez needed its own school. First, Jemez Springs had to be incorporated because an incorporated entity is needed to form a school district. But a school was built and today houses a modern elementary, middle, and high school. The Native Americans on the pueblo have started their own charter high school.

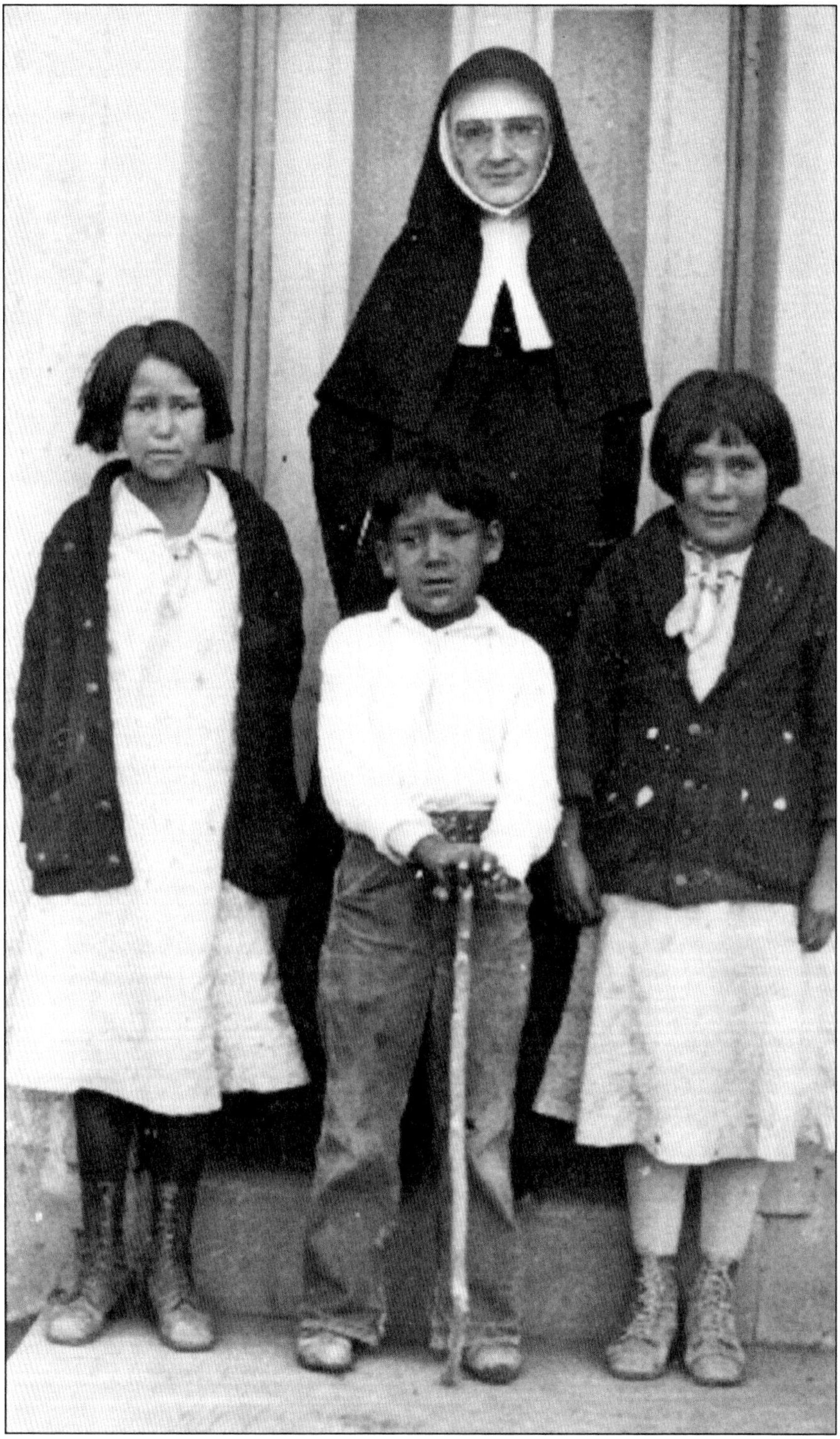

Sister Stephania, one of the first teachers at the mission school, stands with three of her students. This photograph is probably from about 1910. (Courtesy Department of Special Collections and University Archives, Marquette University Libraries.)

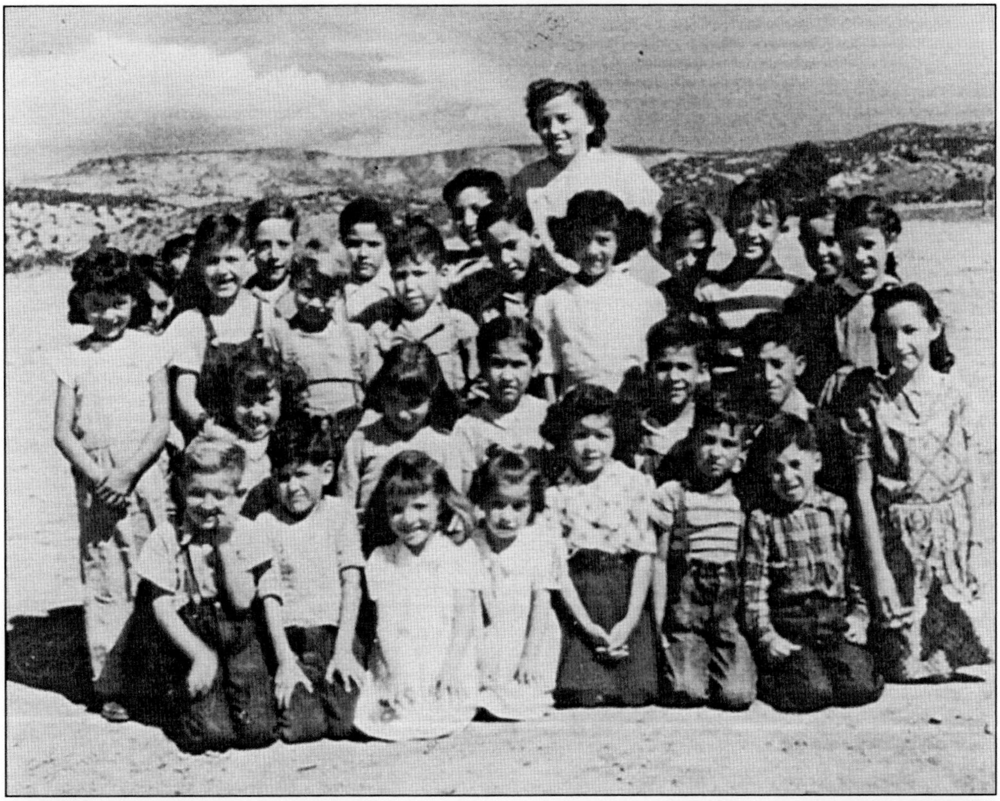

Students of the Ponderosa Grade School pose for their picture in 1947. (Courtesy Susan Diggle.)

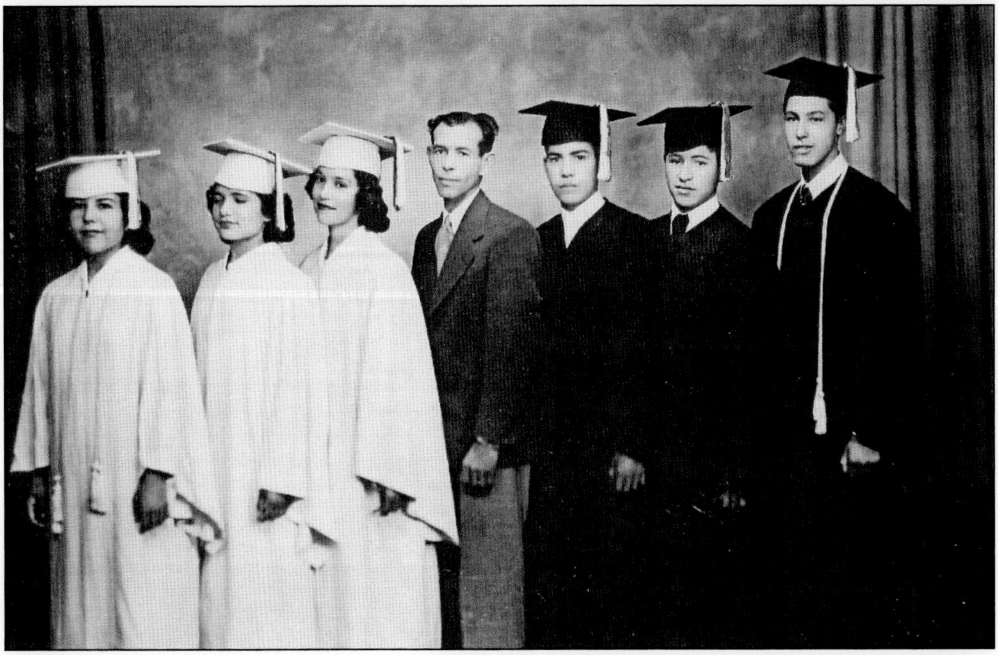

In 1950, Ponderosa eighth graders, resplendent in cap and gown, look forward to graduation. Ponderosa could take its students through only the eighth grade. (Courtesy Susan Diggle.)

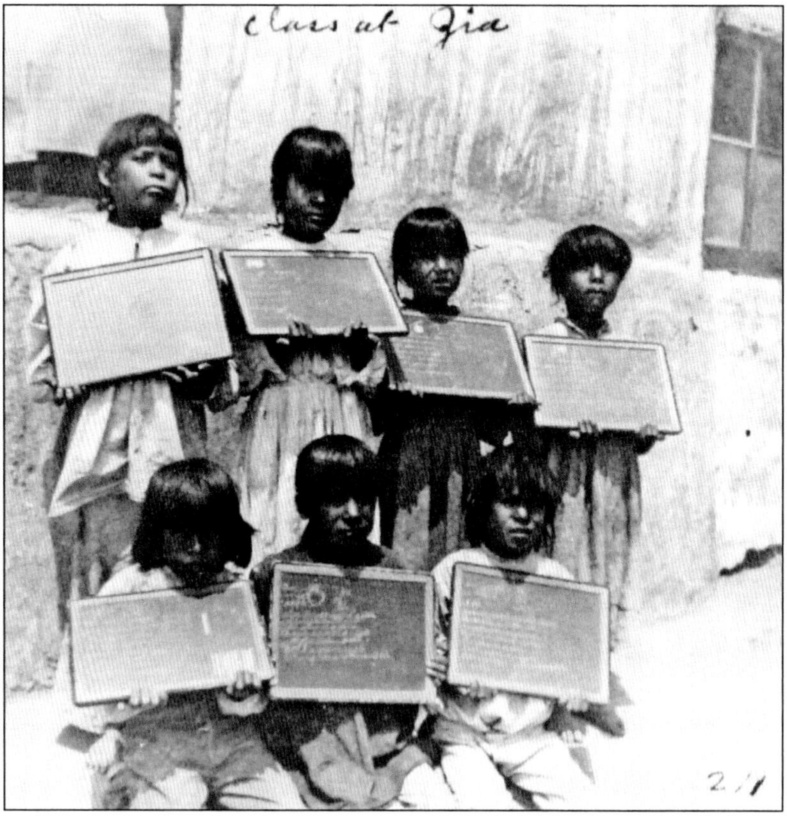

The students of Zia Pueblo Mission School hold up their slates to show their work. Zia is only about 5 miles from San Ysidro. (Courtesy Susan Diggle.)

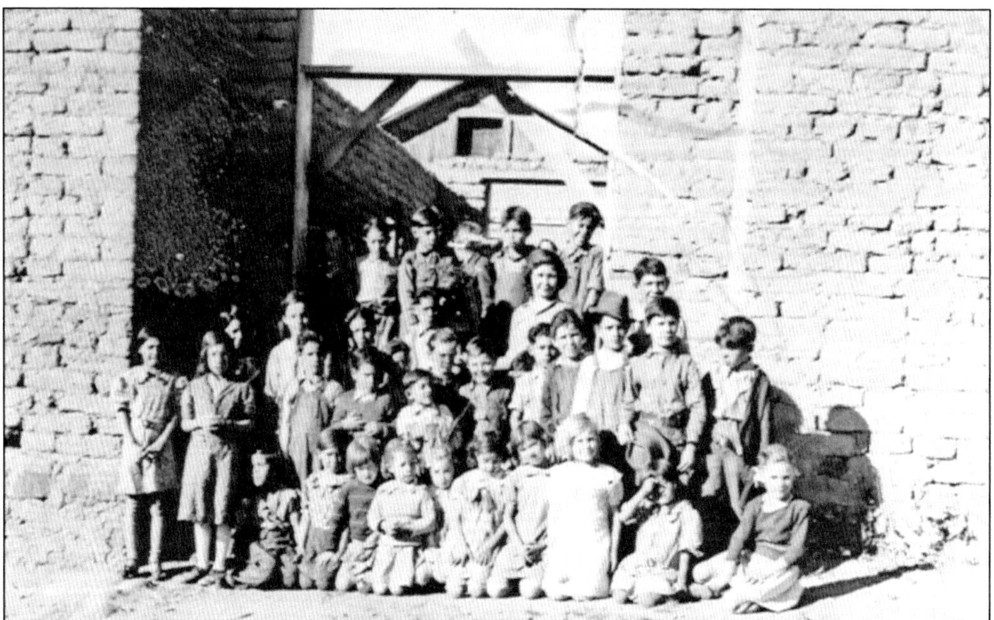

Behind this class in Cañon is the new school being built by the WPA in 1936. (Courtesy Susan Diggle.)

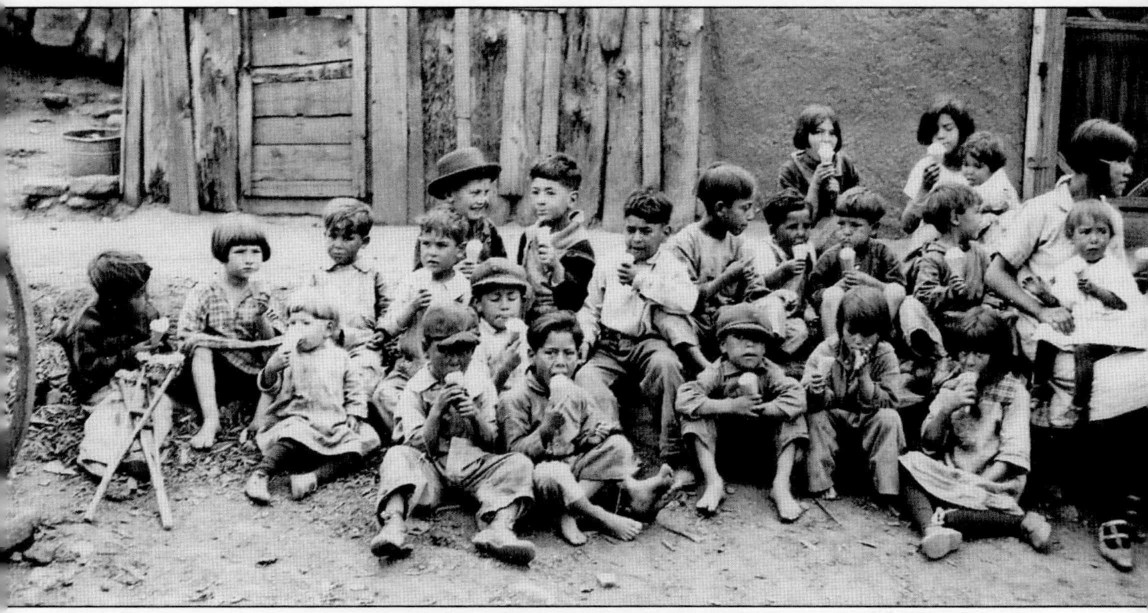

This photograph was taken around 1916 in front of the first schoolhouse in Jemez Springs, where the Jemez Mountains Electric Cooperative Office is now. The teacher (far right) is either Josephine Shepard or Barbara Abousleman. The children are enjoying ice cream cones, thanks to a friend of Shepard. (Courtesy 2005 July 4th Committee.)

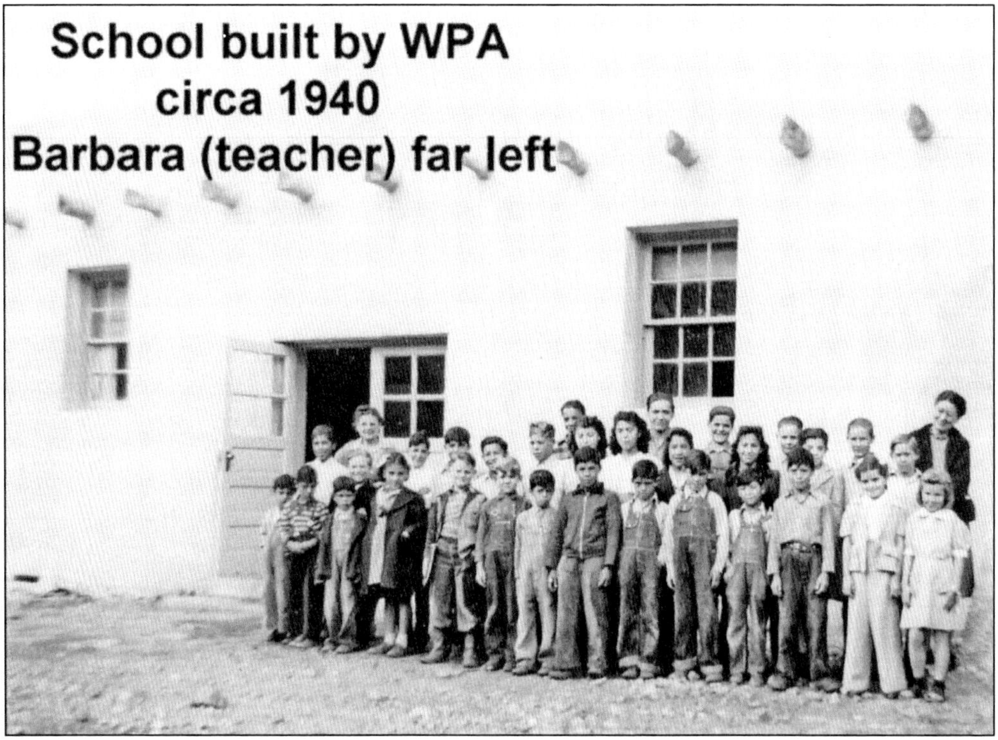

Notice that the girls in this photograph of Sister Stephania and her classes, taken in 1931, all wear dresses made from the same material. It was not uncommon for dresses to be made from the same bolt of material. (Courtesy Department of Special Collections and University Archives, Marquette University Libraries.)

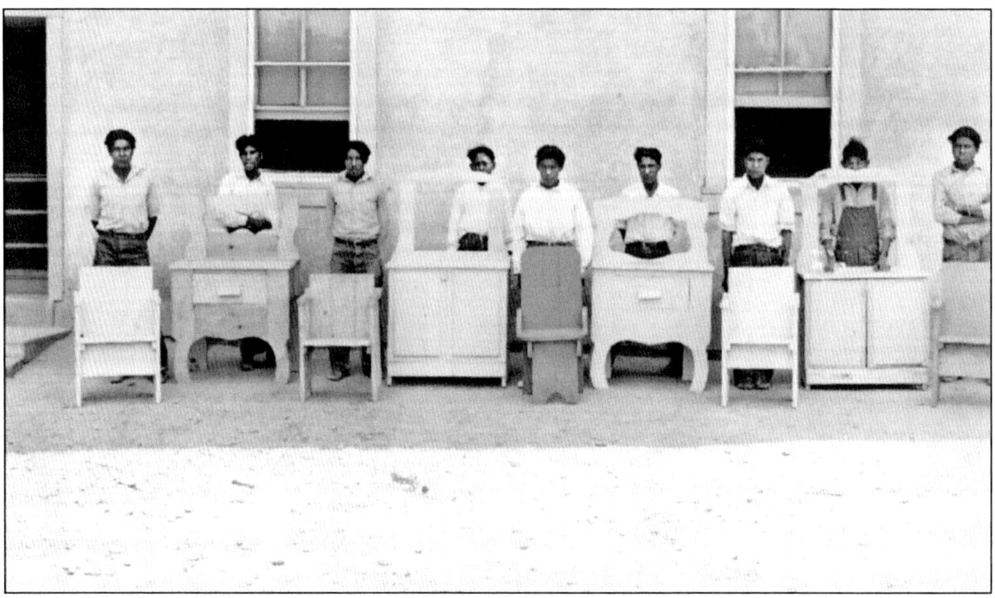

Boys at the pueblo school were taught appropriate skills such as woodworking, as this lineup of dressers and chairs shows. (Courtesy Department of Special Collections and University Archives, Marquette University Libraries.)

Nine

The Arts in the Jemez

Artists are drawn to the Jemez because of its scenery, colors, and the quality of light. Often people see painters with easels set up along the side of the road painting a mesa or a stand of cottonwoods. Over the years, arts organizations have come and gone. The one place that has kept art going consistently is the Hummingbird Music Camp, started by Lloyd and Wanda Higgins in 1959. Students come to the camp for a week, where they hone their musical abilities. Parents who were Hummingbird students often send their children to the camp. Like other camps, there are group meals in the spacious dining room and free time to explore the area or participate in games. Every Sunday before heading for home, the students perform a concert in the Hummingbird band shell for parents and others. The students also perform a concert in the Jemez Springs Park every Saturday evening during the summer and lead off the Fourth of July parade. Nationally known sculptor Rollie Grandbois, of Jemez Springs, has been running a sculpture symposium since 1995. He invites well-known stone carvers as teachers for the weeklong symposium, which attracts not only experienced sculptors but also first-timers. Artists exhibit their work for the local community at the end of the week. Jemez Springs can also lay claim to two famed authors. N. Scott Momaday won the Pulitzer Prize for his novel *House Made of Dawn*. His parents taught in the Jemez Pueblo schools, and Momaday grew up in the pueblo before coming to Jemez Springs. Rudolfo Anaya has been called the "father of Hispanic literature" for his many books that feature Hispanic characters or Hispanic traditions. One of his books is aptly named *Jemez Spring*. The Jemez has painters, potters, folk artists, and jewelry makers.

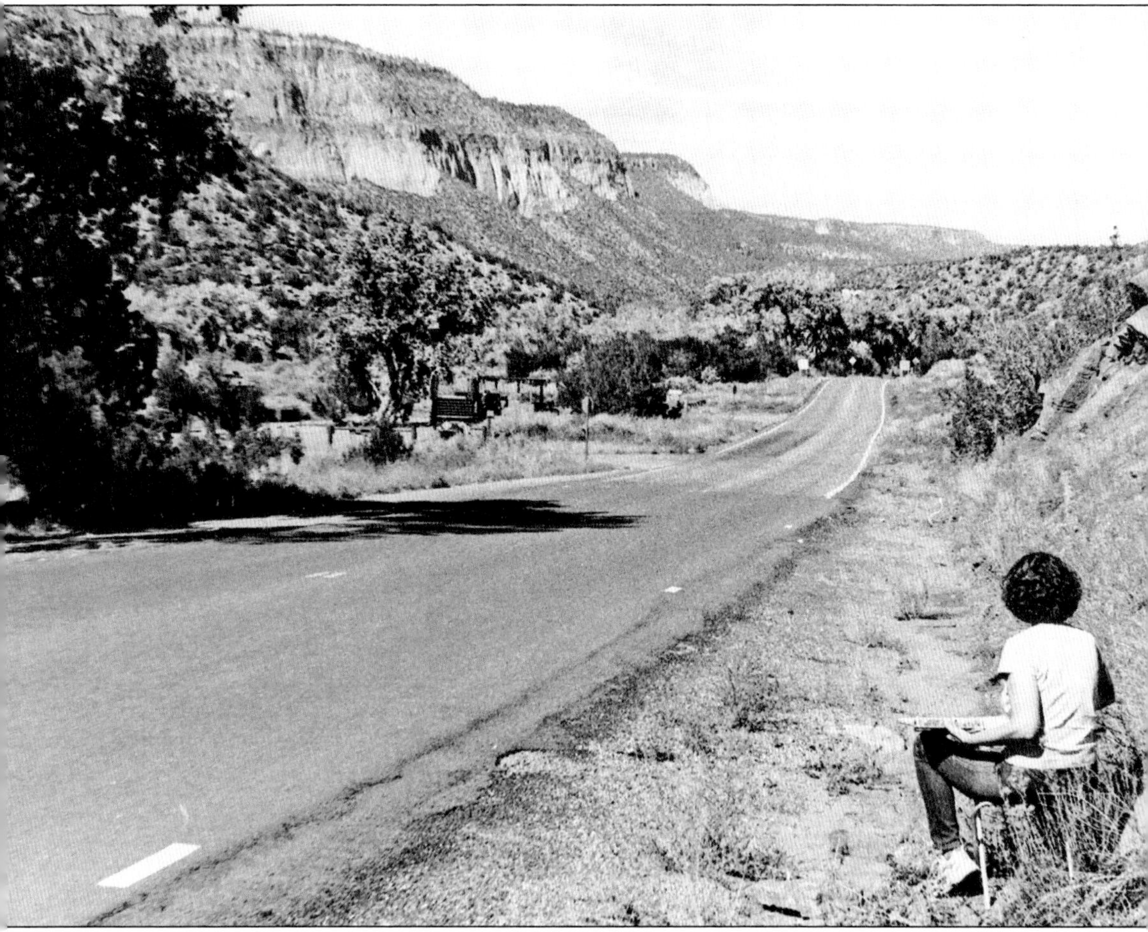

An empty road and soaring mesas are what many artists seek and find in the Jemez, whether they want to sketch or paint. Photographers, too, find the special quality of light perfect for taking prize-winning photographs. (Courtesy Robert Borden.)

Hummingbird Music Camp celebrated its 50th birthday in 2008. It was started by Lloyd and Wanda Higgins to provide a camp for children interested in music and the arts. Lloyd was motivated by his association with the National Music Camp at Interlochen, Michigan. (Courtesy Hummingbird Music Camp.)

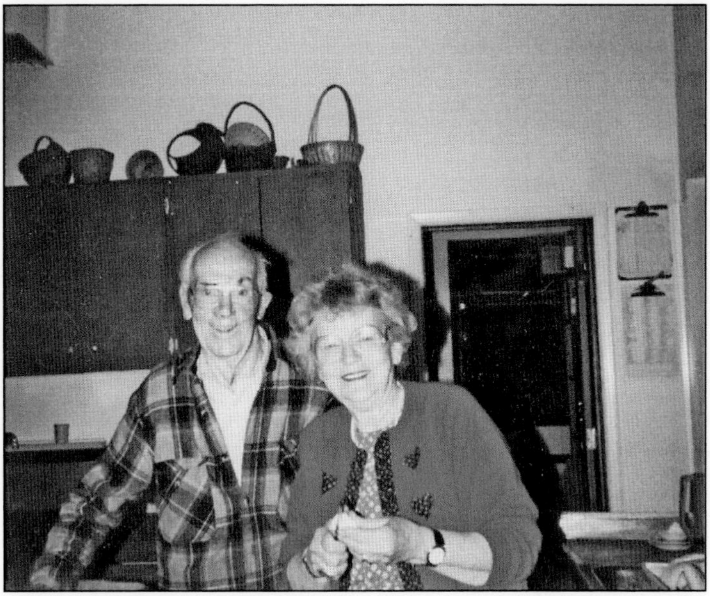

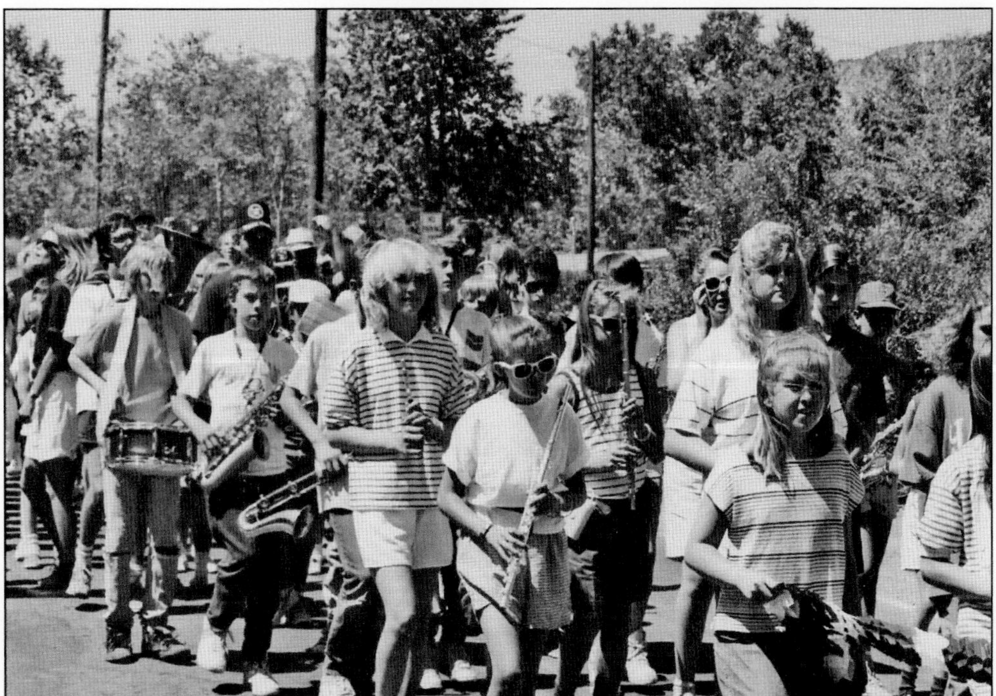

Traditionally Hummingbird Music Camp students lead the annual Fourth of July parade in Jemez Springs with rousing John Phillip Sousa marches. (Courtesy Hummingbird Music Camp.)

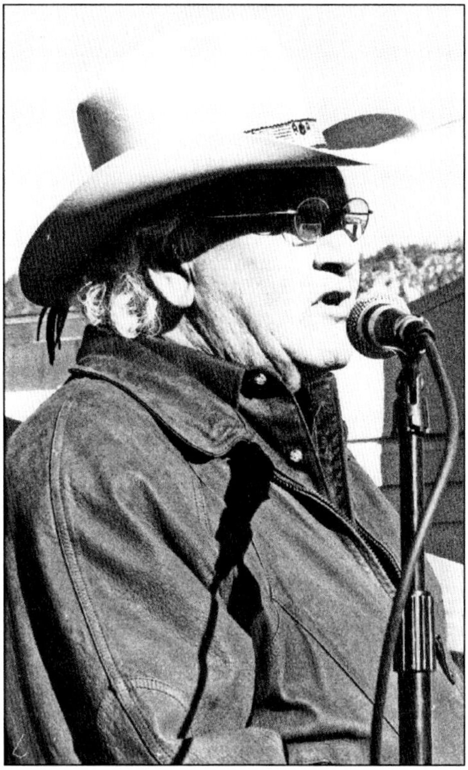

N. Scott Momaday, who won a Pulitzer Prize for his book *House Made of Dawn*, is a part-time resident of Jemez Springs. He has done numerous readings of his poetry and prose in Jemez Springs and shown his paintings at local galleries. Both his mother, Natachee, and father, Alfred Morris Mammedaty, were teachers at Jemez Pueblo and owned a house in Jemez Springs. (Courtesy Robert Borden.)

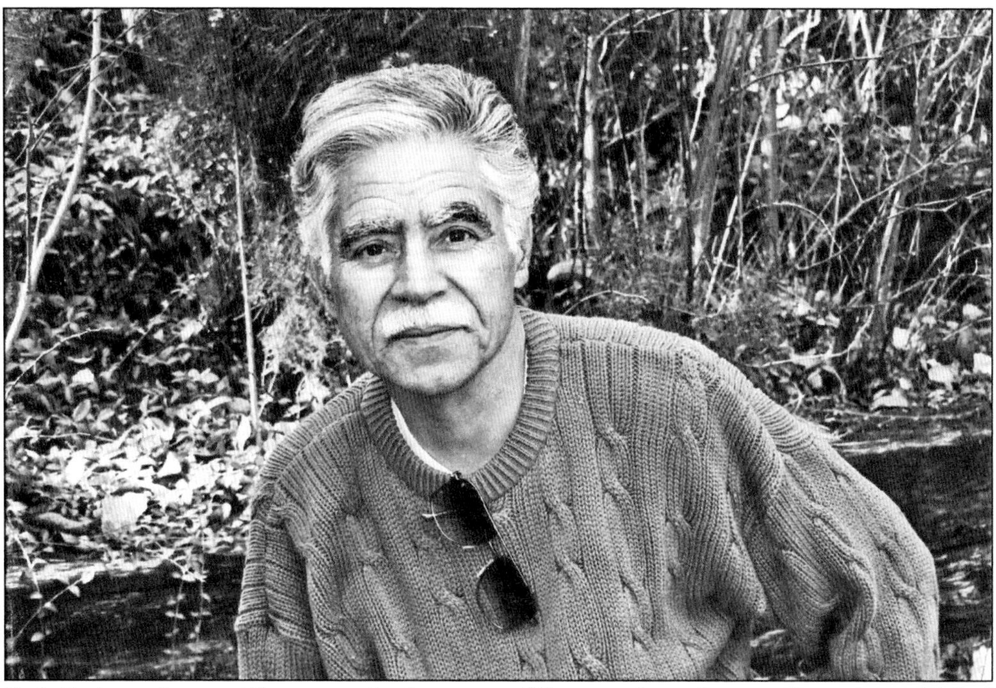

Rudolfo Anaya lives in Albuquerque but keeps a small house in Jemez Springs. Anaya has published a large number of books, most concerning the Hispanic culture. He received a National Medal of Arts from Pres. George W. Bush in 2001. (Author's collection.)

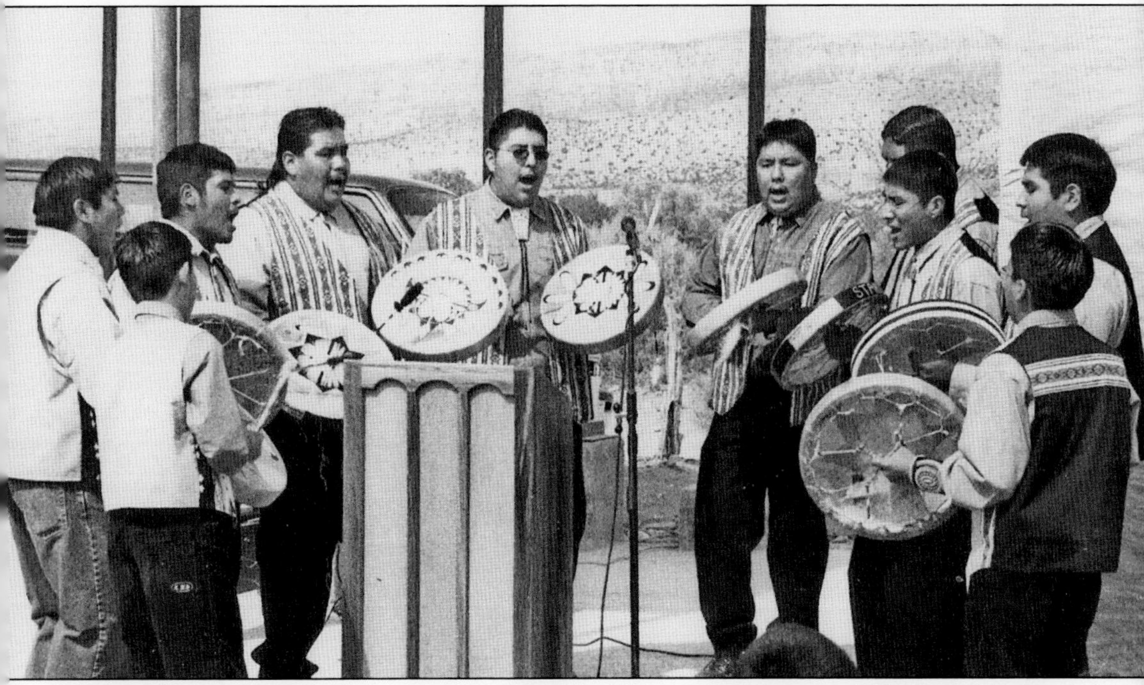

Black Eagle, a traditional drum group from Jemez Pueblo, won a Grammy in 2004 in the Native American music category with its album *Flying Free*. Malcom Yepa started the group in 1989. (Courtesy Robert Borden.)

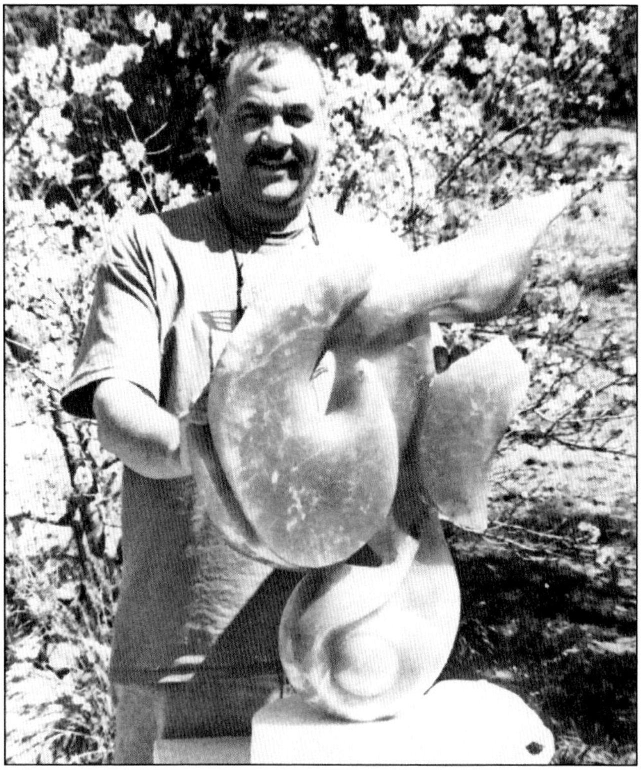

Rollie Grandbois conducts a stone-carving symposium every fall that attracts amateurs as well as professionals on the grounds of Hummingbird. Rollie, a Turtle Mountain Chippewa, is known for his large pieces that are often placed outdoors. (Courtesy Robert Borden.)

Former New Mexico governor Gary Johnson meets Cliff Fragua at his studio in May 2002 to celebrate the start of Fragua's 7-foot-tall sculpture of Popay, the Native American leader of the 1680 pueblo revolt. The sculpture is now one of the two distinguished New Mexicans in Statuary Hall in Washington, D.C. (Courtesy Robert Borden.)

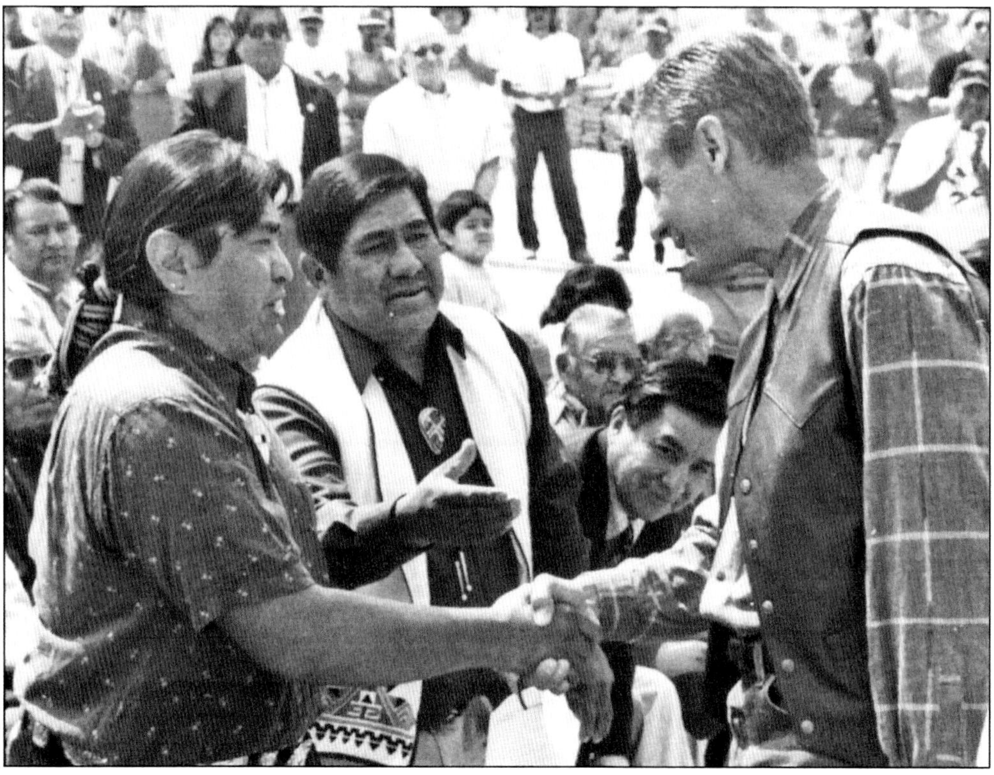

Local artist Raymond Sandoval created this giant Elvis float for the 2005 Fourth of July parade. The theme that year was "The 50s," and Elvis not only sang but also swiveled his hips in time to the music to the delight of the poodle-skirted girls. (Courtesy Robert Borden.)

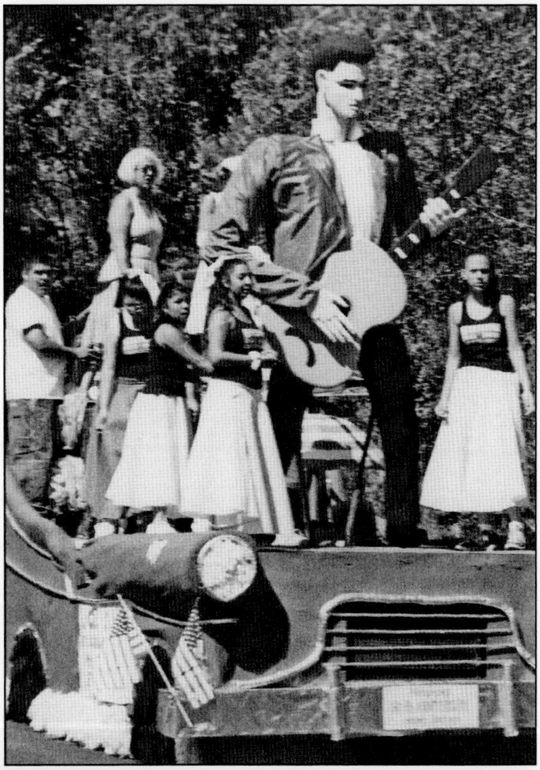

Jemez Pueblo is noted internationally for its pottery. Different types include storytellers, wedding vases, and polished pots. (Courtesy Robert Borden.)

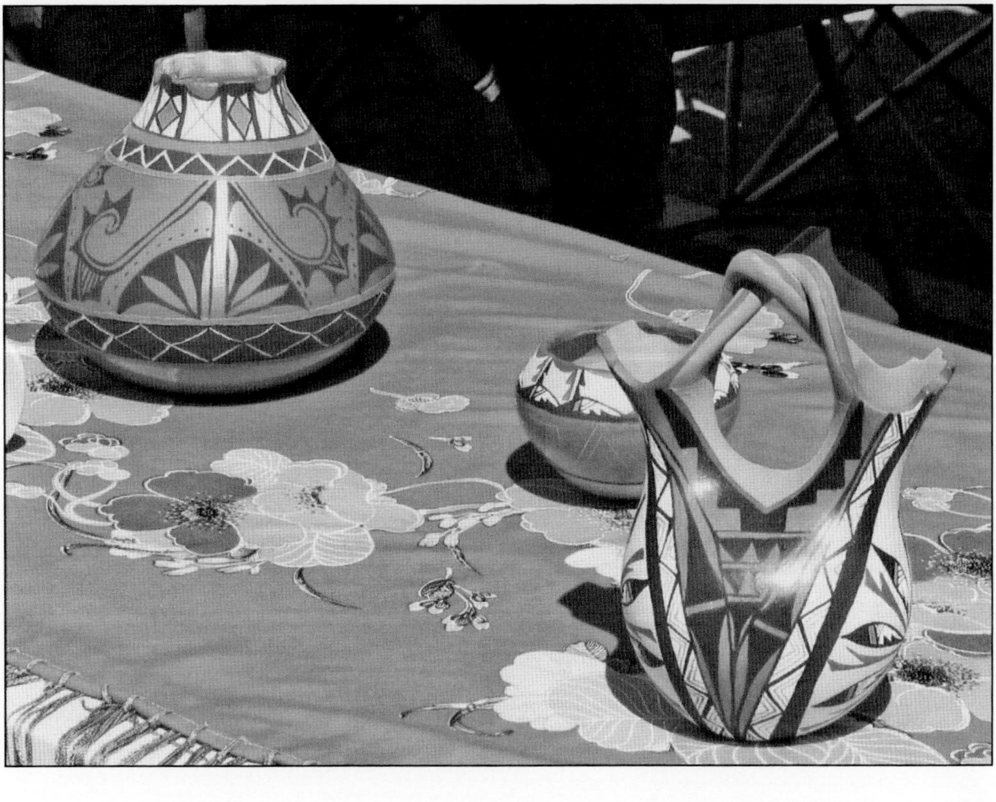

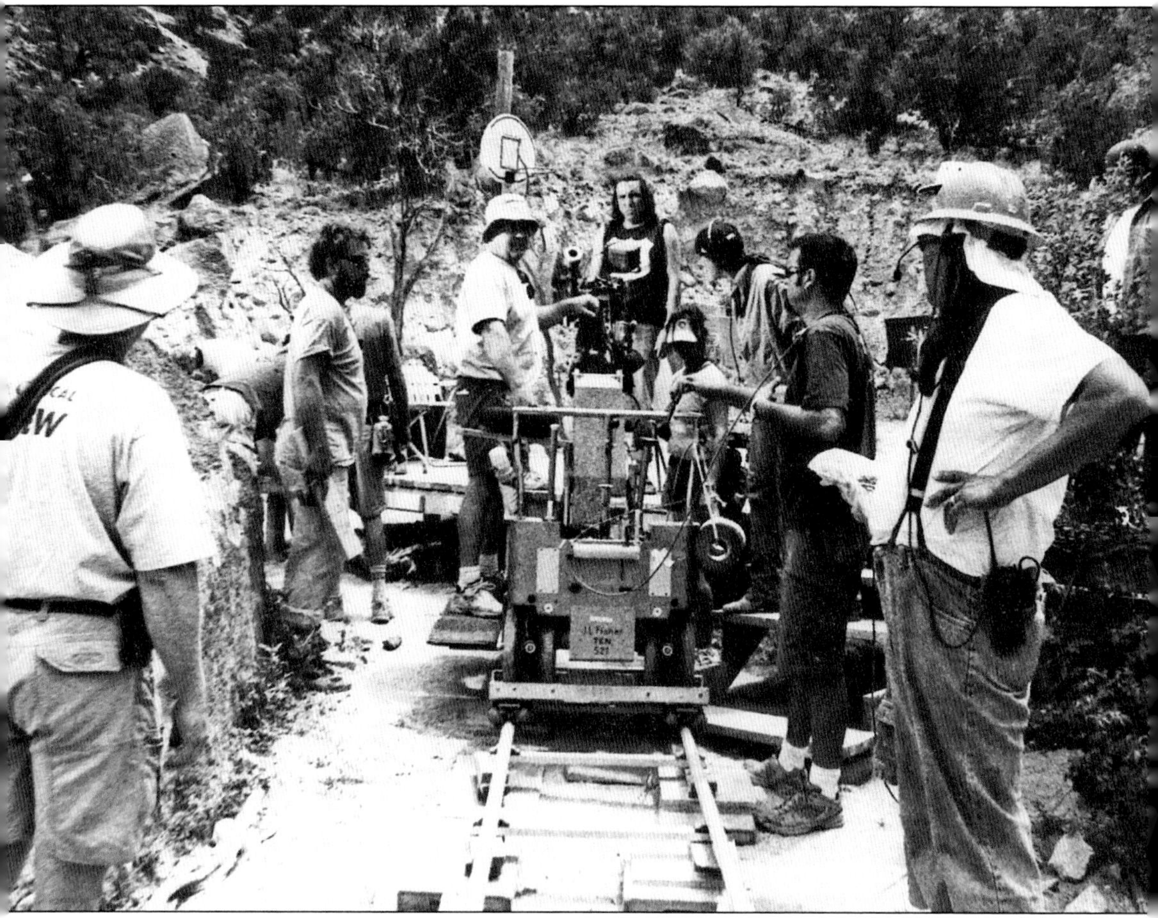

Filmmakers have discovered the Jemez for its red rock scenery, which can substitute for a number of other places in the West. In this photograph, a film crew works at the home of Damon and Sue Stephens in 2003, shooting a PBS film of Tony Hillerman's book *Coyote Waits*. (Courtesy Robert Borden.)

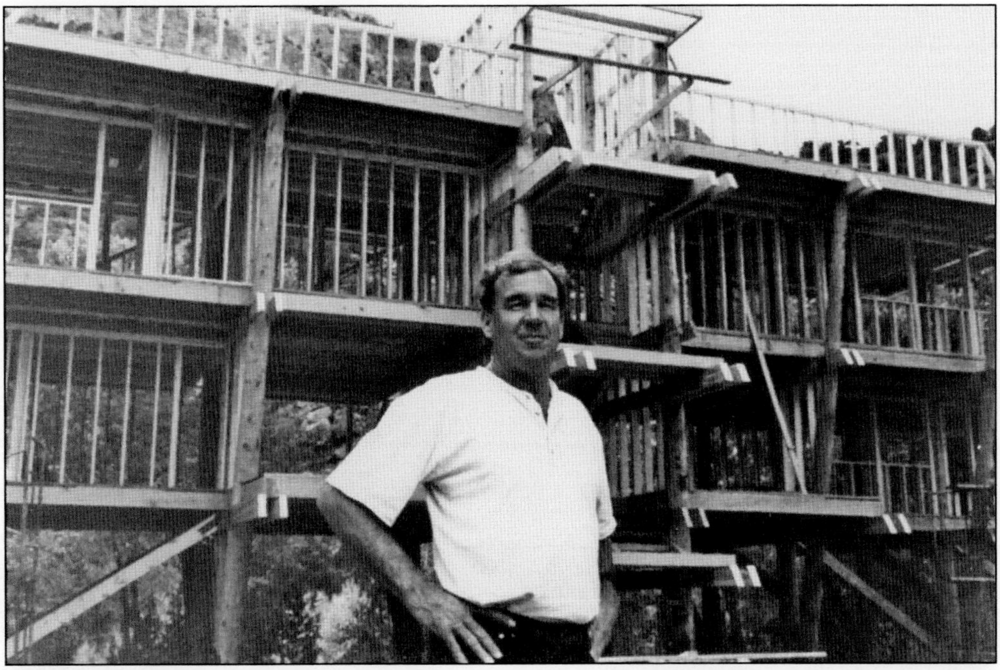

For such a small town, some great architects have done work in Jemez Springs. Bart Prince, whose grandfather was the governor of the New Mexico territory, designed a house along the Jemez River just south of the village. (Courtesy Robert Borden.)

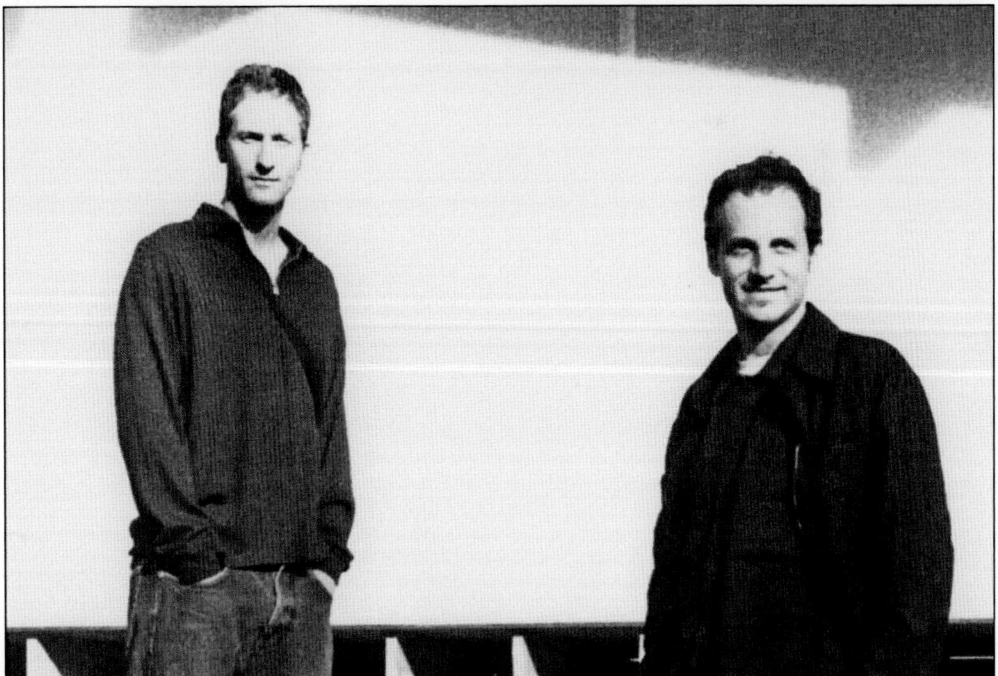

Pictured here, John Frane (left) and Hadrian Predock received the Institute Honor Award from the American Institute of Architects for the Foundation Hall they designed for the Bodhi Manda Zen Center. The building opened in April 2003. (Courtesy Robert Borden.)

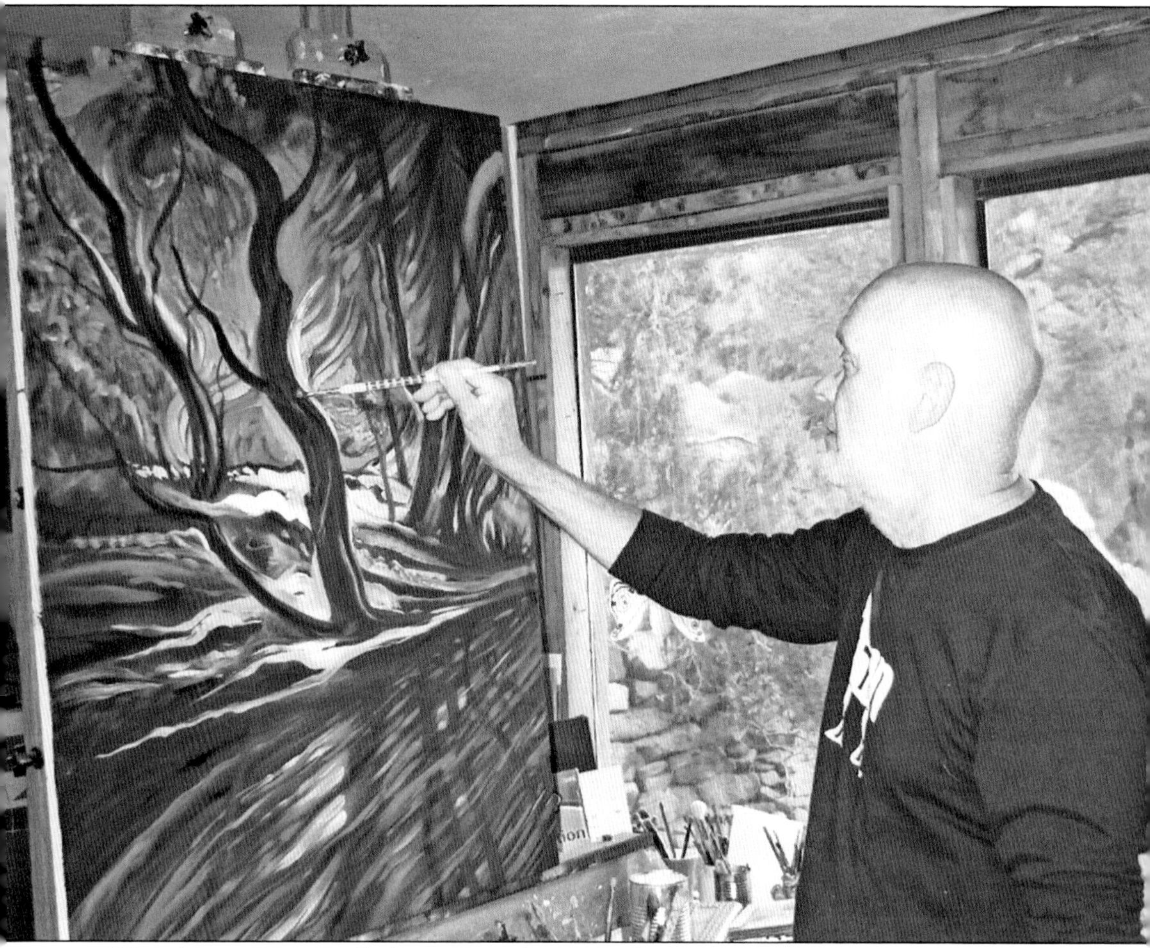

Edward Samuels, originally from New York City, has lived in Gilman since the early 1980s, creating hundreds of landscape paintings, sculptures, and jewelry. (Courtesy Robert Borden.)

Ten

Modern Times

Strictly speaking, the village of Jemez Springs is only 53 years old. That's because the village did not incorporate until December 1955. The actual reason for incorporation was that in order to have a school, they needed a school district, and to have a school district, they needed an incorporated entity. All the small villages in the Jemez said "no thanks," so Jemez Springs stepped up to the plate. And Jemez Springs has done pretty well as far as small villages go. It has a pretty village park where there are concerts every Saturday in the summer, a newly remodeled library, and a historic bathhouse. Los Ojos provides live music on the weekends, and the Laughing Lizard Café uses its walls for art shows. The credit union provides drive-up banking and an ATM. The post office is new and spacious. There is electricity (except when there is a particularly bad electric storm), telephone service (except when someone shoots a cable out with a gun), running water (except when a pipe breaks), and Internet access (except when there isn't). It sounds like any other city, only here everything happens on a small scale.

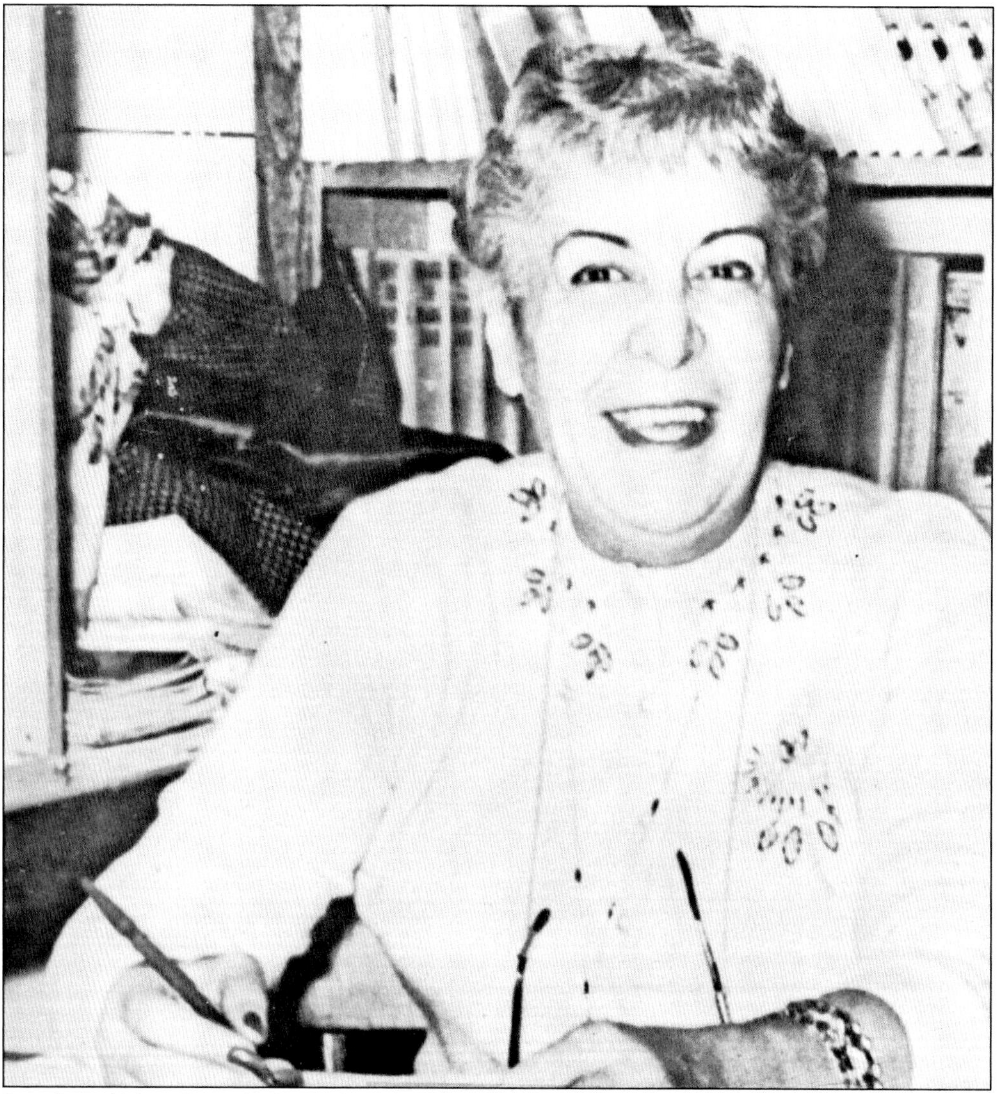

Josephine (Abousleman) Shepard was long active in civic affairs. She was instrumental in getting the village incorporated so there would be a school closer than Bernalillo, 40 miles away. She was a classroom teacher in a one-room school where the electric cooperative is today. She herself had attended a one-room school in the Presbyterian church. She was among the first female mayors in the state, serving three terms from 1970 to 1978 as well as several terms on the village council. As mayor, she instigated a sewage treatment plant and took part in such civic projects as the clinic, firehouse, and procuring Father Fitzgerald Park. She was made an honorary life member of the New Mexico League for all these services to her community. She died at the age of 94 but not before serving as the grand marshal of the Fourth of July parade, which also happened to be her birthday. (Courtesy Village of Jemez Springs.)

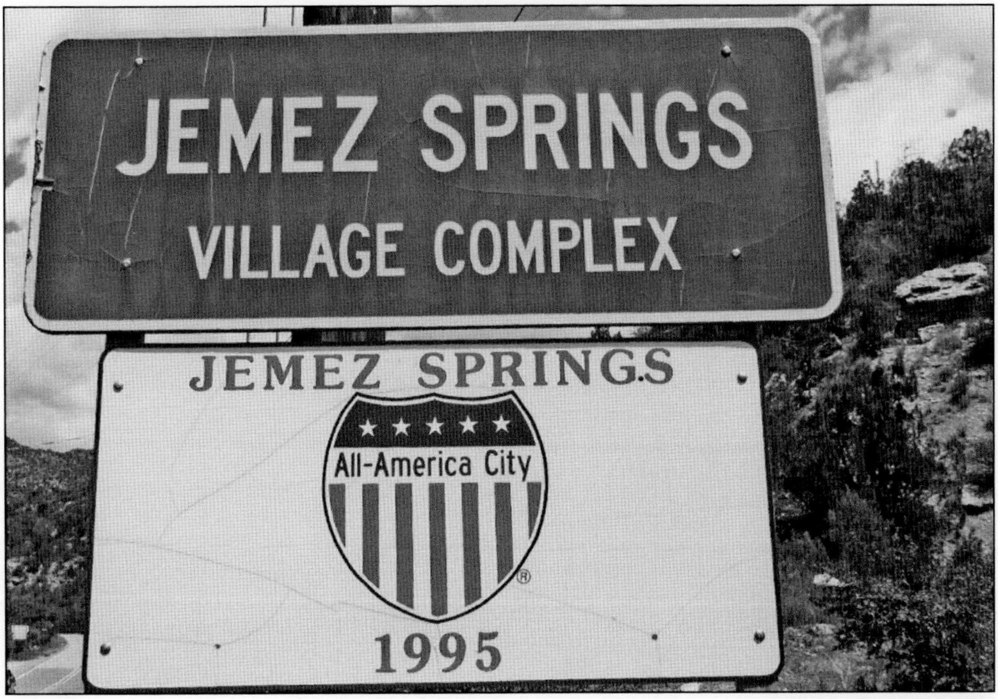

In 1995, the National Civic League named Jemez Springs an All-America City. A total of 145 cities representing 39 states applied for the award. Out of those 145 applicants, 30 were picked on the basis of written applications that detailed three community-building projects. Then each of those 30 entities made a personal presentation to the judges. In the end, 10 cities received the All-America City Award. While some cities brought large contingents, Jemez Springs only had four presenters. Mayor David Sanchez joked that he had brought 1 percent of the population of Jemez Springs. (Courtesy Robert Borden.)

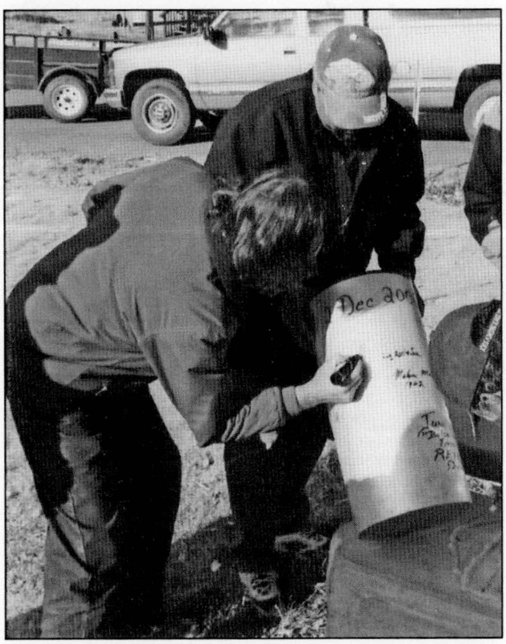

In 2005, Jemez Springs celebrated its 50th anniversary with an event every month of the year. There were chili cook-offs, potlucks, and scavenger hunts. Here Robert Borden (left) and Rollie Grandbois are signing the time capsule that went into a stone bench carved by Grandbois. The signing event actually took place in 2006 as a result of some technical difficulties in 2005. It is supposed to be opened in 2055, when the village is 100 years old. (Courtesy *Jemez Thunder*.)

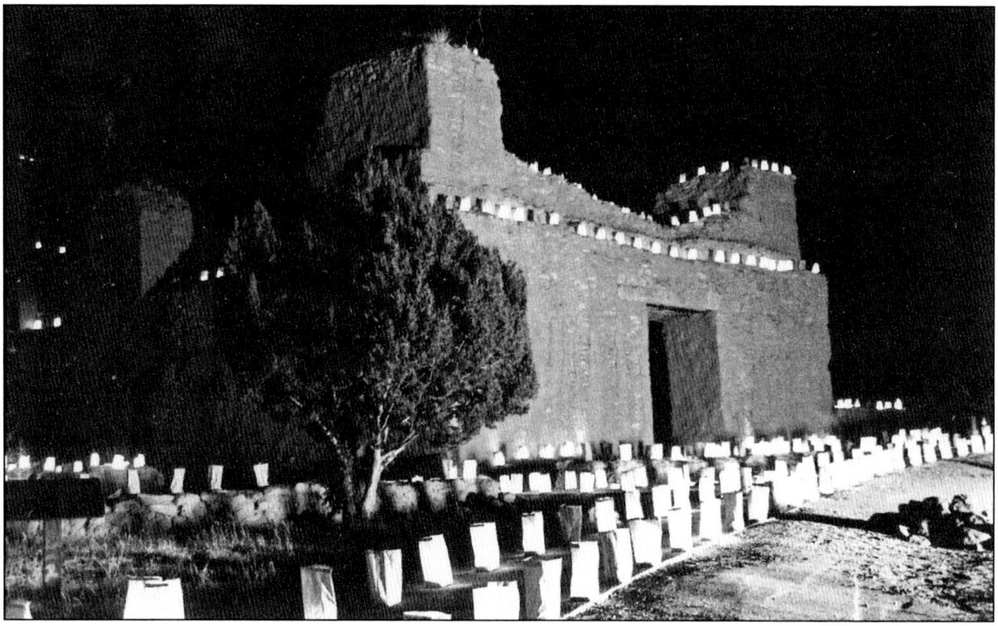

At Christmas, the Jemez State Monument is decorated with over 1,000 luminaries that outline the old mission church and the walkways. There are music, hot drinks, and bonfires to keep people warm. The evening draws people from Albuquerque and Bernalillo as well as locals. (Courtesy Robert Borden.)

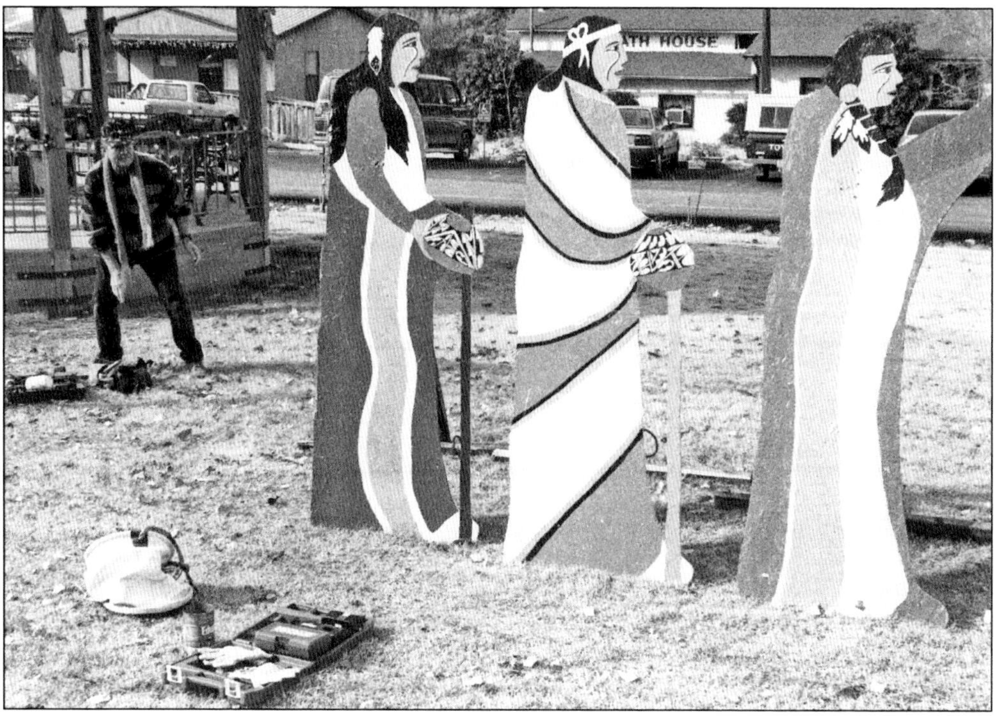

In December 1997, a group of volunteers set out to reproduce the wooden figures Al Momaday had created for the village park in 1968. The nativity figures were represented by Native American figures, as were the three wise men in their Native American blankets. (Courtesy Robert Borden.)

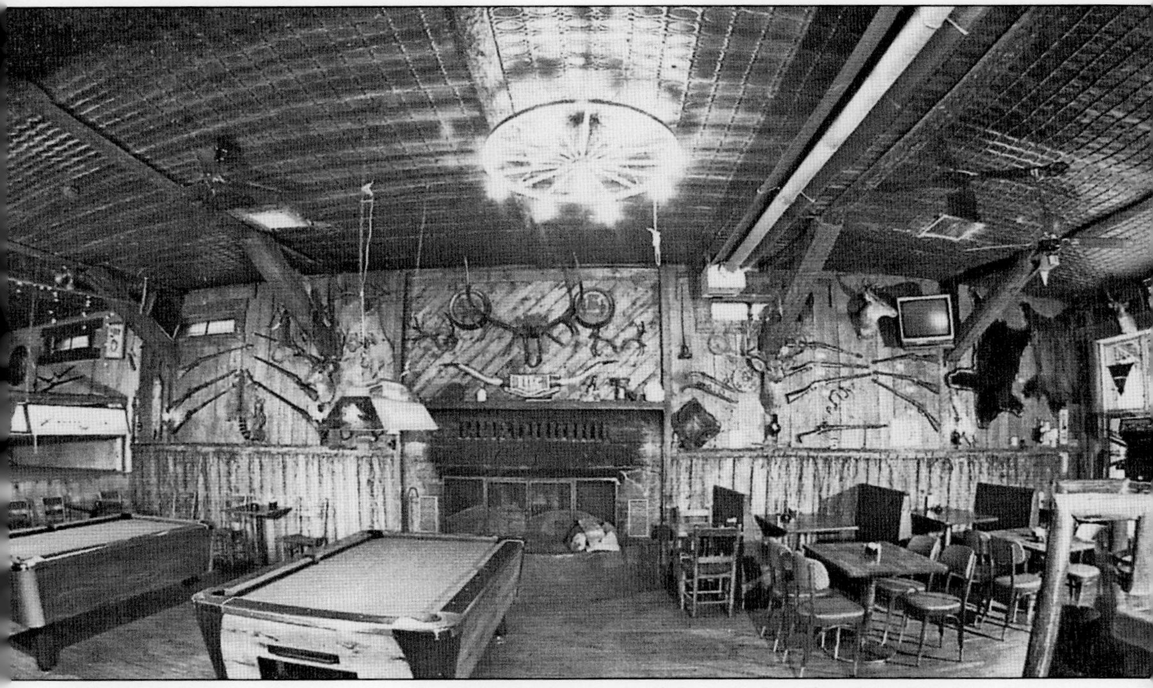

In 2006, Los Ojos was named by *Esquire* magazine one of the "ten best bars" in America. Tom Abousleman, whose father had started the bar, donated the guns that still hang there. Tom himself is a gun collector. (Photograph by Frank Sarnol.)

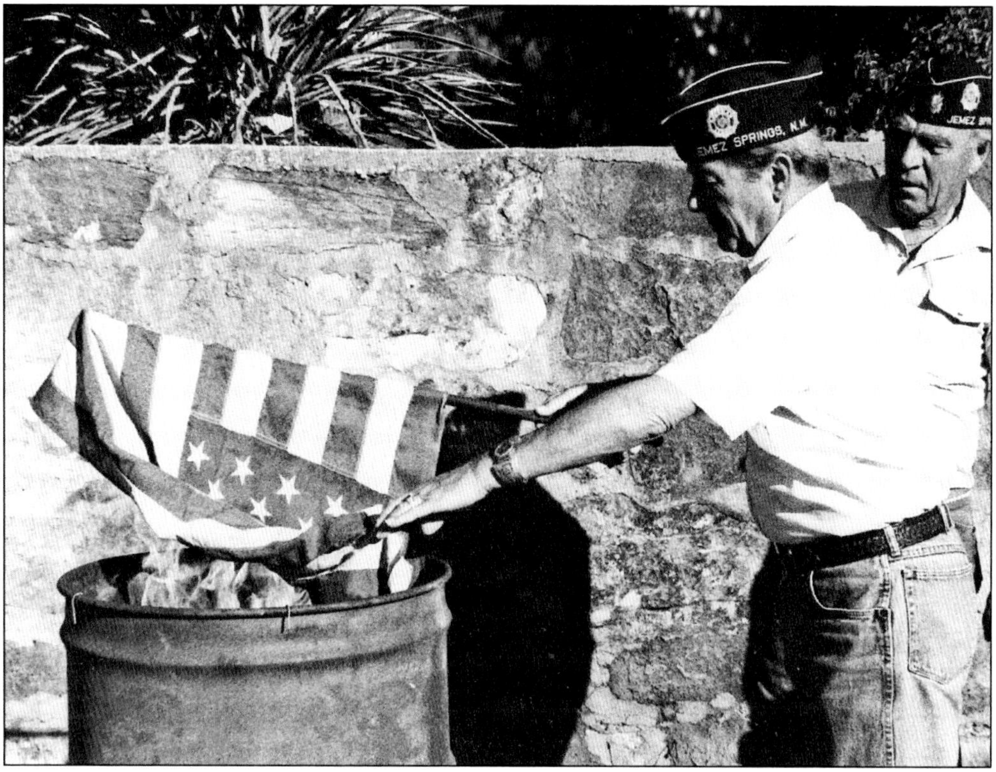

Every year, the American Legion honors Flag Day by burning old flags. In 2004, however, the Legion Hall itself burned to the ground, and the 50-year-old Legion is now leasing space from the village. The Legion Hall (while temporary) still provides a meeting place for many in Jemez Springs. It serves breakfasts and steak dinners once a month and holds special social hours for members. (Both photographs by Robert Borden.)

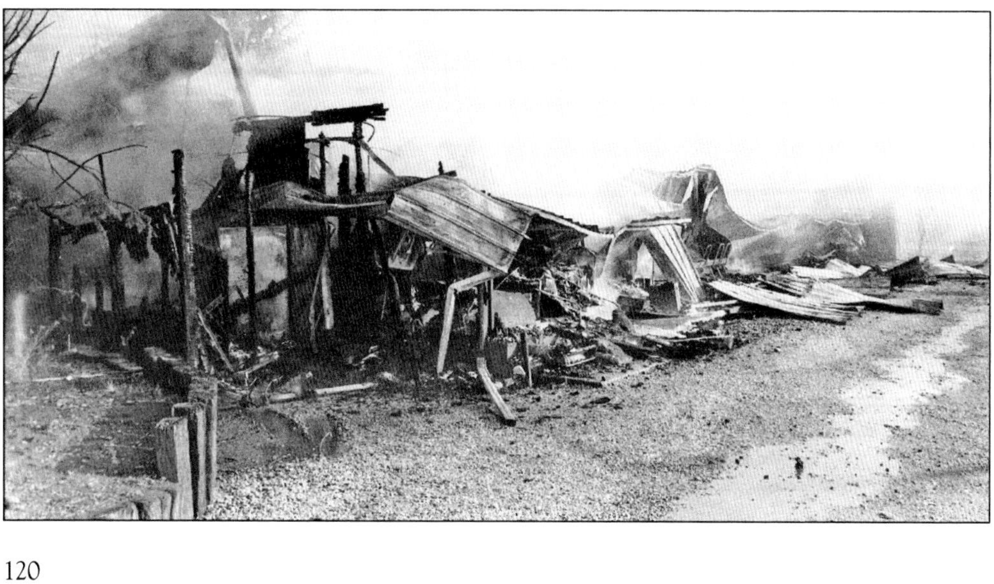

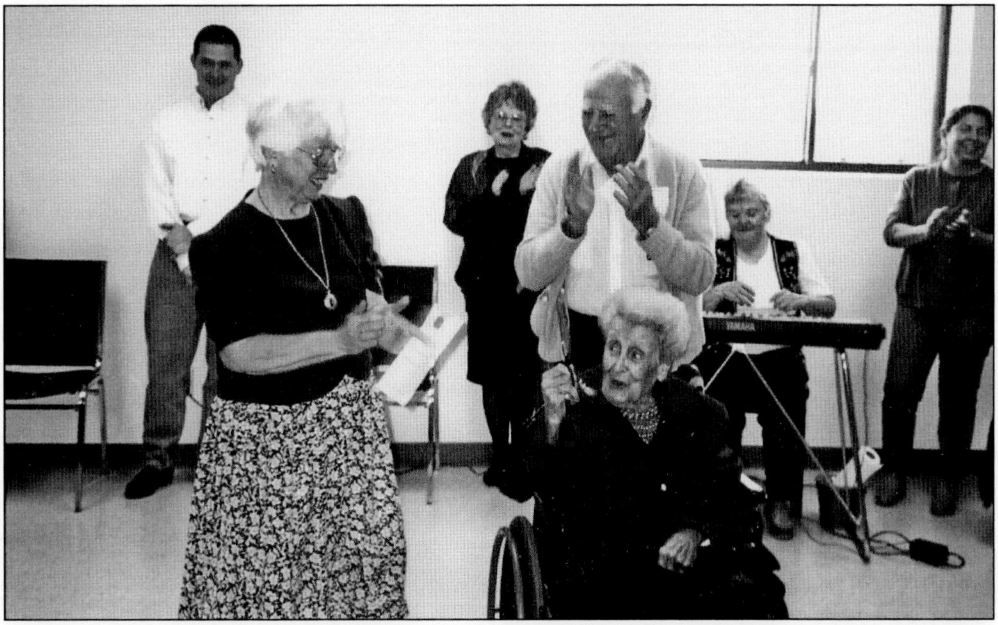

Josephine Shepard was one of the driving forces behind the creation of a new clinic in the Jemez. She also spearheaded the drive for a clinic in 1972, using $1 memberships and fried chicken dinners to raise funds to buy medical equipment and keep the clinic running. The first clinic occupied a back room at the Presbyterian church. Here she cuts the ribbon at the opening of the new clinic in 1998. (Courtesy Esther Smedley.)

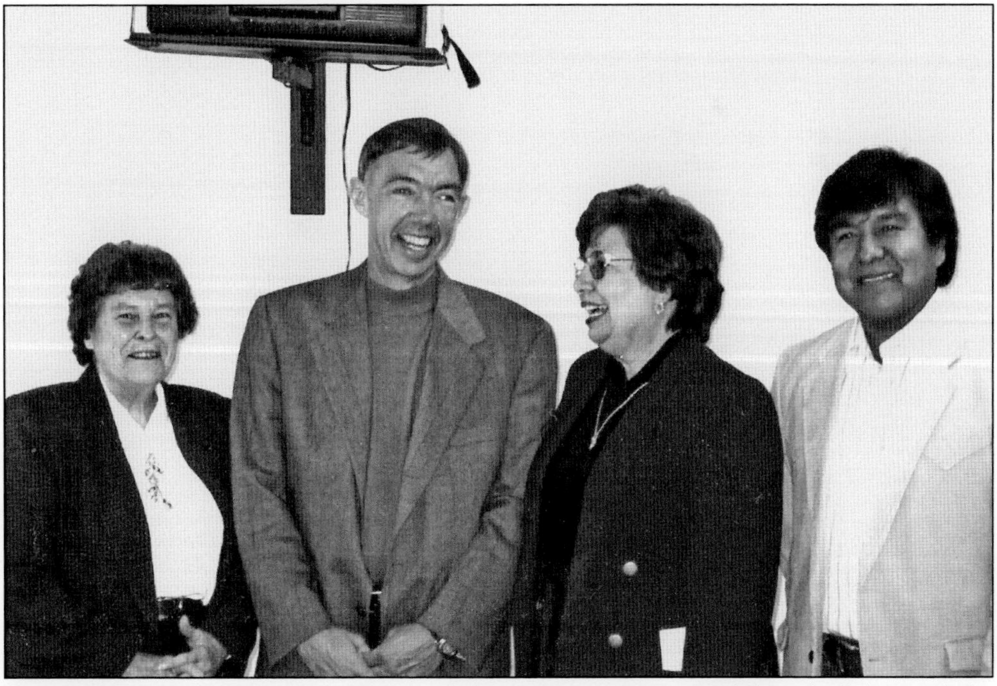

State representatives Jeannette Wallace (left) and James Roger Madalena (right) attend the opening of the Jemez Valley Medical Clinic in 1998, along with Jim Riebsomer, the president of Presbyterian Medical Services, and Esther Smedley. (Courtesy Esther Smedley.)

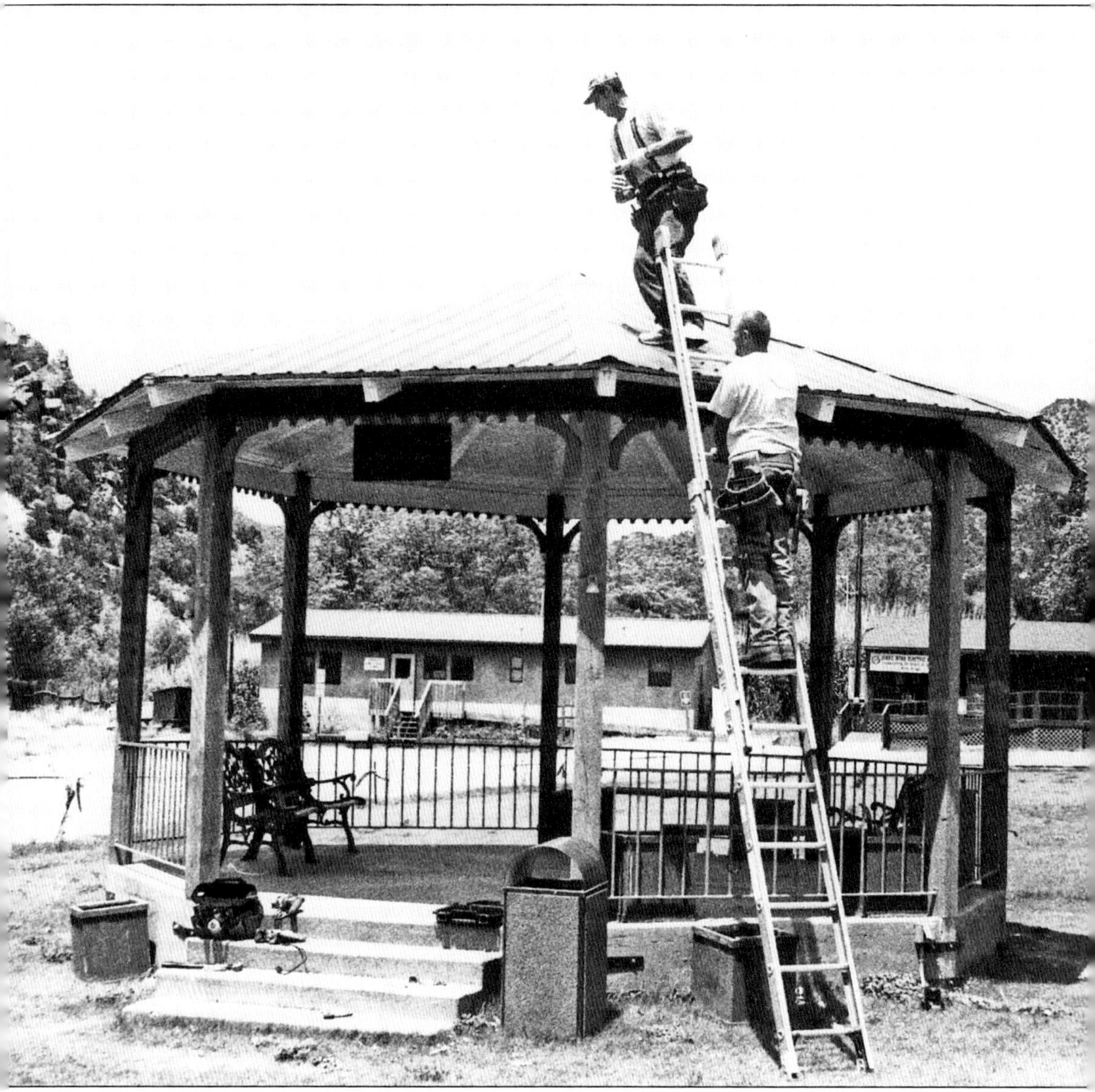

The gazebo in Father Fitzgerald Park gets a reroofing. Father Fitzgerald donated the land for the park, and money for the gazebo came from the widow of a man killed in an automobile accident. Perhaps it was only coincidence that she made the donation after having lunch with Josephine Shepard. (Courtesy Robert Borden.)

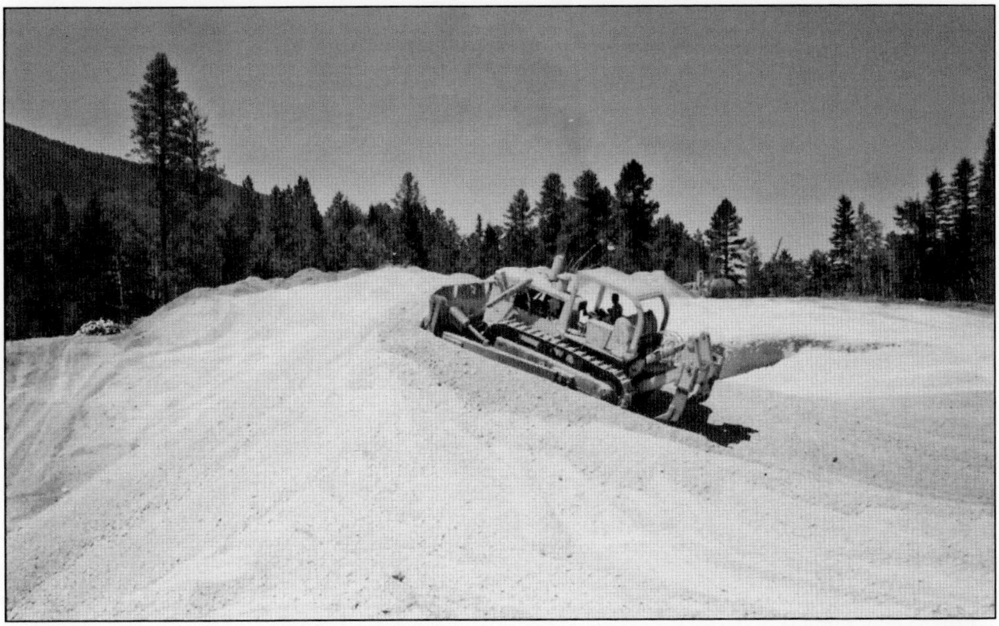

Copar Pumice Company of Española has been operating mines in the Jemez Mountains for years. In 1991, Congressman Bill Richardson proposed the creation of the Jemez National Recreation Area, which became law in 1993. One of the provisions of the legislation was to prohibit all new mining claims within the recreation area. Copar's owner has been constantly in court trying to get the forest service to let him expand. (Courtesy David Torney.)

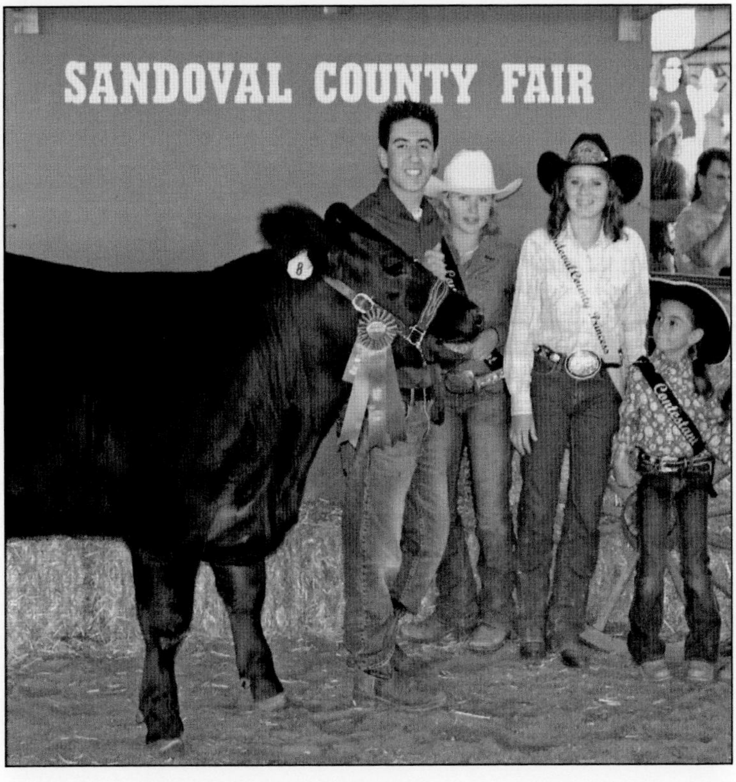

Stephen Montoya poses with his grand champion steer at the 2008 Sandoval County Fair in Cuba. (Photograph by Steve Lucero.)

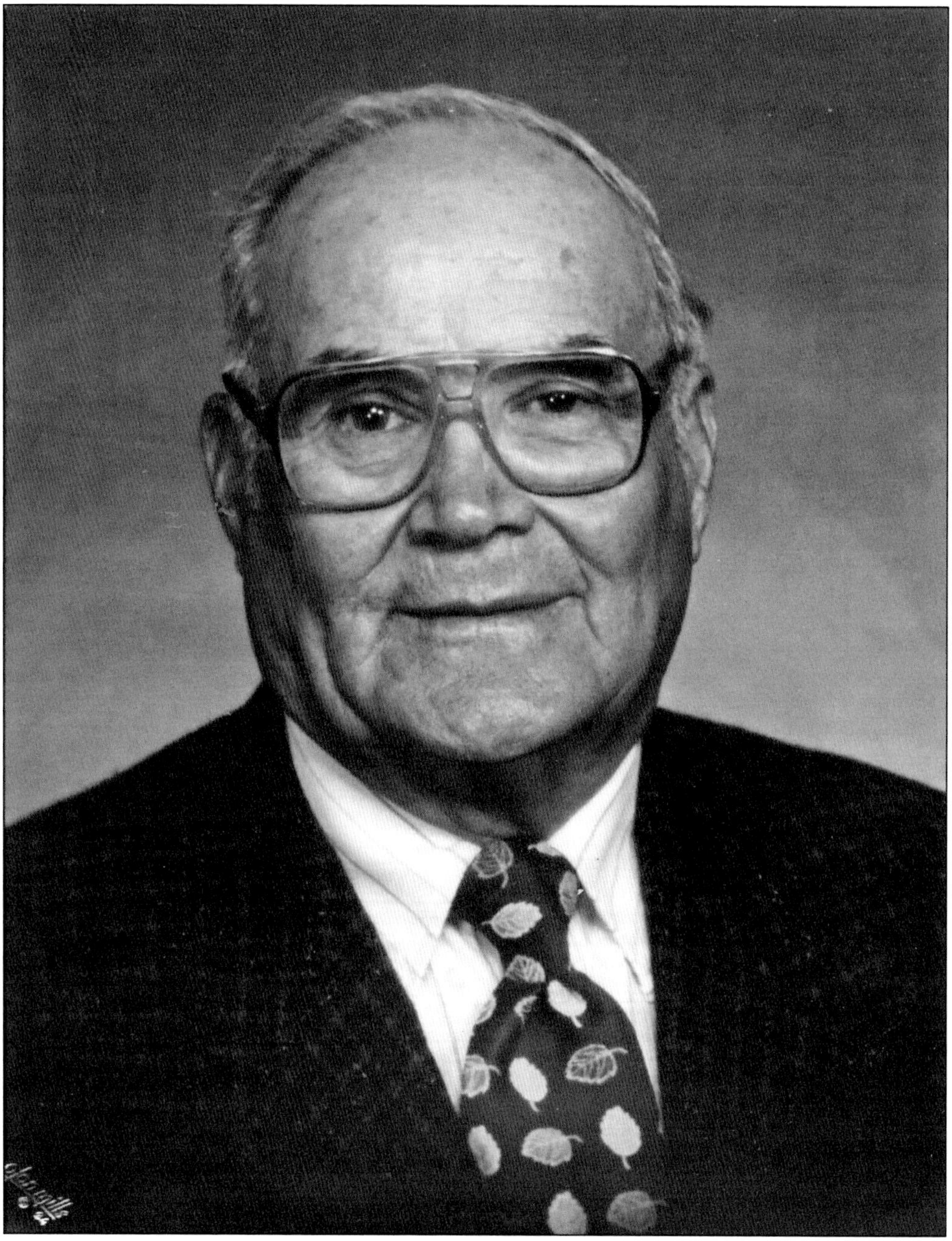

Luciano Garcia was the first mayor of Jemez Springs. Garcia was a colorful character who always wore a black hat and smoked a cigar. He never learned to drive a car, but walked everywhere. He died in 1982 at the age of 91. (Courtesy Village of Jemez Springs.)

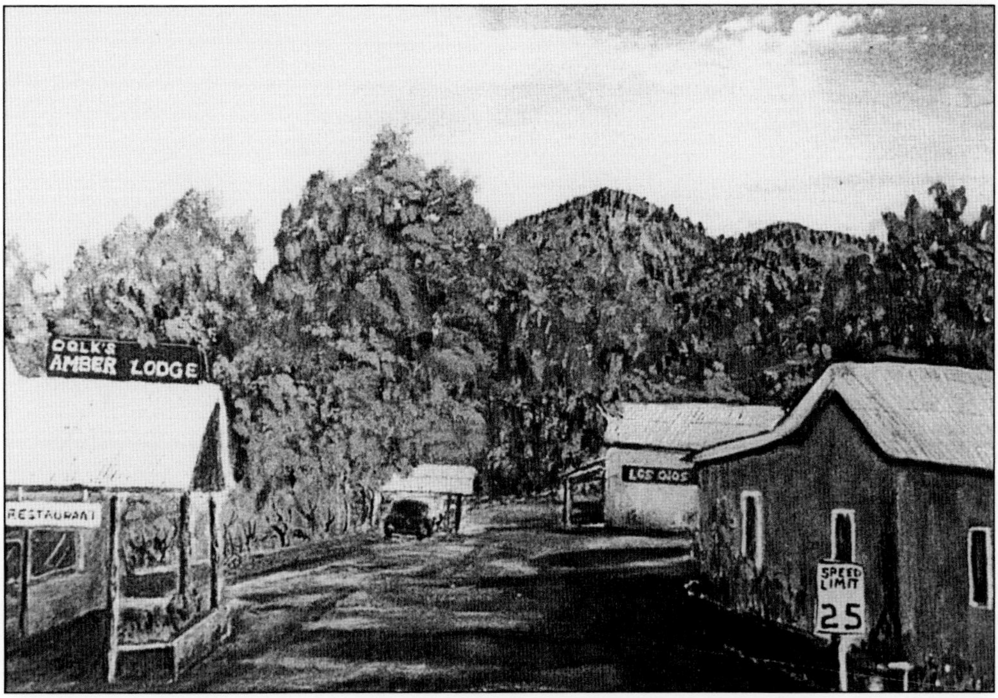

To get an idea of how few changes have occurred to the center part of Jemez Springs, compare these two images. Joann Dolk painted the one above in 1975, and the photograph below is from 2008. Dolk's Amber Lodge is now the Jemez Mountain Inn. The Presbyterian church and Los Ojos are the same. The Mercantile at the back left is now Deb's Deli. Gas can no longer be purchased at Deb's, but the speed limit through the village is still 25 miles an hour. The village has received funding from the New Mexico Legislature to build a walkway along the highway so people do not have to risk life and limb walking on the side of the narrow road. (Above, painting by Joann Dolk; below, courtesy Robert Borden.)

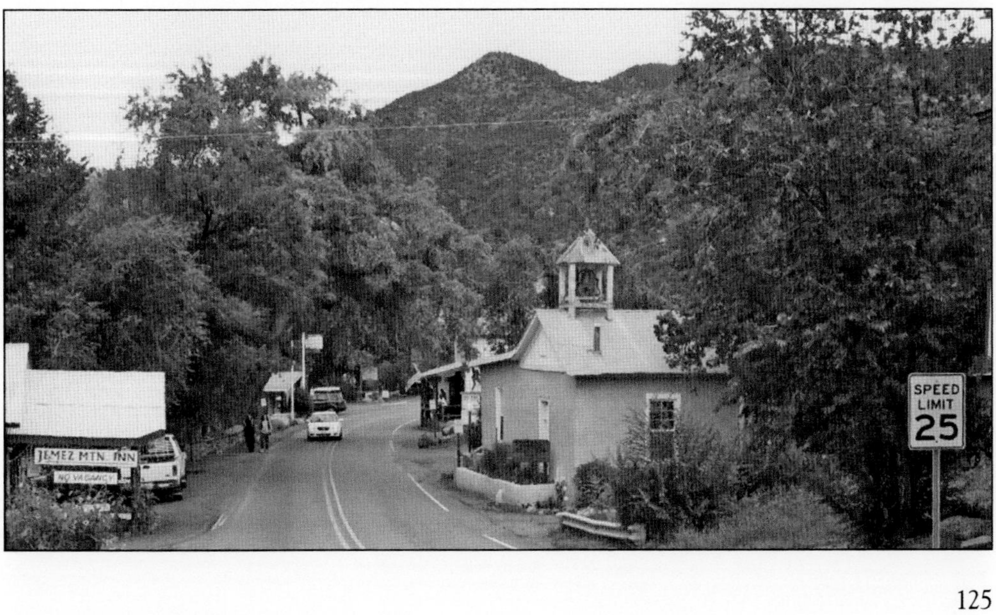

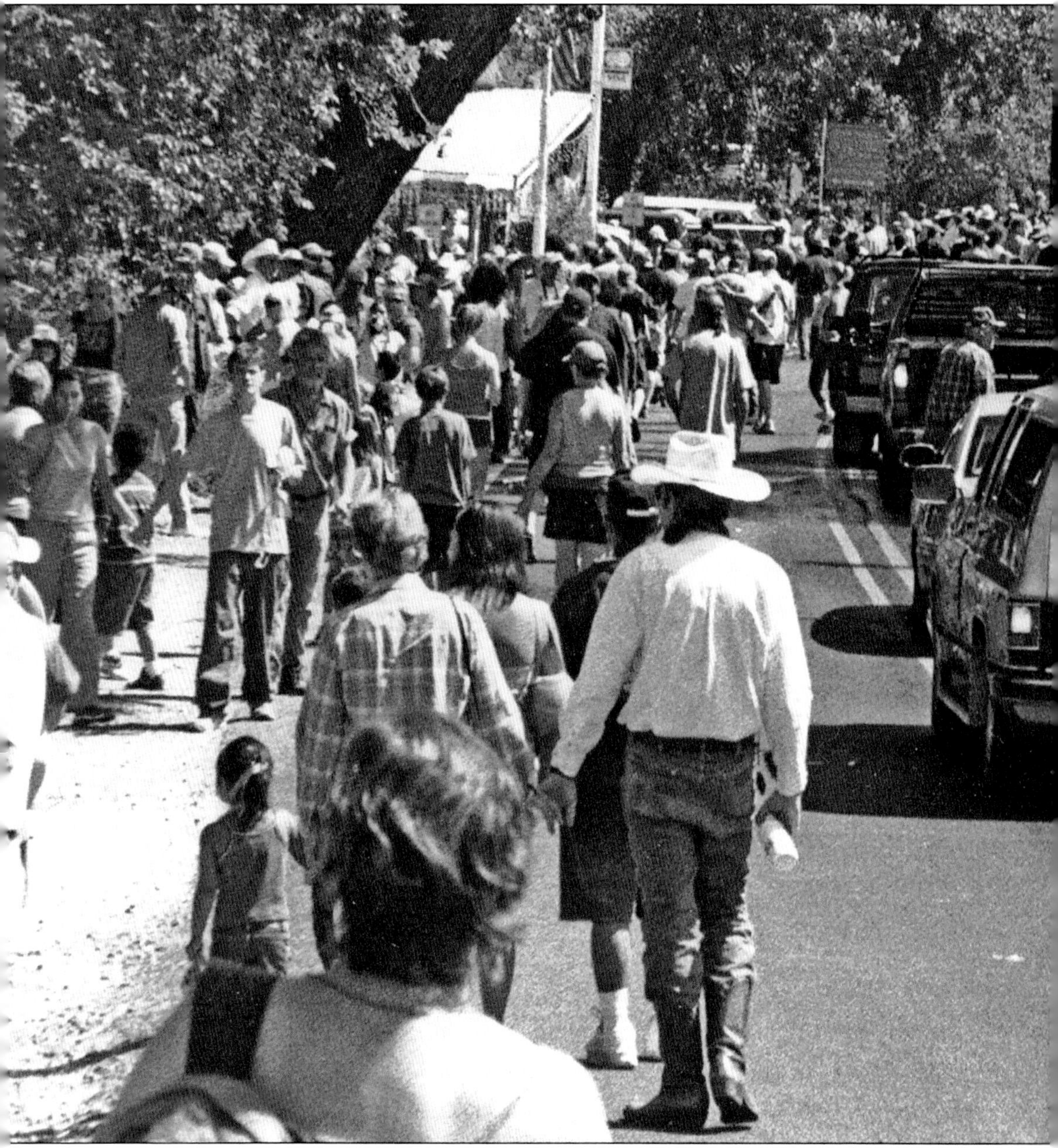

After Christmas, the Fourth of July is the biggest holiday in Jemez Springs. The Fourth of July parade consists of the Hummingbird Music Camp students, the American Legion, fire trucks and emergency vehicles, antique cars, Smokey the Bear in a U.S. Forest Service truck, little kids on bicycles, big kids on motorcycles, and individual floats made by nonprofit groups and local

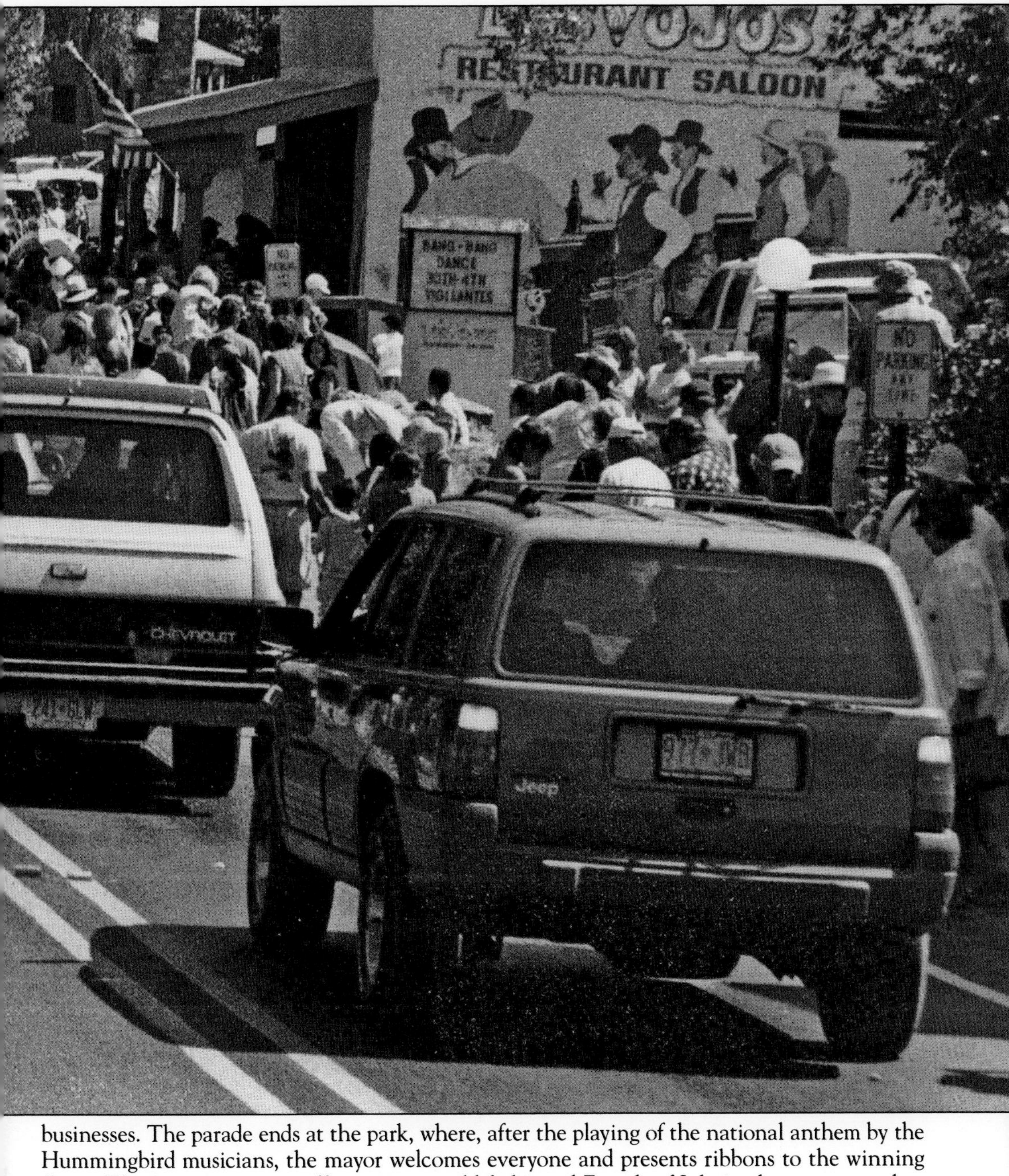

businesses. The parade ends at the park, where, after the playing of the national anthem by the Hummingbird musicians, the mayor welcomes everyone and presents ribbons to the winning floats. Then everyone goes off to enjoy an old-fashioned Fourth of July in the manner only a small town can provide. (Courtesy Robert Borden.)